FOURTH EDITION

Field Experience Guide

Resources for Teachers of Elementary and Middle School Mathematics

FOR

ELEMENTARY AND MIDDLE SCHOOL
MATHEMATICS
Teaching Developmentally
EIGHTH EDITION

JOHN A. VAN DE WALLE
KAREN S. KARP   JENNIFER M. BAY-WILLIAMS

Jennifer M. Bay-Williams
University of Louisville

PEARSON

Boston • Columbus • Indianapolis • New York • San Francisco • Upper Saddle River
Amsterdam • Cape Town • Dubai • London • Madrid • Milan • Munich • Paris • Montreal • Toronto
Delhi • Mexico City • São Paulo • Sydney • Hong Kong • Seoul • Singapore • Taipei • Tokyo

Senior Acquisitions Editor: *Kelly Villella Canton*
Senior Development Editor: *Christina Robb*
Editorial Assistant: *Annalea Manalili*
Senior Marketing Manager: *Darcy Betts*
Senior Production Editor: *Gregory Erb*
Editorial Production Service: *Electronic Publishing Services Inc.*
Manufacturing Buyer: *Megan Cochran*
Electronic Composition: *Jouve*
Interior Design: *Electronic Publishing Services Inc.*
Cover Designer: *Jennifer Hart*

10 9 8 7 6 5 4 3 2 1

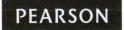

ISBN-10: 0-13-282113-3
ISBN-13: 978-0-13-282113-1

Contents

PART II RESOURCES ORGANIZED BY CONTENT

What Is New in the *Field Experience Guide?*

This fourth edition of the *Field Experience Guide* has a number of new features:

- **Focus on Common Core State Standards content throughout.** First, there are a number of field experiences throughout Part I that include a focus on the *Standards for Mathematical Practice*. All lessons and activities have grade level recommendations that are consistent with the CCSS content recommendations. These lessons are now listed at the beginnings of Chapters 9 and 10 for easy reference.
- **New Field Experience Activities.** New activities were added to several of the Part I chapters (see, for example, 2.3, Level of Cognitive Demand, and 4.7, Classroom Discussions—Talk Moves). As noted previously, several new field experiences are focused on the *Common Core State Standards* (2.5, 3.4, 7.8).
- **Revised rubrics in Part I chapters**. These focus on teaching skills and are intended to be broad enough that they can be used with any task in that chapter.
- **More activities.** Three new activities were added to Chapter 10 to provide more choices and to provide a more comprehensive content coverage in Chapters 9 and 10.
- **Increased focus on diversity.** Lessons now have specific strategies for English language learners (ELLs) and students with disabilities.

Part *1*

Menu of Field Experiences

The purpose of the *Menu of Field Experiences* is to provide a variety of templates and reflective questions so that you can get the most out of your field experience. Each activity is designed to support learning within a classroom or school. Field experiences vary for many reasons, so each chapter has a set of experiences that range in the task and in the level of engagement. Collectively, each section has opportunities to observe, interview (teachers and students), and do (teach, assess, etc.). Each chapter focuses on one aspect of mathematics teaching. These areas have been identified by National Council for Accreditation of Teacher Education (NCATE), which accredits teaching institutions, and by the National Council of Teachers of Mathematics (NCTM), which offers vision on effective mathematics teaching through the *Professional Standards for Teaching Mathematics* (NCTM, 1991) and its revision *Mathematics Teaching Today* (NCTM, 2007). The Teaching Standards, as they are often called, provide what continues to be an excellent guide for what knowledge and skills a teacher should have.

You can use the following two recording sheets that can be used for all of your field experiences:

- Field Experience Cover Sheet
- Field Experience Activity Log

Field Experience Cover Sheet

When you conduct any field experience assignment, attach this as a cover sheet (or provide this information on a cover page).

Your name: _____ Date: _____

School visited: _____

Cooperating teacher: _____ Grade(s) of students: _____

Activity completed (if it is a Field Guide task, give the number): _____

Type of experience

_____ Observation   _____ Teaching

_____ Interview   _____ Project

_____ Reflection   _____ Other: _____

Other pertinent information:

Field Experience Activity Log

Use this log to record the date, time, purpose, and descriptions of each visit to the school. The first table gives an example. You may use this page, or create one of your own.

Activity Log

Name: _____

Date	Times	Purpose of Visit	Brief Description of Visit
3/6/13	8:30–9:00	Observe questioning strategies	I observed Ms. Bergen's second-grade lesson on adding two-digit numbers. After the lesson I asked her a few follow-up questions.
3/7/13	1:00–2:00	Teach an inquiry math lesson	I cotaught a second-grade lesson on growing patterns (with my teaching partner). After the lesson, we met with our supervisor and received feedback.
	2:00–2:30	Assist students as they worked on end-of-quarter portfolios	Ms. Bergen invited me to stay and help students select their "best" work to illustrate what they had learned on specific objectives.

Field Experience Activity Log

Date	Times	Purpose of Visit	Description of Visit

1.1 Observation: Physical Environment

As you enter a classroom, imagine you are a prospective parent visiting for the first time and trying to decide if it's the right environment for your child. As you walk around, jot down your responses to these questions:

1. Describe the mathematics pictures, posters, or other displays. What do they depict?

2. Describe any bulletin boards that have math information or interactive math activities.

3. What manipulatives and tools are evident? Are they accessible to the students (can students get tools at any time, or does the teacher determine when they are available)?

4. Are there any computers or calculators in the class? Describe.

5. Draw a sketch of the location of the desks, calculators, computers, overhead projector, whiteboard (or chalkboard), and other math-related resources.

6. What physical aspects of the classroom do you feel "create a spirit of inquiry, trust, and expectation"? See "A Classroom Environment for Doing Mathematics" on page 14 of *Elementary and Middle School Mathematics* to assist in answering this question.

1.2 Observation: NCTM Professional Teaching Standards

The following template can be used with a live or videotaped math lesson. As described in *Elementary and Middle School Mathematics*, *Mathematics Teaching Today* describes six "Shifts in Classroom Environment" (NCTM, 2007). During your observation, note the evidence that the teacher is modeling each shift in his or her practice and note ideas for incorporating the shifts in your own practice.

Six Shifts in Classroom Environment Toward . . .	Evidence of the Shift in Lesson Observed	Observer's Ideas for Future Actions to Incorporate Shift
Communities that offer an equal opportunity to learn to all students		
A balanced focus on conceptual understanding as well as on procedural fluency		
Active student engagement in problem solving, reasoning, communicating, making connections, and using multiple representations		
Well-equipped learning centers in which technology is used to enhance understanding		
Incorporation of multiple assessments that are aligned with instructional goals and practices		
Mathematics authority that lies within the power of sound reasoning and mathematical integrity		

1.3 Observation: Productive Classroom Culture

This observation reflects the expectations that are often cited as ones that support students in doing mathematics (CCSSO, 2010; Clarke & Clarke, 2004; Hiebert et al., 1997; NCTM, 2007). (See Chapter 2 in *Elementary and Middle School Mathematics*.)

Classroom Feature	Evidence Through Teacher Moves	Evidence Through Student Moves
1. *Persistence, effort, and concentration are important in learning mathematics.*		
2. *Students share their ideas.*		
3. *Students listen to each other.*		
4. *Errors or strategies that didn't work are opportunities for learning.*		
5. *Students look for and discuss connections.*		

1.4 Teacher Interview:
An Environment for Learning

Ask a practicing teacher if you may interview him or her about how he or she organizes the mathematics classroom or the environment for mathematical learning (questions adapted from *Professional Standards for Teaching Mathematics*, NCTM, 1991, p. 57).

1. Describe how a typical lesson is organized. What is your role? What is the students' role?

2. How do you decide how much time to provide learners to explore a math task?

3. How does the way you've arranged the room (e.g., the seating, location of materials) affect the students' learning of mathematics?

4. How important do you think it is to use real contexts or problem situations in teaching a math concept or skill? How do you use contexts or situations to develop mathematical skills and proficiency?

5. What do you do about the learner who says that he or she doesn't like math or is anxious about doing math?

6. Do learners ask questions or make conjectures during your math instruction? Do you encourage this? How?

7. What do your learners do that helps you understand that they are making sense of math? How do you foster and encourage those actions?

1.5 Student Interview: Attitudes and Environment

In this interview you will prepare interview questions in three areas: (1) students' attitudes toward mathematics, (2) the typical math environment, and (3) what learning environment preferences students have. In advance, write two or three questions in each area. You may want to pull some of your questions from the ones below. Each question can be followed with a "Why?" or "Why not?"

<table>
<tr><td colspan="2" align="center">Fourth-Grade Attitudinal Questions</td></tr>
<tr>
<td>
1. Do you think everybody can do well in math if they try?
2. Are you good at mathematics?
3. Do you like solving mathematics problems?
4. What do you notice about other students who you think are good at math?
5. Is math mostly memorization?
6. Is math useful for solving everyday problems?
</td>
<td>
7. Is there only one correct way to solve most math problems?
8. Do people use math in their jobs?
9. If you get stuck on a math problem, what should you do?
10. Can someone not good at math get better at math? How?
</td>
</tr>
</table>

Interview Questions	Responses from Student
Student's attitude	
Typical math class	
Learning preferences	

Answer these questions after completing the interview.

1. How do you think the classroom environment affects students' attitudes?

2. How do you think students' attitudes toward mathematics affect their success in learning mathematics?

1.6 Teaching: Implementing Mathematical Practice 1

Mathematical Practice 1: Make sense of problems and persevere in solving them.

Mathematically proficient students start by explaining to themselves the meaning of a problem and looking for entry points to its solution. They analyze givens, constraints, relationships, and goals. They make conjectures about the form and meaning of the solution and plan a solution pathway rather than simply jumping into a solution attempt. They consider analogous problems, and try special cases and simpler forms of the original problem in order to gain insight into its solution. They monitor and evaluate their progress and change course if necessary. . . . Mathematically proficient students check their answers to problems using a different method, and they continually ask themselves, "Does this make sense?" They can understand the approaches of others to solving complex problems and identify correspondences between different approaches.*

For this experience, the goal is to teach a lesson that focuses on making sense and on perseverance for all students. This means that you plan ways to ensure that all students contribute to every lesson. Specifically, your lesson or activity should have these characteristics:

1. The task has multiple entry points (different ways it can be solved).
2. The task is complex enough that students must make decisions about how to solve the problem (the constraints, relationships of aspects within the problem).
3. The task and your planned questions require students to make conjectures (e.g., Does this always work? When will it work? When is this true?).
4. The task and your lesson plan encourage students to use a different strategy to check their work.
5. Your questions focus students' attention on analyzing and comparing each other's strategies for solving the problem and seeing connections among the strategies.

What you need to do:

1. Find an appropriate task for the age and experiences and needs of your students.
2. Create a three-phase lesson (before, during, and after).
3. In each lesson phase, include question prompts related to the task and to Mathematical Practice 1.
4. Teach the lesson to the class.
5. Write a brief reflection on (1) how successful the lesson was in meeting its objectives and (2) how the activity served to communicate expectations that all students are to be engaged in making sense of mathematics and persevering in solving math problems.

Possible alternative or addition: Try out the lesson with one small group of students.

*Excerpt from *Common Core State Standards.* Copyright © 2010 National Governors Association Center for Best Practices and Council of Chief State School Officers. All rights reserved.

Title of Lesson:	Source/Citation:

Mathematics Learning Objectives:

Lesson Plan

Before

Questions focused on Mathematical Practice 1:

During

Questions focused on Mathematical Practice 1:

After

Questions focused on Mathematical Practice 1:

Reflection

1. Did each student learn what you intended for the math objectives? Describe evidence and include samples of student work.
2. Did each student learn what you intended for Mathematical Practice 1? What is your evidence?

1.7 Project: Assessing School Environment

The focus of this project is to find out the ways the school advocates for the learning of mathematics. Use the prompts below to help you prepare a report on the way your school promotes the importance of learning mathematics. You may interview teachers and/or the principal. Some of the questions you will be able to answer simply by walking around the school and observing. Once you have completed your inquiries in the school, prepare a brief report highlighting the ways the school supports the learning of mathematics and your suggestions for additional support.

Areas of Inquiry	Descriptions and Notes
Parent/community involvement • How are families involved in math instruction (e.g., Back to School Nights, Family Math, tutoring, problems of the week)?	
Displays of math • How are hallway and classroom bulletin boards used to showcase math? • Based on the displays, what seems to be important about math?	
Views of faculty/staff • What do the principal and/or teachers feel are the priorities for math in the school?	
Resources • Does the library have resources for teaching math? Children's books for teaching math? Support for students? • Does the school have classroom sets of calculators? Manipulatives? Computers? • What is the school's math curriculum based on (e.g., problem-based, aligned with standards, skill practice)?	
School goals • What are the school objectives for math for the year? • How do they plan on meeting these goals? • How are students assessed and their progress monitored?	

2 Professional and Pedagogical Knowledge: Planning

Field Experiences

2.1 Teacher Interview: Selecting Goals and Objectives

2.2 Observation: Evidence of Higher-Level Thinking

2.3 Teaching: Level of Cognitive Demand

2.4 Teaching: Worthwhile Task Evaluation

2.5 Teaching: Incorporating the Standards for Mathematical Practice

2.6 Teaching: Planning a Problem-Based Lesson

2.7 Teaching: Using Children's Literature in Math Teaching

Standards Alignment

NCATE

Standard 1: Knowledge, Skills, and Professional Dispositions
1c. Professional and Pedagogical Knowledge and Skills

Teacher candidates reflect a thorough understanding of professional and pedagogical knowledge and skills delineated in professional, state, and institutional standards. They develop meaningful learning experiences to facilitate learning for all students. They reflect on their practice and make necessary adjustments to enhance student learning. They know how students learn and how to make ideas accessible to them. They consider school, family, and community contexts in connecting concepts to students' prior experience and applying the ideas to real-world problems (NCATE, 2008, p. 18).*

NCTM

Learning Principle

Students must learn mathematics with understanding, actively building new knowledge from experience and prior knowledge (NCTM, 2000, p. 20).

Curriculum Principle

A curriculum is more than a collection of activities: it must be coherent, focused on important mathematics, and well articulated across the grades (NCTM, 2000, p. 14).

The revised standards for teaching and learning mathematics in *Mathematics Teaching Today* (NCTM, 2007) addresses classroom environment in **Standard 2 (Knowledge of Student Mathematical Learning):**

Teachers of mathematics must know and recognize the importance of—

- What is known about the ways students learn mathematics;
- Methods of supporting students as they struggle to make sense of mathematical concepts and procedures;
- Ways to help students build on informal mathematical understandings;
- A variety of tools for use in mathematical investigation and the benefits and limitations of those tools; and
- Ways to stimulate engagement and guide the exploration of the mathematical processes of problem solving, reasoning and proof, communication, connections, and representations. (p. 25)[†]

Elementary and Middle School Mathematics

Chapters 3 and 4 provide many suggestions and strategies for effective planning.

*Excerpts from the *Professional Standards for the Accreditation of Teacher Preparation Institutions* (2008) reprinted with permission from the National Council for Accreditation of Teacher Education. All rights reserved.

†Excerpts from *Principles and Standards for School Mathematics* listed with the permission of the National Council of Teachers of Mathematics (NCTM). Copyright © 2000 by the National Council of Teachers of Mathematics. All rights reserved. NCTM does not endorse the content or validity of these alignments.

Name: _____

Title of field experience: _____

Rubric

Note: This rubric is focused on planning, and can be used to assess/provide feedback for any of the field experience activities in Chapter 2.

Indicators	Target	Acceptable	Developing
1. Aligning goals and objectives with standards	Accurately and articulately describes appropriate goals and objectives aligned to standards (local/state/national) and is coherent and focused on important mathematics.	Accurately and articulately describes appropriate goals aligned to standards (local/state/national), though detail or depth related to focus on important mathematics could be more specific.	Provides limited or no evidence of goals and objectives aligned to standards (local/state/national), or the goals and objectives are aligned but do not focus on important mathematics.
2. Selecting tasks for critical thinking	Describes a learning activity appropriate for student learning that will foster higher-level thinking, multiple entry points, and opportunities for students to justify, make conjectures, and make connections among mathematical ideas.	Identifies a learning activity appropriate for student learning, but is not clear on how the task will promote higher-level thinking.	Provides limited or no evidence of a learning activity appropriate for student learning and higher-level thinking is not addressed.
3. Linking learning to students' prior knowledge and experiences	Plans questions and activities that elicit students' prior knowledge and experiences.	Plans questions and activities that elicit students' prior knowledge and experiences.	Makes some connections to students' experiences in at least one phase of the lesson plan.
4. Designing a problem-based lesson	Designs a lesson that has a clear structure, and there is strong coherence across the lesson phases (before, during, and after), each phase supports the learning goals, and each phase includes explicit attempts to engage all learners.	Designs a lesson that has a clear structure, the lesson phases (before, during, and after) are mostly coherent and focused on the learning goals; engaging students in each phase is addressed, but it is not clear how all students will be engaged.	Designs a lesson that has elements of a coherent lesson, but lacks details to ensure that it (a) is well structured, (b) is aligned across lesson phases (before, during, and after); (c) that each phase focuses on the learning goals; or (d) that all students will be engaged.

Comments: _____

_____

_____

_____

2.1 Teacher Interview: Selecting Goals and Objectives

The following is the beginning of an interview protocol to learn how a teacher determines goals and objectives of lessons. You may want to add your own questions, based on your state's specific standards and testing.

1. In your long-term planning, what resources do you use in deciding the topics that you will cover in a year?

2. Are you familiar with the NCTM *Principles and Standards*? Are they used in your planning? How?

3. Are you familiar with [our state standards]? Are they used in your planning? How?

4. Does [this school district] have grade-level expectations or other guidelines about what to teach?

5. Can you describe goals and objectives you would have for a single lesson (like one you are teaching this week)?

6. How is student learning used to determine your lesson objectives?

7. How do you make the objectives accessible and challenging for the wide range of skills and interests of students in your classroom?

2.2 Observation: Evidence of Higher-Level Thinking

Incorporating higher-level thinking into teaching requires careful planning. Higher-level thinking can be defined in a variety of ways. Most commonly, it is used to distinguish between knowledge questions and those that involve analysis, application, and so on. You can usually distinguish between higher-level and lower-level thinking by the level of discussion and effort that is required to solve the task. In this observation, focus on the opportunities for students to engage in higher-level thinking.

1. Did the teacher encourage higher-level mathematical thinking? If so, what were some of the teacher's actions? Cite specific examples and strategies (questions posed, tasks presented, etc.).

2. Did the students make conjectures or engage in mathematical arguments? Were they expected to defend or support their arguments and conjectures? How do you know? Describe the students' actions in this lesson.

3. Circle any of the verbs below that you think describe the activities students were asked to do during the lesson.

explore	investigate	conjecture	solve	justify
represent	formulate	discover	construct	verify
explain	predict	develop	describe	use

4. To what extent were *all* students expected to use higher-level thinking? In other words, when a question or task was posed, what did the teacher do to ensure all students were thinking about and answering the question? How was the classroom structured so that all students were engaged?

5. What tools (technology, manipulatives, visuals, etc.) were used to support higher-level thinking?

2.3 Teaching: Level of Cognitive Demand

Use the levels of cognitive demand (see pages 36–37 of *Elementary and Middle School Mathematics* for details) to evaluate a task or lesson. You can find tasks or lessons in the textbook used in the classroom or school where you are placed, a K–8 math textbook series available at your college or university, a mathematics teacher resource book (such as the *Navigations* series), and websites that post K–8 mathematics activities.

Review the descriptors below. Highlight the elements that are true for the task or lesson you have reviewed.

Levels of Cognitive Demand
Low-Level Cognitive Demand
Memorization Tasks   • Involve either producing previously learned facts, rules, formulas, or definitions or memorizing   • Are routine—involving exact reproduction of previously learned procedure   • Have no connection to related concepts
Procedures Without Connections Tasks   • Specifically call for use of the procedure   • Are straightforward, with little ambiguity about what needs to be done and how to do it   • Have no connection to related concepts   • Are focused on producing correct answers rather than developing mathematical understanding   • Require no explanations or explanations—focus on the procedure only
High-Level Cognitive Demand
Procedures with Connections Tasks   • Focus students' attention on the use of procedures for the purpose of developing deeper levels of understanding of mathematical concepts and ideas   • Suggest general procedures that have close connections to underlying conceptual ideas   • Are usually represented in multiple ways (e.g., visuals, manipulatives, symbols, problem situations)   • Require that students engage with the conceptual ideas that underlie the procedures in order to successfully complete the task
Doing Mathematics Tasks   • Require complex and nonalgorithmic thinking (i.e., nonroutine—there is not a predictable, known approach)   • Require students to explore and to understand the nature of mathematical concepts, processes, or relationships   • Demand self-monitoring or self-regulation of one's own cognitive processes   • Require students to access relevant knowledge in working through the task   • Require students to analyze the task and actively examine task constraints that may limit possible solution strategies and solutions   • Require considerable cognitive effort

Source: Adapted from Smith, M. S., & Stein, M. K (1998). Selecting and Creating Mathematical Tasks: From Research to Practice. *Mathematics Teaching in the Middle School*, 3(5): 344–350. Reprinted with permission.

1. Describe your overall evaluation of whether this task/lesson has the potential to engage students in higher-level thinking._____

   _____

   _____

2. What adaptations can you make to the task or lesson in order to increase the higher-level thinking potential?_____

   _____

2.4 Teaching: Worthwhile Task Evaluation

Using the prompts below, adapted from the *Professional Standards for Teaching Mathematics*, Standard 1 (NCTM, 1991), rate an activity from an elementary or middle school mathematics textbook series. Add comments, as appropriate. You can also use this template to contrast a parallel activity in another textbook series as a way to compare textbook programs.

1 = No evidence of this element in the lesson/activity, and/or the activity does not lend itself to having this element built in.
2 = This element is included in minor ways, or it appears that incorporating this element is possible.
3 = This element is evident in this lesson and is important to the success of the lesson.
4 = This element is central to this lesson or explicit in the design of the lesson.

Standard 1: Worthwhile Mathematical Tasks	Score				Comments
Task is based on . . .					
1. Sound and significant mathematics	1	2	3	4	
2. Knowledge of students' understandings, interests, and experiences	1	2	3	4	
3. Knowledge of the range of ways that diverse students learn mathematics	1	2	3	4	
And . . .					
4. Engages students' intellect	1	2	3	4	
5. Develops students' mathematical understanding and skills	1	2	3	4	
6. Stimulates students to make connections and develop a coherent framework for mathematical ideas	1	2	3	4	
7. Calls for problem formulation, problem solving, and mathematical reasoning	1	2	3	4	
8. Promotes communication about mathematics	1	2	3	4	
9. Represents mathematics as an ongoing human activity	1	2	3	4	
10. Displays sensitivity to and draws on students' diverse background experiences and dispositions	1	2	3	4	
11. Promotes the development of all students' dispositions to do mathematics	1	2	3	4	

2.5 Teaching: Incorporating the Standards for Mathematical Practice

Select one of the Standards for Mathematical Practice (for details, see Appendix A in *Elementary and Middle School Mathematics* or go to www.corestandards.org/the-standards/mathematics/introduction/ standards-for-mathematical-practice). For the practice you have selected, design a lesson with questions in each lesson phase that address the development of the related student proficiencies. The following table (which is also Table 1.2 in *Elementary and Middle School Mathematics*) provides guidance in what students must be doing in order to develop proficiency in each practice. Use the lesson plan template in 1.6 (set up to focus on Mathematics Practice 1, so easily adapted to any practice) or the one in 2.6.

The Standards for Mathematical Practice from the *Common Core State Standards*	
K–8 Students Should Be Able To:	
Make sense of problems and persevere in solving them	• Explain the meaning of a problem • Describe possible approaches to a solution • Consider similar problems to gain insights • Use concrete objects or illustrations to think about and solve problems • Monitor and evaluate their progress and change strategy if needed • Check their answers using a different method
Reason abstractly and quantitatively	• Explain the relationship between quantities in problem situations • Represent situations using symbols (e.g., writing expressions or equations) • Create representations that fit the problem • Use flexibly the different properties of operations and objects
Construct viable arguments and critique the reasoning of others	• Understand and use assumptions, definitions, and previous results to explain or justify solutions • Make conjectures by building a logical set of statements • Analyze situations and use counterexamples • Justify conclusions in a way that is understandable to teachers and peers • Compare two possible arguments for strengths and weaknesses
Model with mathematics	• Apply mathematics to solve problems in everyday life • Make assumptions and approximations to simplify a problem • Identify important quantities and use tools to map their relationships • Reflect on the reasonableness of their answer based on the context of the problem
Use appropriate tools strategically	• Consider a variety of tools and choose the appropriate tool (e.g., manipulative, ruler, technology) to support their problem solving • Use estimation to detect possible errors • Use technology to help visualize, explore, and compare information
Attend to precision	• Communicate precisely using clear definitions and appropriate mathematics language • State the meanings of symbols • Specify appropriate units of measure and labels of axes • Use a degree of precision appropriate for the problem context
Look for and make use of structure	• Explain mathematical patterns or structures • Shift perspective and see things as single objects or as composed of several objects • Explain why and when properties of operations are true in a context
Look for and express regularity in repeated reasoning	• Notice if calculations are repeated and use information to solve problems • Use and justify the use of general methods or shortcuts • Self-assess to see whether a strategy makes sense as they work, checking for reasonableness prior to getting the answer

Source: Adapted from Council of Chief State School Officers. (2010). *Common Core State Standards.* Copyright © 2010 National Governors Association Center for Best Practices and Council of Chief State School Officers. All rights reserved.

2.6 Teaching: Planning a Problem-Based Lesson

Use the ten-step procedure to help you plan a problem-based lesson. Refer to *Elementary and Middle School Mathematics*, pages 59–63, for explanations of each step.

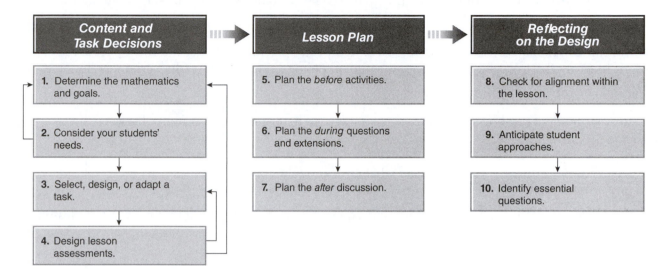

The next page provides a lesson planning template for a problem-based lesson. Keep in mind that it may not be developed sequentially. Typically, as stated above, you start with a math goal. A teacher to whom you've been assigned may say, "Please do a lesson on area of rectangles." Or you may not have any restrictions on what to teach, in which case, you will likely start with the state standards (or national standards) for that grade level.

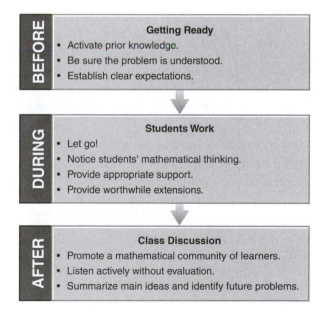

Lesson Planning Template

Lesson Title: _____   **Grade:** _____

Alignment with State Standards: List the grade level expectations from your state that align with this lesson.

Mathematics Goals: Describe the exact learning expectations for students. You must phrase the expectations in a way that you will be able to say a student did or did not learn it (the verb must be something you can observe).

> **Example:** Students will be able to *explain* a strategy for determining if a number between 10 and 50 is even or odd.
>
> **Non-example:** Students will *understand* what even and odd numbers are.

Students' Needs: What prior knowledge and experiences do students have that relate to the lesson goals?

Materials: List transparencies, manipulatives, handouts, and so forth.

> **Lesson Plan**
>
> **Before:** Describe how you will introduce the activity or problem. Consider questions that will elicit students' prior knowledge needed for this activity, get students curious about the task, and/or relate to their personal background or interests. In addition, consider giving directions for getting started on the focus task.
>
> **During:** Describe the expected actions of the students during this phase. What are they to be doing? How are you making sure each child is accountable? What will you ask students as you observe? (Ask good questions related to your objectives; don't just say "good job!") Describe possible extensions or challenges you will have ready for early finishers.
>
> **After:** This is the most important part of a problem-based lesson! What questions will you ask students that will help them understand the mathematics they explored in their task or activity? How will you structure those questions (e.g., think-pair-share, share with an "elbow partner") so that all students will participate in answering each question? Will students be presenting findings? How will this be structured?

Assessment: How will you determine who knows which objectives? Describe the tools, handouts, and techniques you will use.

Accommodations: What strategies will you use to support the diverse needs of students in the class?

2.7 Teaching: Using Children's Literature in Math Teaching

For this teaching experience, you will share a piece of children's literature as an entry point into a problem-based lesson. There are hundreds of excellent books at every grade level. Preferably, you will start by identifying a math topic. The teacher may suggest a topic. Then you will find a book that is a good match. The book will serve as the first part of the *before* part of your lesson, followed by a problem that you will pose from the book. A shortened lesson plan template is provided on the next page to help you.

Resources

Where do you find the right book? There are many places to find lists of children's books for teaching mathematics. Here are a few:

1. See "Literature Connections" sections at the ends of Chapters 8–23 in *Elementary and Middle School Mathematics*.
2. The NCTM journals *Teaching Children Mathematics* and *Mathematics Teaching in the Middle School* often have articles offering good children's books to use in math instruction.
3. Go to University of Missouri eThemes (http://ethemes.missouri.edu/themes/1154) to view their links for math in children's literature, or search online for other sources.
4. Use the Math & Literature books originated by Marilyn Burns (Math Solutions Publications). Also, the Math Solutions website has many ideas.
5. The librarian in your school's media center can be a great resource. Describe the lesson you want to teach and he or she can often point you to several books that are in the library.

Recommendations

Remember that children's literature is not just picture books or fictional stories. Students enjoy poetry, news articles, and nonfiction books (like World Records books).

In selecting the book, poem, or article that you are going to read, it is important to consider the experience and interests of your students. If, for example, you have many Latino/a students, you might pick a book that has a Latina heroine. Be sensitive to the cultural, economic, and family backgrounds of your students.

A book (or poem) is to be enjoyed. Try not to stop repeatedly during the story. If you want students to pick up a detail, go back after you have read and reread particular passages.

If the literature is too long, which is more likely a problem in grades 4–8, you can read the start of the book and skip to the aspect you want to read, but provide opportunities for students to read the entire book. Another option is to tell the story as a storyteller, reading only the passage related to the math problem you have selected.

Literature and Math Lesson Template

Lesson Title: _____   Grade: _____

Children's Book: _____

Author(s): _____

Brief Description of Story:

Goal of the Lesson (math concept):

Objectives:

Materials:

Lesson Plan

Before: What will you ask students prior to reading the book? What will you ask them following the story?

Write the problem-solving task as you will pose it to the students (it must relate to the book you read):

During:

After: How will students be presenting findings? How will this be related to the story that was read to them?

Field Experience Guide: Resources for Teachers of Elementary and Middle School Mathematics © Pearson Education, Inc., 2013

3 Content Knowledge

Field Experiences

3.1 Observation: Conceptual and Procedural Knowledge

3.2 Observation: Mathematical Proficiency

3.3 Teacher Interview: Selecting a Worthwhile Task

3.4 Student Interview: Assessing Mathematical Proficiency

3.5 Teaching: Create a Web of Ideas

3.6 Teaching: Design (and Teach) a Lesson

3.7 Reflection: Student Understanding

Standards Alignment

NCATE

Standard 1: Knowledge, Skills, and Professional Dispositions
1a. Content Knowledge

Teacher candidates have in-depth knowledge of the content that they plan to teach as described in professional, state, and institutional standards. They demonstrate their knowledge through inquiry, critical analysis, and synthesis of the subject (NCATE, 2008, p. 16).*

NCTM

NCTM Content Standards: Number, Algebra, Geometry, Measurement, Data Analysis and Probability

The revised standards for teaching and learning mathematics in *Mathematics Teaching Today* (NCTM, 2007) addresses content in two standards:

Standard 1 (Knowledge of Mathematics and General Pedagogy)

Teachers of mathematics should have a deep knowledge of—

- Sound and significant mathematics;
- Theories of student intellectual development across the spectrum of diverse learners;
- Modes of instruction and assessment; and
- Effective communication and motivational strategies. (p. 19)

Standard 3 (Worthwhile Mathematical Tasks)

The teacher of mathematics should design learning experiences and pose tasks that are based on sound and significant mathematics and that—

- Engage students' intellect;
- Develop mathematical understandings and skills;
- Stimulate students to make connections and develop a coherent framework for mathematical ideas;
- Call for problem formulation, problem solving, and mathematical reasoning;
- Promote communication about mathematics;
- Represent mathematics as an ongoing human activity; and
- Display sensitivity to, and draw on, students' diverse background experiences and dispositions. (pp. 32–33)†

*Excerpts from the *Professional Standards for the Accreditation of Teacher Preparation Institutions* (2008) reprinted with permission from the National Council for Accreditation of Teacher Education. All rights reserved.

†Excerpts from *Mathematics Teaching Today* listed with the permission of the National Council of Teachers of Mathematics (NCTM). Copyright © 2007 by the National Council of Teachers of Mathematics. All rights reserved. NCTM does not endorse the content or validity of these alignments.

Elementary and Middle School Mathematics

Chapter 2 provides lots of suggestions for developing content knowledge.

- Teaching should reflect constructivist learning theory, allowing students opportunities to construct or build meaning.
- Understanding can be defined as a measure of the quality and quantity of connections that an idea has with existing ideas.
- Mathematical knowledge includes both conceptual knowledge and procedural knowledge.
- Manipulatives and physical materials can support students' development of new knowledge.

Part II of the Field Guide includes lessons for each content standard that may be used for the experiences provided in this section.

Name: _____

Title of field experience: _____

Rubric

Note: This rubric is focused on content knowledge, and can be used to assess/provide feedback for any of the field experience activities in Chapter 3.

Indicators	Target	Acceptable	Developing
1. Displaying current knowledge of content and pedagogy through instructional practices	Describes specific aspects of content related to a task or lesson that demonstrates strong content knowledge through critical analysis and synthesis of the subject.	Identifies some aspects of content related to a task or lesson that demonstrates content knowledge through critical analysis and synthesis of the subject.	Describes limited analysis of content related to a task or lesson; limited evidence to demonstrate content knowledge through critical analysis and synthesis of the subject.
2. Using instructional practices to promote student engagement for development of mathematical proficiency	Describes specific and significant opportunities for students to develop conceptual and procedural mathematical knowledge and mathematical proficiency.	Identifies opportunities for students to develop conceptual and procedural mathematical knowledge and mathematical proficiency.	Identifies some opportunities for students to develop conceptual and procedural mathematical knowledge or mathematical proficiency.
3. Applying relational understanding of content to address student prior knowledge and misconceptions	Describes the relational understandings of the content and explicitly connects this analysis to related prior knowledge or experiences for developing the relational understanding for students.	Describes the relational understandings of the content and includes prior knowledge or experiences for developing the relational understanding for students, though connections are not explicitly made.	Describes the relational understandings of the content but does not connect this analysis to related prior knowledge or experiences for developing the relational understanding for students.

Comments: _____

_____

_____

_____

3.1 Observation: Conceptual and Procedural Knowledge

This observation is for a whole class math lesson. Take notes throughout the lesson, recording the questions and tasks the teacher poses and the actions and responses of the students.

> *Conceptual knowledge* of mathematics consists of logical relationships constructed internally and existing in the mind as a part of a network of ideas.
>
> *Procedural knowledge* of mathematics is knowledge of the rules and the procedures that one uses in carrying out routine mathematical tasks and also the symbolism that is used to represent mathematics.

Learning Objectives

1. After watching the lesson, list what you determined to be the learning objectives of the lesson.

2. Which of the objectives are conceptual? Procedural? Both? Explain.

Questioning

3. In what ways do the teacher's questions promote conceptual knowledge? Give examples of questions the teacher used.

4. In what ways do the teacher's questions promote development of procedural knowledge? Give examples of questions the teacher used.

Student Engagement

5. What were the students doing during the lesson that would help them develop conceptual knowledge? Give examples of activities, actions, or explanations you observed students doing.

6. What were the students doing during the lesson that would help them develop procedural knowledge? Give examples of activities, actions, or explanations you observed students doing.

Analysis

Read your notes on this lesson and your responses to the questions above. Respond to the following:

1. Do you feel there was an appropriate balance between concepts and procedures? Explain.

2. What would you do to enhance students' conceptual knowledge in this lesson?

3. What would you do to enhance students' procedural knowledge in this lesson?

3.2 Observation: Mathematical Proficiency

Record notes throughout a lesson in the appropriate box in the table. After completing the observation, add to your notes, as appropriate. You may want to focus on just one category, or a subset of the five strands.

Mathematical Proficiency from *Adding It Up* (National Research Council, 2001)
Conceptual Understanding Standards for Mathematical Practice* 1. Make sense of problems and persevere in solving them 7. Look for and make use of structure To what extent do the learners understand the concepts, operations, or relations in the lesson?   What evidence do you see that students are generating their own strategies based on what they know and that they are seeking to understand other students' strategies?   To what extent are students noticing generalized ideas based on the problems they are working?
Procedural Fluency Standards for Mathematical Practice: 2. Reason abstractly and quantitatively 6. Attend to precision 7. Look for and make sense of structure To what extent do students carry out procedures flexibly, accurately, efficiently, and appropriately?   In what ways are students connecting procedures to concepts?   To what extent are students applying their own strategies to solving procedures and deciding when those approaches are going to work and when they will not?

* Excerpts from Council of Chief State School Officers. (2010). *Common Core State Standards.* Copyright © 2010 National Governors Association Center for Best Practices and Council of Chief State School Officers. All rights reserved.

Mathematical Proficiency from *Adding It Up* (National Research Council, 2001)

Strategic Competence

Standards for Mathematical Practice:

4. Model with mathematics

5. Use appropriate tools strategically

To what extent do students demonstrate that they can formulate, represent, and solve problems?

To what extent do students select and use appropriate tools (e.g., manipulatives, calculators, drawings) to support their thinking?

Adaptive Reasoning

Standards for Mathematical Practice:

2. Reason abstractly and quantitatively

3. Construct viable arguments and critique the reasoning of others

8. Look for and express regularity in repeated reasoning

In what ways does the lesson provide opportunities for students to consider each other's approaches to the problem and determine if the solutions are reasonable?

In what ways are tasks or questions used to help students find patterns or generalizations in their solutions?

Productive Disposition

Standards for Mathematical Practice

1. Make sense of problems and persevere in solving them

8. Look for and express regularity in repeated reasoning

To what extent do students demonstrate a "habit of mind" that mathematics makes sense and is useful?

What strategies are used to encourage students to stick with a problem, try different strategies, and consider if their solution makes sense?

Reflection: Write a summary paragraph on the inclusion of the mathematical proficiencies and practices in this lesson, including strengths and what you may have added to further emphasize mathematical proficiency.

3.3 Teacher Interview: Selecting a Worthwhile Task

The following is an interview that should take no more than 30 minutes. When asking if and when you might conduct an interview, tell the teacher that the interview will focus on a task, activity, or lesson they have recently selected to use with their students. You may use any or all of the questions below, or you can add your own questions.

1. Describe the mathematics task that you recently selected to use with your students.

2. Why did you select this particular task?

3. What do you expect students to learn once they have participated in this lesson?

4. Do you feel that it represents the concepts and procedures appropriately? Explain.

5. Is this task appropriately challenging for all the students? Explain.

6. In what ways were/are the students engaged in the task? In what ways are they "doing" mathematics?

7. What student characteristics did you consider when you chose this task? In other words, how does this task fit your students' background, including their prior knowledge, culture, and learning needs?

8. Does the task appeal to your students' interests, dispositions, and experiences? Will you/did you alter it in any way to make it more appealing?

9. In general, what do you feel are the most important considerations when selecting a math activity, lesson, or task? What makes a task worthwhile?

Add your own questions:

10.

11.

12.

3.4 Student Interview: Assessing Mathematical Proficiency

Knowing how to calculate 23×4 and understanding multiplication are not synonymous. In fact, the former is a subset of the latter. This interview involves finding out what a student knows about one of the operations for whole numbers or for rational numbers.

1. Select a type of number and an operation from the lists below.

Type of Number:	**Operation:**
Whole Number	Addition
Fractions	Subtraction
Decimals	Multiplication
Integers	Division

2. Complete the Link Sheet on the following page yourself.

3. Prepare questions and materials. Review the Mathematical Proficiency table (p. 20) and design questions to see the extent to which the student has developed proficiency for this topic. Collect materials that students may wish to use in completing the Link Sheet (grid paper, base ten blocks, etc.). Young students will need more room to write, so you will need to adapt the template accordingly.

4. Ask the student to complete the Link Sheet.

5. Write a summary of the knowledge the student has related to the topic you selected, including the following points:

   - Student's understanding (related to the content and the mathematical practices)
   - Gaps in the student's understanding
   - What experiences you believe the student needs, based on these results

For more about Link Sheets, see Shield, M. J., & Swinson, K. V. (1996). The link sheet: A communication aid for clarifying and developing mathematical ideas and processes. In P. C. Elliott & M. J. Kenney (Eds.), *Communication in Mathematics, K–12 and Beyond: 1996 Yearbook.* Reston, VA: NCTM.

Link Sheet

Topic: _____

Mathematics Example	Situation/Context

Illustration/Model/Picture	My Explanation of the Operation

Source: Adapted from Shield, M. J., & Swinson, K. V. (1996). "The Link Sheet: A Communication Aid for Clarifying and Developing Mathematical Ideas and Processes." In P. C. Elliott & M. J. Kenney (Eds.), *Communication in Mathematics, K–12 and Beyond: 1996 Yearbook* (pp. 35–39). Reston, VA: NCTM.

3.5 Teaching: Create a Web of Ideas

In order to assist students in using prior knowledge and developing a relational understanding, it is essential that the teacher first analyzes and understands the relationship among mathematics concepts. See *Elementary and Middle School* Mathematics, pages 24–26, for more details on relational understanding.

For this field experience, you will be creating a Web of Ideas, sometimes called a Concept Map. Your topic may be one that fits any of the following criteria:

1. A topic you plan to teach in your field experience this semester
2. A topic provided in Part II of this book
3. A topic in the chapter you are reading in *Elementary and Middle School Mathematics Methods*
4. A topic assigned by your supervisor or instructor

Web of Ideas for _____

(Mathematics Concept)

3.6 Teaching: Design (and Teach) a Lesson

The purpose of this lesson is to engage students in a conceptually based activity and to assess what they know about the topic prior to and after the activity. You may select an activity from Part II of this book, or from any other resource. For guidance on what to write for each lesson part, see *Elementary and Middle School Mathematics*, "Planning a Problem-Based Lesson," pages 59–64.

Title of Activity:	
Mathematics Concept(s)	
Conceptual knowledge:	
Procedural knowledge:	
Before	
Questions/input to determine student understanding (prior knowledge) of selected concept:	
How I will engage the students in the lesson:	
How I will introduce the focus task (communicate clear expectations):	
During	
Questions I will ask as students are working on their task to help them focus on the objectives (e.g., probe their understanding, help them get through a "struggle point"):	
How I will observe and assess:	
After	
Questions I will ask to see if they know the concepts and procedures listed above (include how students will respond to questions so that every child is accountable):	
How I will have students summarize the main ideas of the lesson:	

3.7 Reflection: Student Understanding

This reflection is a natural follow-up to the lesson plan provided in this section, but can also be used to follow any teaching experience.

Upon completion of teaching your lesson, respond to the following questions. Attach your lesson plan to this reflection.

1. What math concepts did you, the teacher, have to understand in order to teach this lesson well?

2. To what extent did students understand the procedures and concepts prior to the start of the lesson? (What did they already know?)

3. What was challenging for the students to understand?

4. What did you notice best supported their development of concepts and/or procedures (e.g., teacher actions, use of tools, aspects of the task itself)?

5. If you were to teach a follow-up to this lesson, what would be the focus of the next lesson? How would you build on what you did in this lesson?

6. Based on your own knowledge and your experience from this lesson, what do you feel is the relationship between conceptual and procedural knowledge?

4 Pedagogical Content Knowledge: Instruction

Field Experiences

Standards Alignment

NCATE

Standard 1: Knowledge, Skills, and Professional Dispositions
1b. Pedagogical Content Knowledge and Skills

Teacher candidates reflect a thorough understanding of the relationship of content and content-specific pedagogy delineated in professional, state, and institutional standards. They have in-depth understanding of the subject matter that they plan to teach and are able to provide multiple explanations and instructional strategies so that all students learn. They present the content to students in challenging, clear, and compelling ways, using real-world contexts and integrating technology appropriately (NCATE, 2008, p. 17).*

NCTM

Teaching Principle

Effective mathematics teaching requires understanding what students know and need to learn and then challenging and supporting them to learn it well (NCTM, 2000, p. 16).

Process Standards: Problem Solving, Reasoning and Proof, Communication, Connections, and Representation

See pages 3–4 of *Elementary and Middle School Mathematics* for a brief description of each process standard. The revised standards for teaching and learning mathematics in *Mathematics Teaching Today* (NCTM, 2007) address instruction across all seven standards, most explicitly in **Standard 5 (Discourse):**

The teacher of mathematics should orchestrate discourse by—

- Posing questions and tasks that elicit, engage, and challenge each student's thinking;
- Listening carefully to students' ideas and deciding what to pursue in depth from among the ideas that students generate during a discussion;
- Asking students to clarify and justify their ideas orally and in writing and by accepting a variety of presentation modes;
- Deciding when and how to attach mathematical notation and language to students' ideas;
- Encouraging and accepting the use of multiple representations;
- Making available tools for exploration and analysis;
- Deciding when to provide information, when to clarify an issue, when to model, when to lead, and when to let students wrestle with a difficulty; and
- Monitoring students' participation in discussions and deciding when and how to encourage each student to participate. (p. 45)[†]

Elementary and Middle School Mathematics

Chapter 3 specifically discusses the problem-based approach to teaching mathematics. In addition, all the chapters in Section II (Chapters 8–23) address the specific pedagogical content knowledge (PCK) areas for teaching mathematics.

Name: _____

Title of field experience: _____

Rubric

Note: This rubric is focused on pedagogical content knowledge (specifically instruction), and can be used to assess/provide feedback for any of the field experience activities in Chapter 4.

Indicators	Target	Acceptable	Developing
1. Demonstrating understanding of the processes and practices that engage students in learning important mathematics	Describes or enacts instruction that explicitly addresses the processes and practices that lead to higher-level thinking and student engagement.	Describes or enacts instruction that explicitly addresses some of the processes and practices that lead to higher-level thinking and student engagement.	Describes or enacts instruction that somewhat addresses the processes and practices, but the connection to higher-level thinking and/or student engagement is not developed.
2. Communicating high expectations for learning	Integrates learning objectives into all learning activities, states what the learning expectations are, and includes opportunities for all students to participate and communicate their learning.	Integrates learning objectives into most of the learning activities, states what the learning expectations are, and includes opportunities for most students to participate and communicate their learning.	Integrates learning objectives into at least some of the learning activities, but learning expectations are not clearly stated, and it is not clear that an attention has been given to ensure all students have learned the intended objectives.
3. Demonstrating skill, knowledge, and reflection in teaching	Attends to or incorporates a range of effective practices that ensure high level of student thinking and participation, including explicit attention to grouping and questioning strategies.	Attends to or incorporates some practices that ensure high level of student thinking and participation, including explicit attention to grouping and questioning strategies.	Attends to or incorporates some practices that ensure high level of student thinking and participation, but lacks connections to grouping and questioning strategies.
4. Reflecting on a standards-based mathematics lesson	Describes lesson effectiveness based on student outcomes of mathematical learning.	Identifies some components of an effective lesson based on student outcomes of mathematical learning.	Provides limited evidence of lesson effectiveness using student outcomes of mathematical learning.

Comments: _____

_____

_____

_____

4.1 Observation: The Process Standards

You may observe a video or live classroom for this experience. As you observe, note evidence of each of NCTM's process standards. Following the observation, consider adaptations or additional ideas for incorporating each process standard. The table below can help you to identify each of the processes.

The Five Process Standards from *Principles and Standards for School Mathematics*	
Problem Solving Standard Instructional programs from prekindergarten through grade 12 should enable all students to—	• Build new mathematical knowledge through problem solving • Solve problems that arise in mathematics and in other contexts • Apply and adapt a variety of appropriate strategies to solve problems • Monitor and reflect on the process of mathematical problem solving
Reasoning and Proof Standard Instructional programs from prekindergarten through grade 12 should enable all students to—	• Recognize reasoning and proof as fundamental aspects of mathematics • Make and investigate mathematical conjectures • Develop and evaluate mathematical arguments and proofs • Select and use various types of reasoning and methods of proof
Communication Standard Instructional programs from prekindergarten through grade 12 should enable all students to—	• Organize and consolidate their mathematical thinking through communication • Communicate their mathematical thinking coherently and clearly to peers, teachers, and others • Analyze and evaluate the mathematical thinking and strategies of others • Use the language of mathematics to express mathematical ideas precisely
Connections Standard Instructional programs from prekindergarten through grade 12 should enable all students to—	• Recognize and use connections among mathematical ideas • Understand how mathematical ideas interconnect and build on one another to produce a coherent whole • Recognize and apply mathematics in contexts outside of mathematics
Representation Standard Instructional programs from prekindergarten through grade 12 should enable all students to—	• Create and use representations to organize, record, and communicate mathematical ideas • Select, apply, and translate among mathematical representations to solve problems • Use representations to model and interpret physical, social, and mathematical phenomena

Source: Reprinted with permission from *Principles and Standards for School Mathematics.* Copyright © 2000 by the National Council of Teachers of Mathematics. All rights reserved. Standards are listed with the permission of the National Council of Teachers of Mathematics (NCTM). NCTM does not endorse the content or validity of these alignments.

NCTM Process Standards Observation Template

Process Standard	Evidence	Additional Ideas
Problem solving		
Reasoning and proof		
Communication		
Connections		
Representation		

Summary Reflection

1. What is the relationship between these processes and student engagement?

2. How do students of diverse backgrounds respond to an environment that incorporates the process standards?

4.2 Observation: Classroom Discourse

Classroom discourse includes the ways of representing, thinking, talking, agreeing, and disagreeing in the classroom. Observe the interactions in a classroom (video or live) and use the statements from the *Professional Standards for Teaching Mathematics* and *Mathematics Teaching Today* standard on Discourse to note evidence of discourse (NCTM, 1991, 2007).

Strategies for Orchestrating Discourse	Evidence
Teacher's Role	(Record teacher statements or actions in the appropriate box.)
Pose questions and tasks that elicit, engage, and challenge each student's thinking.	
Listen carefully to students' ideas.	
Ask students to clarify and justify their ideas orally and in writing.	
Decide when and how to attach mathematical notation and language to students' ideas.	
Monitor students' participation in discussions and decide when and how to encourage each student to participate.	
Students' Role	(Record student statements or actions in the appropriate box.)
Listen to, respond to, and question the teacher and each other.	
Use a variety of tools to reason, make connections, solve problems, and communicate.	
Initiate problems and questions.	
Make conjectures and present solutions.	
Explore examples and counterexamples to explore a conjecture.	
Try to convince themselves or others of the validity of particular representations, solutions, conjectures, and answers.	

What do you feel are key teacher actions to develop a classroom with a high level of student involvement in the discourse?

4.3 Observation: Cooperative Groups

Ask your teacher if you can observe the class on a day that he or she is using cooperative groups. The purpose of this observation is twofold: first, for you to identify management strategies for ensuring that each child participates and learns, and second, to analyze the ways cooperative groups can support student learning.

Introducing the Cooperative Learning Activity

1. **Organization.** Describe how the teacher organizes groups (e.g., how many students are in a group? Is there an ability mix? Gender mix? Do students pick their groups?).

2. **Accountability.** Describe what the teacher does to have individual accountability within group work (e.g., are group roles assigned to individuals in each group? Are other strategies used to make sure each individual contributes to the group?).

3. **Management.** Discuss how the teacher organizes the classroom to facilitate cooperative groups (e.g., how does the teacher transition between the whole class and small groups? What does the teacher do while students are working in groups? Are materials accessible to students?).

Choose one group to observe during the cooperative group task. The following questions refer to just the group you selected.

1. **Interaction.** Describe how the members of the group interact (e.g., do students listen to, respond to, and question one another? Does everyone contribute equitably? Do students pose and explore conjectures?).

2. **Support for Learning.** Describe how members of the group interact with someone who doesn't understand or is struggling with an idea (e.g., are they left out? Helped? Does the teacher assist, or expect the team members to help? Does the teacher coach the students on how to help each other?).

3. **Accountability.** Describe the actions of the individuals within the group (e.g., do they interact to make sure each person learns, or do some students rely on others to do the work for them? How do the groups record and report their answers?).

4. **Assessment.** Explain strategies that are used to identify what each individual child has learned (e.g., does the teacher informally interview students while they work? Does he or she use a checklist? Individual recording sheets? How does the teacher know who learned the objectives of the lesson?).

Postobservation Analysis

Based on this observation, readings in *Elementary and Middle School Mathematics*, and your own experiences, respond to the following two questions.

1. Take a position on whether students should or should not learn a new concept in cooperative groups and defend your answer.

2. Describe what you believe to be the critical features for cooperative groups to serve as effective learning communities.

4.4 Teacher Interview: Teaching for Understanding

The purpose of this interview is to learn, from the teacher, how a topic he or she is about to teach ties into other mathematics concepts. In addition, you are to explore the way in which he or she is going to develop the topic so that students make those connections. These two objectives are worded in general questions below, but prior to your interview, you will need to plan three to five more specific questions for each. Chapter 2 in *Elementary and Middle School Mathematics* is a good resource to help you plan and implement this interview.

1. How does the concept relate to the other mathematics concepts that students have learned and will be learning?

    a.

    b.

    c.

    d.

    e.

2. What experiences are you planning/have you planned for the students so that they connect this concept with prior learning and/or real-life contexts?

    a.

    b.

    c.

    d.

    e.

Following your interview, you will need to write up the responses the teacher gave to each question and conclude with a brief paragraph explaining what you learned about (1) the topic you discussed, (2) instructional strategies for that topic that were new, and (3) ideas of your own that would enhance a student's understanding of the topic.

4.5 Student Interview: Learning Mathematics Developmentally

The purpose of this interview is to find out how a student who is learning through a developmental approach views mathematics. You can use this interview with any student. Comparison of the responses from a student using a different approach could be very interesting. Some questions are provided below, but you will need to adapt them for phrasing appropriate for the age level of the student.

Introduce yourself and your purpose: "I am learning how to teach math. You can help me by telling me what you know and think about math. Can I ask you some questions?"

Interview Prompts	Additional/Adapted Questions
Mathematics as a Subject	
If I had no idea what math meant, what would you tell me? What is math?	
What are the important math topics?	
Why do you think you are learning math? How will you use it? Can you give some examples?	
Is there usually one way to solve a problem or more than one way?	
Your teacher says, "It's time for math." What is going to happen (what will you be doing, what will the teacher be doing)?	
Attitudes/Beliefs about Mathematics	
When you visualize someone who is good at math, what kinds of things can this person do?	
Do you think everybody can do well in math if they try?	
Who is good at math?	
Is math something that is useful to know? Why or why not?	
Are you good at math? Why do you think so?	
How is math best learned?	
How do you best learn math?	
Is math your favorite subject?	

4.6 Teaching: Teaching a Small Group

The purpose of this field experience is to give you an opportunity to practice posing a quality task, using good questioning, and observing student thinking. Use this page as a guide in completing this experience. You will turn in (1) your lesson plan, (2) the task you used, and (3) a one- to two-paragraph reflection describing your students' reactions to the task and your own reflections on the task.

1. **Selecting a worthwhile task.** Select one problem that will engage students and lends itself to working together (you might consult the teacher for ideas). You can select from:
   a. Lesson outlines in Part II of this guide
   b. Activities that are provided in Activity boxes in *Elementary and Middle School Mathematics*
   c. A problem-based resource, such as the NCTM *Navigations* series or Illuminations website
2. **Identify the learning objective for the activity.** Describe what students will be able to do after they complete the activity you have selected.
3. **Determine exactly how you will implement the activity for the small group.** Complete a short version of the lesson plan format:

Lesson Plan

Before: Describe how you will introduce the activity or problem. Record questions that you will pose. Plan directions for getting started on the focus task.

During: Describe the expected actions of the students during this phase. What are they to be doing? How will you redirect them if they are stuck, without giving away the challenge of the task? What questions will you ask to extend their thinking?

After: How will students show what they learned from the task? Will each student be presenting what he or she learned?

---

4. **Ask students questions regarding their reactions to the task.** For example, "How difficult did you think the problem was? Did you like being challenged?"

4.7 Teaching: Classroom Discussions—Talk Moves

As described in Chapter 3 of *Elementary and Middle School Mathematics*, using specific talk moves leads to increased student participation (and thinking). For this experience, you are going to incorporate talk moves into a lesson you are teaching. Here are the steps:

1. Review the talk moves below.
2. Select which one(s) you are going to make a point to use (you may want to start with just one).
3. Consider where in your plan you will have opportunities to use this move.
4. Teach the lesson. Audio- or videorecord, if possible.
5. Reflect (see prompts below).

<table>
<tr><th colspan="3">Talk Moves for Classroom Discussions</th></tr>
<tr><th>Talk Moves</th><th>What It Means and Why</th><th>Example Teacher Prompts</th></tr>
<tr><td>1. Revoicing</td><td>This move involves restating the statement as a question in order to clarify, apply appropriate language, and to involve more students. It is an important strategy to reinforce language and enhance comprehension for ELLs.</td><td>"You used the hundreds chart and counted on?"<br>"So, first you recorded your measurements in a table?"</td></tr>
<tr><td>2. Rephrasing</td><td>Asking students to restate someone else's ideas in their own words will ensure that ideas are stated in a variety of ways and encourage students to listen to each other.</td><td>"Who can share what Ricardo just said, but using your own words?"</td></tr>
<tr><td>3. Reasoning</td><td>Rather than restate, as in talk move 2, this move asks the student what they think of the idea proposed by another student.</td><td>"Do you agree or disagree with Johanna? Why?"</td></tr>
<tr><td>4. Elaborating</td><td>This is a request for students to challenge, add on, elaborate, or give an example. It is intended to get more participation from students, deepen student understanding, and provide extensions.</td><td>"Can you give an example?"<br>"Do you see a connection between Julio's idea and Rhonda's idea?"<br>"What if . . ."</td></tr>
<tr><td>5. Waiting</td><td>Ironically, one "talk move" is not to talk. Quiet time should not feel uncomfortable, but should feel like thinking time. If it gets awkward, ask students to pair-share and then try again.</td><td>"This question is important. Let's take some time to think about it."</td></tr>
</table>

Source: Based on Chapin, S., O'Conner, C., & Anderson, N. (2009). *Classroom Discussions: Using Math Talk to Help Students Learn* (2nd ed.). Sausalito, CA: Math Solutions. Reprinted with permission.

Reflection

1. **Using the talk move.** Describe your successes and challenges in implementing this talk move. What will you try next time?
2. **Impact of talk move.** Describe what you noticed in terms of how the talk move altered student engagement and learning in the lesson.

4.8 Teaching: Teaching a Standards-Based Lesson

The focus of this experience is on teaching. Most of the time, teachers do not create a lesson from scratch, but rather take an activity from a textbook or other resource and determine how they will use it with a whole class of students. That is what you will be doing in this field experience.

1. Select one of the Expanded Lessons in Part II of this guide. As an alternative, you can use a full lesson plan from another source that uses a developmental approach to teaching.
2. Consider each component of the lesson, and think of what **teaching strategies** you can use to make the component effective with students. For example, will you have students discuss a key question with a partner? Will you have students write down an idea before asking them to share? Will they use manipulatives?
3. Consider **management** of the lesson. In particular, how long do you plan to spend on each part? How will you plan for transitions from whole class to small groups and back to whole group again? What exact instructions will students need?
4. What **resources** will the students need? Are they easily accessible?
5. After teaching the lesson, reflect on the instructional strategies, management, and resources you planned. What worked? What would you do differently if you were to teach it again? (See 4.9, "Reflection: Reflecting on Teaching and Learning" for a lesson reflection template.)

Putting It All Together

To do a complete lesson cycle using the *Field Experience Guide*, you can:

1. Work with the teacher to determine the mathematics topic and/or the state standard that will be the focus of your lesson.
2. Complete the lesson plan (see 2.6, "Teaching: Planning a Problem-Based Lesson").
3. Submit the lesson to your teacher and/or supervisor for feedback.
4. Teach the lesson to the students.
5. Use 4.10, "Feedback on Teaching" template to get input from the teacher.
6. Complete 4.9, "Reflection: Reflecting on Teaching and Learning." Alternatively, see 3.7, "Reflection: Student Understanding," 5.5, "Reflection: Reactions to Learning with Technology," and 8.7, "Reflection: Meeting the Needs of All Learners."

4.9 Reflection: Reflecting on Teaching and Learning

1. To what extent did the lesson tasks, activities, and/or discussion support the lesson objectives?

2. To what extent was each child engaged throughout the lesson?

3. What instructional strategies seemed effective? Ineffective?

4. What management strategies seemed effective? Ineffective?

5. To what extent were you able to determine if each child learned the objectives? Be specific.

6. What do you feel were the most successful aspects of this lesson?

7. What would you do differently if you were to teach this lesson again?

4.10 Feedback on Teaching

This form is to be used by the classroom teacher and/or your supervisor to observe your teaching (see Chapter 2 of *Elementary and Middle School Mathematics* for more background on each of these categories).

Category	Evidence	Suggestions
Creating a mathematical environment • Students try out ideas • No passive observers • Students take risks		
Posing worthwhile tasks • Task is problematic to students • Students actively look for relationships • Task leads to students learning important math concepts		
Using variety of grouping structures • Pairs, small groups allowed to work together • Individuals in groups are participating • Teacher observing and questioning		
Using models • Manipulatives, calculators, and/or visuals support objectives • Management of tools is effective		
Using discourse and writing • Opportunities to explain thinking verbally • Opportunities to write and/or illustrate ideas • Effective questioning		
Justification of student responses • Students explain how they arrived at the solution • Students justify why it works		
Listening actively • Lesson child centered, not teacher centered • Adequate wait time • Prompts extend students' explanations		
Other		

Observer's Final Comments
Strengths:

Goal(s) for next teaching experience:

5 Pedagogical Content Knowledge: Technology

Field Experiences

5.1 Project: Learning Online
5.2 Project: Evaluating Mathematics Software or Websites
5.3 Teaching: Using a Calculator to Support Learning

5.4 Teaching: Develop a Calculator Learning Center
5.5 Reflection: Reactions to Learning with Technology

Standards Alignment

NCATE

Standard 1: Knowledge, Skills, and Professional Dispositions
1b. Pedagogical Content Knowledge and Skills

Teacher candidates reflect a thorough understanding of the relationship of content and content-specific pedagogy delineated in professional, state, and institutional standards. They have in-depth understanding of the subject matter that they plan to teach and are able to provide multiple explanations and instructional strategies so that all students learn. They present the content to students in challenging, clear, and compelling ways, using real-world contexts and integrating technology appropriately (NCATE, 2008, p. 17).*

NCTM

Technology Principle

Technology is essential in teaching and learning mathematics; it influences the mathematics that is taught and enhances students' learning (NCTM, 2000, p. 24).†

Elementary and Middle School Mathematics

Chapter 7 offers suggestions for using technology.

Name: _____

Title of field experience: _____

Rubric

Note: This rubric is focused on use of technology, and can be used to assess/provide feedback for any of the field experience activities in Chapter 5.

Indicators	Target	Acceptable	Developing
1. Using resources for teaching with technology	Describes high quality mathematical technology resources and software accessible to students and teachers and provides detailed and critical analysis of how the technology can support student learning.	Identifies high quality mathematical technology resources and software accessible to students and teacher, with some critical analysis of how the technology can support student learning.	Identifies mathematical technology resources and software accessible to students and teacher, but no critical analysis of how technology can support student learning.
2. Integrating technology in classroom learning	Selects appropriate technology to support learning goal, and describes specific ways in which that technology will be used to engage students in learning that content.	Selects appropriate technology to support learning goal, and generally describes the ways in which that technology will be used to engage students in learning that content.	Selects technology to support learning goal, but technology may not be the best match for the learning goals, or description does not make the connection between the technology and student learning.
3. Reflecting on teaching and learning with technology	Specifically describes lesson effectiveness related to the use of technology, and connects this reflection to specific data on student learning.	Specifically describes lesson effectiveness related to the use of technology, and connects this reflection to general observations about student learning.	Specifically describes lesson effectiveness related to the use of technology, but does not connect reflection to student learning.

Comments: _____

_____

_____

_____

_____

Field Experience Guide: Resources for Teachers of Elementary and Middle School Mathematics © Pearson Education, Inc., 2013

5.1 Project: Learning Online

For this experience, you may complete Part I, Part II, or both. The NCTM Illuminations website (http://illuminations.nctm.org) and e-Examples (www.nctm.org/standards/content.aspx?id=24600) have various interactive applets that enable you to explore mathematics concepts. In addition, see the resources listed in Chapter 7 of *Elementary and Middle School Mathematics* and in the "Online Resources" at the end of every chapter for excellent online explorations. For this field experience, you will select one of these tasks and explore it.

Part I: Personal Reflections on Online Applets

1. Describe the applet that you explored.
2. What was the learning goal of the applet?
3. Compare and contrast a parallel task that could be done without the use of technology. What would be gained or lost?
4. How do you believe students at the appropriate grade level would respond to doing this applet as their activity for learning about the intended objective(s)?

Part II: Observe a Student Exploring an Online Applet

Find a student (grade 3–8) who is willing to be interviewed. The student might be from the class you have been assigned or another student you know.

1. Explain to the student how to use the applet (not how to solve the problems in the applet).
2. Ask the student to take some time to explore and see if he or she can figure out the task.
3. Upon completion, ask the student (1) what he or she learned from using the applet and (2) what he or she thinks of learning using the computer.
4. Write up your observations of what the student did while exploring the applet, what the student told you, and what you learned about students using technology.

5.2 Project: Evaluating Mathematics Software or Websites

In order to complete this field experience, you will need to ask what math software is used in your assigned school and/or consult your university library to see if there is pre-K–8 math software available to review. The purpose of this experience is to think critically about the learning opportunities that a particular software offers. There is a wide range of quality and as a teacher, you will need to be discerning in making choices for your students. The criteria below are adapted from *Elementary and Middle School Mathematics*, pages 123–124.

Name of software or website: _____

URL for website or publisher of software: _____

Scale: 1 = False   2 = Probably false   3 = Neutral   4 = Probably true   5 = True

Criteria	Rating	Comments
The software or website provides better opportunities to learn than alternative approaches.	1 2 3 4 5	
Students will be engaged with the math content (not the frills).	1 2 3 4 5	
The software or website provides opportunities for problem solving.	1 2 3 4 5	
The program develops conceptual knowledge and supports student understanding of concepts.	1 2 3 4 5	
The program develops procedural knowledge and supports student understanding of skills.	1 2 3 4 5	
The software or website allows the teacher to assess student learning through records and reports.	1 2 3 4 5	
The program is challenging for a wide range of skill levels.	1 2 3 4 5	
The program is equitable in its consideration of gender and culture.	1 2 3 4 5	
The software or website promotes good student interaction and discussion.	1 2 3 4 5	
The software or website has quality supplemental materials, such as blackline masters.	1 2 3 4 5	

5.3 Teaching: Using the Calculator to Support Learning

The calculator is so much more than a tool to improve the speed and accuracy of computation; it is a tool for challenging students and helping them learn. In this field experience, you will teach a lesson that uses the calculator as a tool for learning. Use the Lesson Plan Template from 2.6, "Teaching: Planning a Problem-Based Lesson."

Resources for finding calculator lessons:

1. See activities throughout *Elementary and Middle School Mathematics* (see calculator icons to find the activities employing calculators).
2. The Math Tools website (http://mathforum.org/mathtools) allows you to search by grade level and by the type of technology you wish to use.
3. Texas Instruments has a collection of calculator activities to review (http://education.ti.com/calculators/downloads/US/Activities/).
4. Casio has several calculator activities to review for elementary and middle school (http://edu.casio.com/support/activity/).

5.4 Teaching: Develop a Calculator Learning Center

In this field experience, you will create a calculator-dependent activity that is appropriate for a learning center. A learning center is usually set up in a classroom so that it is always accessible to students who have extra time and are looking for an interesting challenge, or it may be part of a series of learning activities. An effective teacher will provide tasks that extend what is being learned in the classroom.

In order for a learning center to be effective, the tasks should have the following characteristics.

1. **Kid-friendly instructions.** The students should be able to read and follow all instructions without needing clarification from the teacher.
2. **Multidimensional and/or repeatable tasks.** If the task has one solution, a student will complete that task and not want to spend more time in the learning center. See, for example, the Range Game (p. 254 of *Elementary and Middle School Mathematics*), in which the activity can be easily extended by having the student create his or her own Start and Range (or do this with a partner).
3. **Promotion of conceptual development, not merely skill practice.** Notice that the Range Game focuses on estimation and promoting students' understanding of multiplication.
4. **Final product.** Completion of the task should result in a tangible product that is turned in to the teacher.

The template on the next page is intended to be a guide. You can also create your own template. The final product should look intriguing to the age group you are targeting. Without much time invested, you can download artwork from the Web or place other illustrations on the page to increase the visual appeal and perhaps help to clarify the task.

Calculator Learning Center Planning Template

Title:

Topic: Grade:

Instructions (written to student):

Tasks/Problems/Examples:

Extension(s)/Alternatives:

Attach a page entitled "Student Recording Sheet," designed to match the task above.

5.5 Reflection: Reactions to Learning with Technology

After teaching or observing a lesson that uses computers or calculators as a means for learning mathematics, respond to the following prompts.

1. What were the learning objectives of the lesson?

2. In what ways did the technology support or inhibit the learning of those objectives?

3. If technology were not available, what impact would that have had on the lesson?

4. How did students respond to using the technology? Did students respond differently? Explain.

5. Based on this lesson, readings, and your personal beliefs, describe what you think the appropriate use of calculators should be for the grade that you taught or observed.

6 Dispositions

Field Experiences

6.1 Teacher Interview: Communicating with Families

6.2 Parent Interview: What Is Important to You?

6.3 Teaching: Prepare a Family Math Take-Home Activity

6.4 Reflection: Professional Growth

Standards Alignment

NCATE

Standard 1: Knowledge, Skills, and Professional Dispositions
1g. Professional Dispositions

Candidates work with students, families, colleagues, and communities in ways that reflect the professional dispositions expected of professional educators as delineated in professional, state, and institutional standards. Candidates demonstrate behaviors that create caring and supporting learning environments and encourage self-directed learning by all students. Candidates recognize when their own dispositions may need to be adjusted and are able to develop plans to do so (NCATE, 2008, p. 20).*

NCTM

The revised standards for teaching and learning mathematics in *Mathematics Teaching Today* (NCTM, 2007) addresses being a reflective practitioner in **Standard 7 (Reflection on Teaching Practice):**

The teacher of mathematics should engage in ongoing analysis of teaching by—

* Reflecting regularly on what and how they teach;
* Examining effects of the task, discourse, and learning environment on students' mathematical knowledge, skills, and dispositions;
* Seeking to improve their teaching and practice by participating in learning communities beyond their classroom;
* Analyzing and using assessment data to make reasoned decisions about necessary changes in curriculum; and
* Collaborating with colleagues to develop plans to improve instructional programs. (p. 60)[†]

In addition, it is important to pursue professional development.

Elementary and Middle School Mathematics

Chapter 1 in *Elementary and Middle School Mathematics* states well the disposition for excellence in teaching:

The best teachers are always trying to improve their practice through the latest article, the newest book, the most recent conference, or by signing up for the next series of professional development opportunities. These teachers don't say, "Oh, that's what I am already doing"; instead, they identify and celebrate one small tidbit that adds to their repertoire. The best teachers never finish learning all that they need to know, they never exhaust the number of new mental connections that they make, and, as a result, they never see teaching as stale or stagnant. (p. 10)

Name: _____

Title of field experience: _____

Rubric

Note: This rubric is focused on dispositions, and can be used to assess/provide feedback for any of the field experience activities in Chapter 6.

Indicators	Target	Acceptable	Developing
1. Communicating with families	Describes varied methods and means for teacher–parent and parent–teacher communication.	Identifies some methods for teacher–parent and parent–teacher communication.	Identifies some methods for teacher–parent OR parent–teacher communication.
2. Engaging families in learning	Describes authentic means (above and beyond homework) for involving families in mathematical projects and learning, and provides evidence of frequency and success.	Identifies some means (above and beyond homework) for involving families in mathematical projects and learning, but provides limited evidence of frequency and success.	Provides limited or no evidence of the means for involving families in mathematical projects other than homework.
3. Understanding students' approach to learning	Describes the value of knowing and communicating (to students and parents) the varied approaches to learning (styles, modalities, intelligence) they exhibit.	Identifies a general understanding of varied approaches to learning (styles, modalities, intelligence) and at least one way to communicate this to students or parents.	Identifies a general understanding of varied approaches to learning (styles, modalities, intelligence) but does not describe how to communicate this to students or parents.
4. Having a reflective disposition	Articulately reflects on practice, connecting reflection to evidence of student learning and engagement with a focus on the unique needs of each student.	Reflects on practice, making some connections to student learning and engagement, but does not focus on the individual needs of each student.	Reflects on teaching, but does not connect to the learning of students.

Comments: _____

_____

_____

_____

6.1 Teacher Interview: Communicating with Families

For this field experience, prepare an interview in which you can learn about what the teacher does to communicate with families, how they do the things that they do (e.g., if they do a newsletter, find out what it looks like, how often it goes out, who contributes to the writing).

Ask a practicing teacher if you may interview him or her about how he or she involves families in their child's math learning. Your interview should address four areas:

1. What communication they use and how they use those approaches (see possible communication strategies below).
2. What they consider most important in terms of communication with parents/guardians (specific to math teaching and learning).
3. What strategies they use to involve parents/guardians who are not likely to show up on their own (due to their own bad experiences in school, cultural background, etc.).
4. How they build support for using reform practices in mathematics (see Chapter 1 in *Elementary and Middle School Mathematics* for details on this). If the teacher is not using reform practices, you may replace this item with asking what they want parents to know as the priorities in their math class.

Parent Communication Strategies

1. Teacher → parent communication
   - Homework
   - Newsletters
   - Notes to individual parents
   - Back-to-school nights

2. Parent → teacher communication
   - E-mails
   - Phone calls
   - Visits to the school

3. Teacher ↔ parent communication
   - Family math nights
   - Student/parent conferences (these can be one-way, but should be two- or three-way)
   - Parent volunteers in classroom

After completing your interview, respond to the questions on the following page.

Summary of Communication with Families

1. Summarize the ways the teacher communicates with parents/guardians.

2. Analyze the ways the teacher communicates with families in terms of one-way and two-way communication.

3. What strategies does the teacher use (or suggest) for communicating with hard-to-reach parents/guardians?

4. What strategies does the teacher use to gain the confidence and support from families in terms of his or her instructional approach to teaching math?

5. What have you learned from this interview that you would prioritize in your own classroom in terms of communicating with families?

6.2 Parent Interview: What Is Important to You?

Find a parent who has at least one child in grades K–8. The purpose of this interview is for you to gain understanding on the perspectives of parents in terms of their children's achievement in math and their own beliefs about math. This background is of critical importance when you consider your own relationship with parents and how you will sell your math program to the families of your students. A few questions are provided for you. Add your own questions that are relevant to the local community.

Interview Questions	Parent Response
1. What do you think are the important things your child will learn this year?	
2. How do you think people learn math? How does your child learn best?	
3. What is your opinion of the use of calculators? Explain.	
4. What is your opinion of students working together on a math problem or assignment?	
5. What math do you think your child needs in order to have access to the career he or she may desire?	
Other questions:	

Summary

After completing your interview, discuss the following:

1. How are the parents' views aligned with or in contrast to how you would teach math?
2. Take one issue for which the parent had a different view. Describe two to three strategies you would use to avoid or address a possible conflict.

6.3 Teaching: Prepare a Family Math Take-Home Activity

For this experience you will put together a family math activity (a Take-Home Kit).

Family Math Nights are common in schools and are excellent for developing parent support for math and getting to know your students' families. A Family Math Night can be done for your classroom, collaboratively for all students at a particular grade, or for the entire school.

The key to the success of a Family Math Night is to have engaging tasks that parents and their children can enjoy and that illustrate important mathematics concepts. Good tasks for Family Math Night are ones that can be used over and over again.

Where can you find these tasks?

1. In this book! See Chapters 9 and 10—many of these lessons and ideas can be adapted to become a Family Math Night activity.
2. Look at the activities throughout *Elementary and Middle School Mathematics*. Select one related to a mathematical topic that is being taught in your assigned classroom. For example, Salute! (Activity 10.12) is a fun activity that can be played over and over again to support reasoning strategies and memorization of the basic facts.
3. National Council of Teachers of Mathematics (NCTM) has high-quality activities and resources available at www.nctm.org/resources/families.aspx.
4. Visit the Family Math Program, which includes a series of books that are full of good ideas, at www.lhs.berkeley.edu/equals. The university or school library may have one of these books. If not, there are a few on the website that can be downloaded. These books are available in English and Spanish.
5. Check out games or activities in the class's math textbook. If you have engaging activities built into your units, this is a great way to have families support their children's math learning and for you to show off the quality of your math program.
6. There are so many teacher resource and activity books. If you select carefully, you can find excellent activities for Family Math Nights.

Family Math Take-Home Activity Example (Adaptation of Activity 14.13)

> ### Predict Down the Line
> In this activity, students and parents will build and predict what happens down the line.
>
> **Take-Home Kit (in a zip-lock bag), including the following:**
>
> 1. Detailed, kid-friendly instruction card. In the instructions, students and families will first predict how many tiles for the fifth or seventh figure for the cards you have in the kit. Then, they will be instructed to create their own. The parent can create the first three steps and ask their child to predict "down the line" (such as step 8); then they can trade roles.
> 2. Several patterns on cards, such as the repeating and growing patterns in Figures 14.10 or 14.11 in *Elementary and Middle School Mathematics*.
> 3. 50–60 1-inch square tiles (cut colored cardstock).
> 4. Optional: laminated card with a table (for recording how many tiles are needed for step 1, 2, 3, . . .) and an overhead nonpermanent marker.

6.4 Reflection: Professional Growth

Constructing knowledge requires reflective thought, actively thinking about or mentally working on an idea. The idea you are working on is the goal of becoming an effective mathematics teacher. This reflection can be used after a single lesson but can also be used to comprehensibly review a series of teaching opportunities. The purpose is for you to consider your strengths and target areas for growth.

This form can be completed by a preservice teacher for self-reflection, a cooperating teacher collaboration with the preservice teacher, or by a university supervisor. Review the rubrics in each chapter in Part I of this book. After reading what it takes to reach the target in each area, complete the table below.

	Strengths	Areas for Continued Growth
Classroom environment		
Planning		
Content knowledge		
Instruction		
Use of technology		
Assessment		
Diversity		

7 Student Learning and Assessment

Field Experiences

7.1 Classroom Observation: Assessing to Inform Instruction
7.2 Diagnostic Interview: Assessing for Understanding
7.3 Student Observation and Interview: Learning Through Problems
7.4 Teaching: Assessing Student Understanding with Rubrics

7.5 Teaching: Creating and Using Rubrics
7.6 Teaching: Using Anecdotal Notes to Assess Students
7.7 Teaching: Using a Checklist to Assess Students
7.8 Teaching: Assessing the Standards for Mathematical Practice

Standards Alignment

NCATE

Standard 1: Knowledge, Skills, and Professional Dispositions
1d. Student Learning

Teacher candidates focus on student learning and study the effects of their work. They assess and analyze student learning, make appropriate adjustments to instruction, monitor student learning, and have a positive effect on learning for all students (NCATE, 2008, p. 19).*

NCTM

Assessment Principle

Assessment should support the learning of important mathematics and furnish useful information to both teachers and students (NCTM, 2000, p. 22). The revised standards for teaching and learning mathematics in *Mathematics Teaching Today* (NCTM, 2007) addresses assessment in **Standard 6 (Reflection on Student Learning):**

The teacher of mathematics should engage in ongoing analysis of students' learning by—

- Observing, listening to, and gathering information about students to assess what they are learning

So as to—

- Ensure that every student is learning sound and significant mathematics and is developing a positive disposition toward mathematics;
- Challenge and extend students' ideas;
- Adapt or change activities while teaching;
- Describe and comment on each student's learning to parents and administrators; and
- Provide regular feedback to the students themselves. (p. 55)†

Elementary and Middle School Mathematics

Chapter 5 provides suggestions and tools for assessment.

Name: _____

Title of field experience: _____

Rubric

Note: This rubric is focused on student learning and assessment, and can be used to assess/provide feedback for any of the field experience activities in Chapter 7.

Indicators	Target	Acceptable	Developing
1. Designing assessment aligned with content/ instructional goals	Selected or identified assessments effectively address all the instructional goals for all learners.	Selected or identified assessments addresses most of the instructional goals.	Selected or identified assessments address some of the instructional goals.
2. Using assessment to provide authentic application of knowledge and understanding for all learners	Assessment provides opportunity for all learners to demonstrate learning for all instructional goals and attention to application and understanding is described.	Assessment provides opportunities for all learners to demonstrate instructional goals, though explicit attention to application and understanding is not provided.	Assessment provides opportunities for some learners to demonstrate instructional goals but no attention to application and understanding is provided.
3. Analyzing student work to determine student learning	Articulately describes student performance related to instructional goals, including what students learned and didn't learn and attention to next steps.	Provides some description about student performance related to instructional goals, and provides some analysis of what students learned or did not learn and possible next steps.	Provides some description about student performance, but not well connected to the instructional goals; provides some analysis of what students learned or did not learn.
4. Using results of assessment to inform instruction	Accurately and articulately describes how student performance will inform instructional goals for next-step lessons.	Uses some knowledge about student performance to describe some instructional goals for next-step lessons.	Provides limited or no evidence, or evidence provided about student learning does not follow a logical sequence for next-step lessons.

Comments: _____

_____

_____

_____

7.1 Classroom Observation: Assessing to Inform Instruction

The goal of this observation is to assess how the students in the classroom are performing on the topic they are learning and later to determine what you feel are the appropriate next steps for this group of students. When you schedule this observation, make sure that they will be learning a new concept.

Begin the observation by asking the teacher what he or she hopes the students will learn in the lesson (these objectives may be posted on the board). These will be the focus of your observation, not behavior, teaching strategies, or anything else.

1. Does each child have the prior knowledge to learn the new topic?

2. Does each student demonstrate evidence of understanding the task or activity they are supposed to be doing? If they do not understand, can you determine the cause of their confusion (e.g., don't understand instructions, don't know the math, are not familiar with the mathematics language)?

3. How successful is each student at demonstrating understanding of the lesson objectives? What is your evidence for this assessment? Be sure to respond to this in terms of individuals (e.g., three of the students . . .) and to use the evidence you used to reach this conclusion (e.g., their work on a handout, their oral explanation).

4. For the students who did not complete the task, what did you see as their gaps in understanding or other reasons for not completing the task?

Postobservation

5. Given what you recorded in your observation, describe what next steps you would take with this class of students (i.e., what you would have as the focus of the lesson the next day).

7.2 Diagnostic Interview: Assessing for Understanding

The goal of a diagnostic interview is to find out where a child is at a particular time in terms of concepts and procedures. Ask your supervising teacher if you can interview a student and then follow the steps below. For more on diagnostic interviews, see page 90 in *Elementary and Middle School Mathematics*.

Preinterview

1. Select a topic that will be in the student's curriculum this year but has not yet been taught.
2. Select or design one to three tasks for the student to demonstrate and/or explain this concept. You must select items so that the student can complete them in 10–20 minutes (depending on student's age). Many of the activities in Part II of *Elementary and Middle School Mathematics* can be developed into tasks for diagnostic interviews, if you add questions. Also, see "Formative Assessment Notes" in each Part II chapter, where ideas are offered for doing diagnostic interviews.
3. Schedule a time to visit with the student.

FORMATIVE Assessment Notes

Interview

4. Introduce yourself to the student and explain the purpose of your discussion. Tell the student that you are interested in learning about his or her thinking, so you will be asking the student to explain what he or she is thinking and doing.
5. Explain each task clearly (preparing a script is recommended). Watch the student solve the task; do not assist the student. Give the student enough time. If the student is stuck, ask the question a different way, simplify the task, or remind the student of something that might help to jog his or her memory.
6. If appropriate, when a student solves a problem, ask if he or she could solve it another way.
7. Thank the student for helping you to learn more about teaching math. Tell the student he or she did a good job.

Postinterview

8. Write a summary of how the student performed on each question you asked. Include any work samples you have from the interview.
9. Describe what future instruction you feel is appropriate for this student (related to your specific topic).

Sample Interview for Primary Grades

MATH: Counting strategies (Grades K–1)

Task 1:
Provide student with 17 counters. Ask the learner, "How many counters are here?"

Observe what strategy the student originally uses (counting by ones, twos, fives, tens).

Possible interview questions:

1. If the student counted by ones, ask "Can you count them another way?" or "Is there a quicker way you could count them?"
2. If student counts by ones and twos, ask what other ways they know how to count.
3. If the counters were placed into piles, say, "Tell me why you chose to do that."
4. Ask the student, "What do you do to remember which counters you already counted?"
5. If counters were counted more than once, present the same counting task with fewer than ten counters. Ask yourself whether the child conserves number (i.e., the child can avoid double-counting despite the arrangement of the counters and knows when to stop counting to have counted them all). The task may be developmentally beyond the learner right now.

Task 2:
Provide student with 42 counters. Ask the learner, "How many counters are here?"

Observe what counting strategy the student uses and how he or she organizes the counters (e.g., were the counters moved into pile(s) as they were counted? How?).

Possible interview questions:

1. If the student begins to count by ones, ask "Can you count them a quicker way?" or "Can you organize the counters so they will be easier to count?"
2. Ask the student, "Can you count by twos (or fives) to find out how many?"
3. Ask the student, "What do you do to remember which counters you already counted?"
4. If student has been successful on these tasks, ask "What if you had a whole box of counters? How would you figure out how many were in the box?"

Sample Interview for Intermediate Grades

MATH: Readiness concepts for finding perimeter of a rectangle (see Expanded Lesson 9.16, "Fixed Areas," in Part II for a possible activity on finding perimeter of rectangles)

Readiness Skill/Concept 1:
Properties of a rectangle (e.g., opposite sides are the same length)

Interview Task 1a:

I am going shopping to buy fencing for a cage I am making for my rabbit (draw a picture of a rectangle). The pet store owner suggested that the long side be 7 feet long and the short side be 4 feet wide.

Related Questions to Probe Student:

Can you label the picture for me?

Can you tell me what the measures of the other sides are, or do we not have enough information?

Interview Task 1b:

Show a collection of rectangles of different shapes (including some squares). Ask student to describe the characteristics of a rectangle.

Related Questions to Probe Student:

What can you tell me that is true for all rectangles?

What is never true for rectangles?

What is sometimes true for a rectangle, but not always?

Readiness Skill/Concept 2:
Addition and being able to double

Interview Task 2a:
What is 26 + 26?

Related Questions to Probe Student:

How did you solve it?

If student solved it with the standard algorithm:

    Can you do it another way?

    Can you do it in your head?

Math Concept: _____

Task 1:

Key Questions

1.

2.

3.

Task 2:

Key Questions

1.

2.

3.

Task 3:

Key Questions

1.

2.

3.

7.3 Student Observation and Interview: Learning Through Problems

The focus of this observation and interview is to observe a student solving a problem and ask questions to see what the student knew in order to solve the task and what was learned as a result of doing the task. You may use any task, but there is a collection of good tasks on pages 81–82 of *Elementary and Middle School Mathematics*. You need to do only one task, but you may want to have an extension ready in case the one you selected is too easy for the student. Prepare two to four questions that extend the problem and ask the child to explain his or her strategy.

After having a student solve the task, respond to the following prompts:

1. What prior knowledge did the student have to have in order to solve this problem?

2. What strategies did the student use to solve the problem? Did the student try different approaches?

3. In what ways did the questions you asked extend the student's thinking?

4. What did the student learn from the task itself and/or the questions you posed?

7.4 Teaching: Assessing Student Understanding with Rubrics

In Chapter 11 of this guide are three balanced assessment items. Balanced Assessment–Mathematics Assessment Resource Service Project (http://balancedassessment.concord.org) was designed to create high-quality performance tasks across the curriculum that could be used to more comprehensively assess what a student knows in mathematics. The tasks and rubrics illustrate how problem-based tasks can be used to assess student understanding.

Select one of the Balanced Assessment Performance Tasks and ask a student or small group of students to complete the task. Be sure they are clear about what they are to do before getting them started on the performance task.

Once they have completed the task, use the rubrics provided and the example assessed work to help you apply the rubric to the students who have completed the task.

Complete the following questions and submit this along with the student-completed tasks and your scoring of each one.

Reflection on Using Balanced Assessment Items

1. As the student worked on the task, what problems were particularly challenging?

2. What strategies did the student use to solve the more challenging tasks?

3. Do you think that the student learned something as a result of doing the performance task? Explain.

4. What did you learn about the student as a result of his or her completion of this task?

7.5 Teaching: Creating and Using Rubrics

For this experience you can use a task from a lesson you plan to teach, a task that your cooperating teacher has used, or one that has not been used.

Assessment is to involve the learner. Rubrics should be shared with students prior to completion of the task, so that they can clearly see what the expectations are. The expectations must be heavily weighted on what the objectives of the lesson are. It is not appropriate to have behavior included in a rubric that is designed to assess students' understanding of area, for example. Neatness and clarity are legitimate items to include, but should not overshadow the learning objectives.

Part I: Develop the Rubric

Using a four-point rubric as a guide, create a rubric that is specific to the task that you have selected.

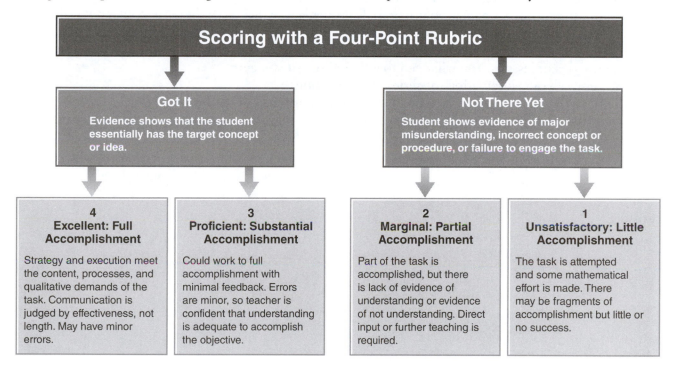

Scoring with a Four-Point Rubric

Got It
Evidence shows that the student essentially has the target concept or idea.

Not There Yet
Student shows evidence of major misunderstanding, incorrect concept or procedure, or failure to engage the task.

4 Excellent: Full Accomplishment	3 Proficient: Substantial Accomplishment	2 Marginal: Partial Accomplishment	1 Unsatisfactory: Little Accomplishment
Strategy and execution meet the content, processes, and qualitative demands of the task. Communication is judged by effectiveness, not length. May have minor errors.	Could work to full accomplishment with minimal feedback. Errors are minor, so teacher is confident that understanding is adequate to accomplish the objective.	Part of the task is accomplished, but there is lack of evidence of understanding or evidence of not understanding. Direct input or further teaching is required.	The task is attempted and some mathematical effort is made. There may be fragments of accomplishment but little or no success.

Part II: Use the Rubric

After using this rubric in the lesson you teach (or the cooperating teacher taught), use it to assess the student work you collected. For all students, you should be able to underline the descriptions of their work in each section of the rubric. This communicates to children what they accomplished and what areas need improvement.

Part III: Reflection and Revision of Rubric

Typically, a first-draft rubric doesn't quite capture what you had hoped and you realize this after struggling over whether a piece of student work is a 3 or a 4. For Part III, revise your rubric. In addition, comment on the impact the rubric had on the quality of the student work.

7.6 Teaching: Using Anecdotal Notes to Assess Students

One strategy teachers use to assess student learning is to keep anecdotal evidence, using note cards or sticky notes. These notes are used throughout a unit. See Figures 5.6 in *Elementary and Middle School Mathematics* for a visual of what this can look like. As students work on the *during* part of a lesson, the teacher observes and keeps notes on who is and is not achieving the objectives.

The goal of this experience is for you to use anecdotal notes to assess student learning. You can attempt to do an entire class of students or a fraction of the class. You can observe one lesson or a series of lessons.

1. Select a style you are going to use to record your notes (note cards on a clipboard, the template provided and sticky notes, or a format the teacher recommends).
2. Prepare cards/notes. Organize your materials in such a way that it will be easy to take notes during the lesson.
3. Record notes on each student. You will want to try to observe them at several points during the lessons/series of lessons. You will need to visit and revisit students.
4. At the end of your observation (or series of observations):
   a. Summarize to what extent each child learned the objectives of the lesson or unit.
   b. Describe what you see as the benefits and limitations of using anecdotal notes to assess student learning.

Rubric Format for Anecdotal Notes

See Figure 5.7 in *Elementary and Middle School Mathematics* to see an example of this format. You may want to use sticky notes in the right column, which allows you to write students' names and brief notes. Using sticky notes means you can move them to new categories or revise their notes without having to erase the form.

Math Concept: _____

Level of Understanding	Names of Students (post students' names)
Above and Beyond Clear understanding. Communicates concept in multiple representations. Shows evidence of using idea without prompting. Specific descriptors: 1. 2.	
On Target Understands or is developing well. Uses designated models. Specific descriptors: 1. 2.	
Not There Yet Some confusion or misunderstands. Only models idea with help. Specific descriptors: 1. 2.	

7.7 Teaching: Using a Checklist to Assess Students

For this field experience, you will use a checklist format to assess student learning. Although it is called a checklist, you can also add anecdotal notes to the form as a way of tracking students. This is intended for a lesson that you have planned but can also be used with a lesson that you are observing.

For this task you will:

1. Observe a lesson using one of the forms provided here or one you have created
2. Record how each student in the class has achieved the objectives of the class
3. Respond to the following reflection prompts

Postobservation Reflection

1. Briefly describe the lesson, in particular describing the goals of the lesson.

2. To what extent did students learn the objectives? In other words, who learned which objectives?

3. Based on your response to item 2, what needs to be planned for these students for their upcoming math lesson?

4. What are the benefits and limitations of using checklists in classroom assessment?

Full-Class Observation Checklist

List student names in the left column. See *Elementary and Middle School Mathematics*, page 89, for a model.

Topic: _____	Objective 1	Objective 2	Objective 3	Notes
1.				
2.				
3.				
4.				
5.				
6.				
7.				
8.				
9.				
10.				
11.				
12.				
13.				
14.				
15.				
16.				
17.				
18.				
19.				
20.				
21.				
22.				
23.				
24.				
25.				
26.				
27.				
28.				
29.				
30.				

7.8 Teaching: Assessing the Standards for Mathematical Practice

Select one of the Standards for Mathematical Practice (see Appendix A in *Elementary and Middle School Mathematics* or go to www.corestandards.org/the-standards/mathematics/introduction/standards-for -mathematical-practice). For the practice you have selected, review the list of related student actions that would indicate that they are demonstrating mathematical proficiency. Table 1.2 from *Elementary and Middle School Mathematics* (also found in this book on page 20) provides guidance in what students must be doing in order to develop proficiency in each practice.

1. Select a task or activity related to something that has already been taught.
2. Use the student actions to develop a set of probing questions (use the template on the next page).
3. Ask the student to solve the task, talking aloud to share their thinking.
4. While listening, note any evidence of mathematical proficiency on the practice.
5. Once the student completes the task, ask your questions to see if the student has mathematical proficiency on the practice.
6. Reflect on the extent to which the student demonstrates mathematically proficiency related to that particular practice.

Assessing the Standards for Mathematical Practice

Complete the first three columns prior to meeting with the student. Record notes in Column 4 during and after the interview.

Mathematical Practice Identified	Student Actions Related to Practice (refer to page 20)	Probing Questions Related to Mathematical Practice	Observations and Responses to Questions That Provide Evidence of Proficiency Related to the Selected Practice

8 Diversity

Field Experiences

Standards Alignment

NCATE

Standard 4: Diversity
4a. Design, Implementation, and Evaluation of Curriculum and Experiences

Curriculum, field experiences, and clinical practice promote candidates' development of knowledge, skills, and professional dispositions related to diversity in the unit's conceptual framework. They are based on well-developed knowledge bases for, and conceptualizations of, diversity and inclusion so that candidates can apply them effectively in schools. Candidates learn to contextualize teaching and to draw upon representations from the students' own experiences and cultures. They challenge students toward cognitive complexity and engage all students, including English language learners and students with exceptionalities, through instructional conversation. Candidates and faculty review candidate assessment data on candidates' ability to work with all students and develop a plan for improving their practice and the institution's programs (NCATE, 2008, p. 34).*

NCTM

Equity Principle

Equity in mathematics education requires equity—high expectations and strong support for all students (NCTM, 2000, p. 12).†

Elementary and Middle School Mathematics

Chapter 6 provides information on the types of diversity one is likely to encounter and strategies for supporting those learners.

---

* Excerpts from the *Professional Standards for the Accreditation of Teacher Preparation Institutions* (2008) reprinted with permission from the National Council for Accreditation of Teacher Education. All rights reserved.

†Excerpts from *Principles and Standards for School Mathematics* listed with the permission of the National Council of Teachers of Mathematics (NCTM). Copyright © 2000 by the National Council of Teachers of Mathematics. All rights reserved. NCTM does not endorse the content or validity of these alignments.

Name: _____

Title of field experience: _____

Rubric

Note: This rubric is focused on diversity, and can be used to assess/provide feedback for any of the field experience activities in Chapter 8.

Indicators	Target	Acceptable	Developing
1. Understanding students' approach to learning	Describes the value of knowing and communicating to students and parents the varied approaches to learning (styles, modalities, intelligence) they exhibit.	Identifies a general understanding of varied approaches to learning (styles, modalities, intelligence) and the importance of communicating with students or parents.	Provides limited description of varied approaches to learning that students exhibit and does not address the value of communicating it to students or parents.
2. Having knowledge of students' backgrounds	Articulately describes the value of knowing and utilizing issues of learners' special needs, including race, ethnicity, culture, gender, language, religion, and social class, in relation to mathematical learning.	Describes general understanding of learners' special needs, including race, ethnicity, culture, gender, language, religion, and social class, in relation to mathematical learning.	Describes general understanding of some learners' special needs, including race, ethnicity, culture, gender, language, religion, and social class, in relation to mathematical learning.
3. Designing or implementing appropriate accommodations/ modifications for all learners	Effectively designs or implements instruction that provides appropriate and specific accommodations and/or modifications for students of diverse backgrounds in such a way that maintains high expectations for all learners.	Effectively designs or implements instruction that provides some accommodations and/or modifications for students of diverse backgrounds that maintain high expectations for all learners.	Designs instruction that has the potential to meet the range of learners, but accommodations or modifications are not provided or the ones provided alter the lesson content in a manner that does not maintain high expectations for all learners.

Comments: _____

_____

_____

_____

8.1 Observation: One Child's Experience

The purpose of this observation is to focus on one child who has a special need (e.g., gifted, LD, ELL) and observe his or her learning in a lesson. You will have to communicate with the teacher about the purpose of the observation and have him or her assist in selecting the student. Also, you will need to be careful that in observing the student, you do not make him or her feel uncomfortable. Use the template below to record notes.

Focus Area	Evidence of Accommodations or Modifications	My Additional Ideas
Physical Environment • Desk arrangement • Placement of student • Bulletin boards, displays, posters • Accessibility of tools		
Instructional Strategies • Explanation of the task • Building on prior knowledge • Use of manipulatives, models, visuals • Use of overheads and whiteboard to write/illustrate		
Classroom Discourse • Asking students to clarify thinking • Student–student and student–teacher communication • Different student approaches to problem • Involving all students in the task and discussion		
High Expectations • Goals of the lesson for each child • Task completion expectations • Support (hints, tools, etc.) offered to students		

Postobservation Reflection

For each of these questions, you are responding in relation to the one student you observed.

1. Describe the specific learning needs of this student.

2. What struggles did this student encounter in the lesson (language was difficult, lesson wasn't challenging, etc.)?

3. What structures or strategies were in place that seemed to best support this child's learning?

4. What additional strategies or ideas do you feel would have enhanced the learning for this child?

8.2 Observation: Culturally Responsive Instruction

This observation can be used to view a video of a lesson (or part of a lesson), to observe a teacher, or to self-reflect on a lesson you have planned or taught. Use the reflection questions below to consider the extent to which a lesson is culturally responsive. For more information on culturally responsive mathematics instruction, read Chapter 6, pp. 102–104 in *Elementary and Middle School Mathematics*.

Reflective Questions to Focus on Culturally Relevant Mathematics Instruction	
Aspect of Culturally Responsive Instruction	**Reflection Questions to Guide Teaching and Assessing**
The content of the lesson is about important mathematics and the tasks performed by students communicate high expectations.	Does the content include a balance of procedures and concepts? Are students expected to engage in problem solving and generate their own approaches to problems? Are connections made between mathematics topics?
The content is relevant.	In what ways is the content related to familiar aspects of students' lives? In what ways is prior knowledge elicited/reviewed so that all students can participate in the lesson? To what extent are students asked to make connections between school mathematics and mathematics in their own lives? How are interests of students (events, issues, literature, or pop culture) used to build interest and mathematical meaning?
The instructional strategies communicate the value of students' identities.	In what ways are students invited to include their own experiences within a lesson? Are story problems generated from students and teachers? Do stories reflect the real experiences of students? Are individual student approaches presented and showcased so that each student sees their ideas as important to the teacher and their peers? Are alternative algorithms shared as a point of excitement and pride (as appropriate)? Are multiple modes to demonstrate knowledge (e.g., visuals, explanations, models) valued?
The instructional strategies model shared power.	Are students (rather than just the teacher) justifying the correctness of solutions? Are students invited to (expected to) engage in whole-class discussions where students share ideas and respond to each other's ideas? In what ways are roles assigned so that every student feels that they contribute to and learn from other members of the class? Are students given a choice in how they solve a problem? In how they demonstrate knowledge of the concept?

8.3 Teacher Interview: Student Diversity

The purpose of this interview is to learn about the individual students in your classroom. It is important to know students' needs and have a good collection of strategies to support their learning.

Learner Subgroups	Number of Students in Subgroup	Teacher Suggestions Ask the teacher to share **three to five** adaptations or instructional strategies she or he uses to make mathematics accessible and meaningful.	Your Additional Suggestions Add **two to three** of your own ideas for adapting/ designing instruction to support each type of learner.
Gender	B: G:		
Intellectual disabilities			
Gifted			
Culturally/ ethnically diverse			
English language learner			
Struggling/ reluctant learner			

Interview Questions

1. In general, what strategies do you use to differentiate a lesson in order to meet the needs of all the diverse learners in your classroom?

2. What strategies do you use to make the content accessible, but still maintain high expectations for learning the intended objectives?

8.4 Teacher Interview: Environment and Students

Ask a classroom teacher if you may interview him or her about how they use knowledge of students, family, and community to make decisions for his or her math teaching.

A classroom environment that nurtures all learners reflects both the best practices in teaching mathematics and the needs of the specific learners. As the NCTM Equity Principle states, we must have "high expectations and strong support for all students." Here you will design five questions to ask a classroom teacher, so that you will learn about how he or she develops an environment with high expectations that supports all learners. This might include, but is not limited to, cultural and/ or linguistic background, involving families' learning styles, learning differences, personalities, skills/backgrounds, local community interests/events, interests of individual students, and seasonal considerations.

Interview Questions	Teacher Response
1.	
2.	
3.	
4.	
5.	
Other:	

Summary

After completing your interview, describe how you believe the teacher keeps expectations high and supports all learners. How does the teacher use the backgrounds and interests of her or his students? Offer suggestions of your own that you would try to incorporate if you were the teacher of this particular classroom.

8.5 Teaching: Lesson Adaptations

The purpose of this experience is for you to apply what you know about students, what you know about adaptations for various special needs, and your knowledge of mathematics teaching. Adaptations include both accommodations and modifications. Accommodations are strategies you use to help a student learn (e.g., showcasing key vocabulary, putting a child in a particular seat, pairing a child with a certain student). Modifications are changes to the lesson itself (e.g., altering the objectives, changing the activity).

In this task, you will develop accommodations and/or modifications that directly relate to the learners in the classroom that you would be teaching and then teach the lesson. The following steps are offered as a suggested approach:

1. Complete the Student Diversity sheet (see 8.3, "Teacher Interview: Student Diversity") or use your own form for finding out what the special needs are within your classroom.
2. Select a task and plan a lesson for the class, or use one of the Expanded Lessons available in this guide.
3. Review your Student Diversity sheet, and for each child, list the strategies you will use to make the lesson accessible to him or her.
4. Teach the lesson.
5. Complete 8.7, "Reflection: Meeting the Needs of All Learners."

Lesson Adaptations Planning Template

Title of Lesson: _____

Mathematics Topic in the Lesson: _____

Name of Student	Description of Special Need	Accommodations or Modifications

Field Experience Guide: Resources for Teachers of Elementary and Middle School Mathematics © Pearson Education, Inc., 2013

8.6 Teaching: Sheltering a Lesson for English Language Learners

The purpose of this field experience is for you to identify and incorporate those instructional strategies that can support an English language learner (ELL). In Chapter 6 of *Elementary and Middle School Mathematics*, you will find a description of the following ways to support ELLs:

1. Write and state the content and language objectives
2. Build background
3. Encourage use of native language
4. Use comprehensible input
5. Explicitly teach vocabulary
6. Use cooperative groups

In addition, Table 4.1 of *Elementary and Middle School Mathematics* offers lesson planning suggestions for ELLs.

For this experience you are going to take an existing lesson from a textbook or teacher resource (you can also use one of the Expanded Lessons in this guide) and "shelter" it. That means that you will take each component of the lesson (the objectives; the before, during, and after; and the assessment) and determine the accommodations or modifications you would make. If you have access to a classroom with English language learners, discuss with the teacher their level of language proficiency so that the adaptations you are making fit the needs of those specific students.

Sheltering a Lesson for English Language Learners

Use this page to record any accommodations or modifications to the lesson you selected. Attach this cover page to that lesson.

Lesson	Accommodations/Modifications for English Language Learners
Mathematics goals	
Thinking about the students	
Materials and preparation	
Lesson Plan	
Before	
During	
After	
Assessment	

What instructional strategies are already embedded in the lesson that will support English language learners?

1.

2.

3.

4.

5.

8.7 Reflection: Meeting the Needs of All Learners

Complete this reflection after teaching a lesson. This could be a lesson you developed for 8.5 or 8.6, or any other lesson.

1. Did all students learn the mathematics you identified in your objectives? How do you know?

2. What instructional strategies enabled your diverse students to be successful? Respond with specific strategies for each type of diversity.

3. In what ways did student interaction support the learning of all students (grouping, discussions, etc.)?

4. The NCTM Equity Principle states that we need high expectations and strong support for all students.

   a. In what ways did your lesson goals and instructional strategies communicate high expectations?

   b. In what ways did your lesson goals and instructional strategies provide strong support (without lowering expectations)?

Bibliography

CCSSO (Council of Chief State School Officers). (2010). *Common core state standards.* Retrieved from http://correstandards.org

Chapin, S., O'Conner, C., & Anderson, N. (2009). *Classroom discussions: Using math talk to help students learn* (2nd ed.). Sausalito, CA: Math Solutions.

Common Core State Standards Initiative (2010). *Common core state standards for mathematics.*

Hiebert, J., Carpenter, T. P., Fennema, E., Fuson, K., Wearne, D., Murray, H., Olivier, A., & Human, P. (1997). *Making sense: Teaching and learning mathematics with understanding.* Portsmouth, NH: Heinemann.

National Council for Accreditation of Teacher Education. (2008). *Professional standards for the accreditation of teacher preparation institutions.* Washington, DC: NCATE.

National Center for Educational Statistics. (2003). *National assessment of educational progress.* http://nces.ed.gov/nationsreportcard.

National Council of Teachers of Mathematics. (1991). *Professional standards for teaching mathematics.* Reston, VA: NCTM.

National Council of Teachers of Mathematics. (2000). *Principles and standards for school mathematics.* Reston, VA: NCTM.

National Council of Teachers of Mathematics. (2002). *Professional standards for school mathematics.* Reston, VA: NCTM.

National Council of Teachers of Mathematics. (2007). *Mathematics teaching today.* Reston, VA: NCTM.

National Research Council. (2001). *Adding it up: Helping children learn mathematics.* J. Kilpatrick, J. Swafford, & B. Findell (Eds.). Washington, DC: National Academies Press.

Shield, M., & Swinson, K. (1996). The link sheet: A communication aid for clarifying and developing mathematical ideas and processes. In P. C. Elliott & M. J. Kenney (Eds.), *Communication in Mathematics, K–12 and Beyond: NCTM Yearbook.* Reston, VA: NCTM.

Smith, M. S., & Stein, M. K. (1998). Selecting and creating mathematical tasks: From research to practice. *Mathematics Teaching in the Middle School, 3*(5): 344–350.

Part II

Resources for Teaching

In this section, we offer many lessons and tasks that can be used with the field experience activities in Part I or on their own. These lessons and activities are organized into three categories: Expanded Lessons (Chapter 9), Mathematics Activities (Chapter 10), and Balanced Assessment Items (Chapter 11). There are lessons and activities for every content chapter in *Elementary and Middle School Mathematics*. The first page of each chapter includes a chart that provides the content objective, and appropriate grade level (based on the *Common Core State Standards*, 2010).

Expanded Lessons

These are detailed lesson plans that provide substantial support in planning, though you will want to adapt the lesson to your particular classroom based on students' backgrounds and interests.

Mathematics Activities

These are short tasks that have been selected because they have the potential for teaching important mathematical concepts, though planning the details is left to you. A brief overview of the lesson is provided as a starting point for planning. This is what often happens in teaching—you are handed an activity and then you determine how to use it with students. If you just hand it out and collect it, you aren't going to see the learning that you will if you carefully plan how you will organize the *before*, *during*, and *after* components of the lesson. Part I, 2.6, "Teaching: Planning a Problem-Based Lesson," can be used as a tool to create a full lesson.

Balanced Assessment Tasks

These are detailed mathematics tasks that include scoring rubrics and sample solutions that have been scored. These items provide guidance on how to assess student learning through performance tasks. You can use these as activities, as diagnostic interviews, or as performance assessments.

All Three Types of Resources: Accommodations and Modifications

Classrooms are diverse. Learners can differ in skills, rates of learning, language proficiency, abilities to abstract, physical abilities, sociability, motivation, and prior knowledge. For each lesson or mathematics task, think about ways to differentiate the task to meet the needs of the diverse learners in your classroom.

9 Expanded Lessons

These lessons, designed in the *before*, *during*, and *after* format, address the Standards for Mathematical Practice. Each lesson includes elements discussed across the practices, including justifying, generalizing, giving examples, using different approaches, mathematical models, use of tools, and so on. It is through daily instruction with lessons designed to incorporate the Mathematical Practices that students will become mathematically proficient.

The lessons are designed for all learners. Suggestions are given for supporting students with intellectual disabilities and students who are English language learners. In addition, tasks are carefully selected so that there are multiple entry points and multiple ways to demonstrate understanding—in other words, differentiated for a range of learners.

The list provided here will help you to find the lesson that best fits the grade and subject you are teaching. If the lesson doesn't fit your students' needs exactly, then adapt it to be a better fit—just leave in the opportunities for higher-level thinking and reasoning so that students will learn the intended objectives!

	Title of Expanded Lesson	Content Focus (related chapter in *Elementary and Middle School Mathematics*)	Grade Level Recommendation (based on *Common Core State Standards*)
9.1	Exploring Subtraction Strategies	To use invented strategies for subtracting two-digit numbers (Ch. 9)	Grade 2
9.2	Close, Far, and In Between	To develop number sense through thinking about relative magnitude of numbers (Ch. 9, 12)	Grades 2–3
9.3	Two More Than/ Two Less Than	To develop the paired relationships of two more than and two less than for numbers to 12 (Ch. 8, 10)	Grades K–1
9.4	Learning about Division	To develop the measurement (repeated subtraction) concept of division (Ch. 9)	Grade 3
9.5	Estimating Groups of Tens and Ones	To connect a count-by-ones understanding to a count based on the number of groups of 10 and leftovers for quantities to 100 (Ch. 11)	Grades 1–2
9.6	Dot-Paper Fraction Equivalences	To develop a conceptual understanding of equivalent fractions; the same quantity can have different fraction names (Ch. 15)	Grade 3
9.7	Multiplication of Fractions Stories	To develop the meaning of multiplication of fractions through various area models (Ch. 16)	Grades 5–6
9.8	Friendly Fractions to Decimals	To connect equivalent decimals to familiar fractions in a conceptual manner (Ch. 17)	Grade 4
9.9	Division of Fractions Stories	To develop the partitive meaning of division with fractions through investigating various contexts (Ch. 16)	Grades 5–6
9.10	How Many In Between?	To develop the concept of density of the rational numbers (Ch. 17)	Grades 4–6
9.11	Comparing Ratios	To develop conceptual strategies for comparing ratios in various contexts; proportional reasoning (multiplicative as opposed to additive) (Ch. 18)	Grades 6–7
9.12	One Up and One Down	To discover and explore number patterns within the context of addition (Ch. 2, 9)	Grades K–1

	Title of Expanded Lesson	Content Focus (related chapter in *Elementary and Middle School Mathematics*)	Grade Level Recommendation (based on *Common Core State Standards*)
9.13	Geometric Growing Patterns: Predict How Many	To explore growing patterns using three representations: pictures or drawings, table of values, and a rule (Ch. 14)	Grades 4–5
9.14	Create a Journey Story	To interpret line graphs and write scenarios that are representative of given graphs (Ch. 14)	Grade 5
9.15	Crooked Paths	To see length as an attribute that need not be in a straight line (Ch. 19)	Grades K–1
9.16	Fixed Areas	To contrast the concepts of area and perimeter (Ch. 19)	Grades 3–4
9.17	Shape Sorts	To develop awareness of the wide variety of ways that two-dimensional shapes can be alike and classify shapes by various properties (Ch. 20)	Grades K–3
9.18	Diagonals of Quadrilaterals	To investigate the properties of the diagonals of quadrilaterals (Ch. 20)	Grades 3–7
9.19	Triangle Midsegments	To investigate the relationship between a triangle's midsegment and its base (Ch. 20)	Grades 7–8
9.20	Using Data to Answer a Question	To determine a question that can be answered through gathering data, gather the data, create graphs, and answer question (Ch. 21)	Grades K–3
9.21	Design a Fair Game	To explore probability of an event with equally likely outcomes; Explore the concept of variation and the Law of Large numbers (Ch. 22)	Grades 7–8
9.22	Bar Graphs to Circle Graphs	To introduce the use of a circle graph (pie chart) to display data and explore the concept of percent (Ch. 21)	Grades 4–7
9.23	Testing Bag Designs	To develop the concepts that some events are more or less likely than others and previous trials do not influence how likely a subsequent event is. And to explore variability in data (Ch. 22)	Grades 5–7
9.24	Toying with Measures of Central Tendency	To develop an understanding of how characteristics of a data set (e.g., distribution of data, outliers) affect the mean, median, and mode (Ch. 21)	Grades 6–8

EXPANDED LESSON 9.1

Exploring Subtraction Strategies

Mathematics Goals

- To use invented strategies for subtracting two-digit numbers
- To use efficient strategies for subtracting two-digit numbers (beyond counting on by ones)

Grade Level Guide

NCTM *Curriculum Focal Points*	*Common Core State Standards*
At grade 2 students are expected to develop fluency and quick recall of two-digit subtraction of whole numbers. There is an expectation that they will develop methods to subtract and, where possible, will be able to estimate and calculate answers mentally.	Students in grade 2 are using their understanding of place value to subtract. They should "fluently add and subtract within 100 using strategies based on place value, properties of operations, and/or the relationship between addition and subtraction (CCSS, 2010, p. 19).

Consider Your Students' Needs

Students should have experience using a variety of invented strategies for adding two-digit numbers. Students should have had experience subtracting with smaller values, and may have had experience subtracting two-digit from two-digit numbers. The assumption is that students have not been taught the standard algorithms for addition and subtraction. Consider using manipulatives or drawings as a tool to support students' thinking.

For English Language Learners

- Reading comprehension is central to this task. If ELLs have limited English, you can modify this lesson, having all the stories be about the same subject (pick one). If

proficiency is stronger, ensuring that the contexts are understood must be part of the "Before" phase.

For Students with Disabilities

- Cut the recording sheet into three pieces to reduce the visual display or put one problem to a page
- If students are struggling explicitly, suggest the use of a particular strategy (such as the empty number line) but do not suggest how to do the problem

Materials

Each student will need:

- "Looking at Collections" recording sheet (FEG Blackline Master 62)
- Manipulatives (for counting)

LESSON

Before

Present the task to the class:

- Read the first problem together with the students. Ask students questions to make sure they understand the situation (not how to solve it). For example, ask "What do we know?" or "Can you put the problem in your own words?"
- Record what students know on the board.
- Ask students to brainstorm ideas on how they might solve the problem. Call on several students and elicit their thoughts. For example, if a student says, "I would start with 35 and count up to 72," ask how he or she will count, or what model he or she might be using to do the problem. It is not sufficient to say, "I would subtract."

- Summarize by encouraging students to use one of the ideas they heard or one of their own ideas. Also, encourage them to use manipulatives or models (e.g., hundreds chart, empty number line) if they would like.

Provide clear expectations:

- Explain to students that they will be working individually (or you may choose to have them work in pairs).
- Explain that they are to show how they solved each problem. They can show with words, drawings, or equations.
- They should provide enough information on their paper that if it were shared with a student in the another second-grade class, that student would understand what they did.
- Tell students to continue to the second and third problems after they finish the first one.

During

Initially:

- Observe that students have access to the materials needed to solve the problem.
- Observe that each student understands the question and is in the process of attempting to solve the first situation.

Ongoing:

- Observe students' work—notice the methods they are using and the models they are using to solve the problem. See the "Assessment" section of this lesson for details. Keep these in mind for selecting who will share in the "After" phase of the lesson.
- As students work, ask them to tell you what the problem is asking and how they are thinking about solving it. See the "Assessment" section at the end of the lesson for details.
- If a student is stuck, try to make a suggestion that builds on the student's ideas. For example, if the student says, "I want to take 35 from 72, but I don't know how to start," you might ask the student if the hundreds chart might help them. Or you might suggest that the student try one of the ideas that was mentioned in the "Before" phase of the lesson. After making a suggestion, walk away and check back later.
- If you notice an error, rather than correct it, ask the student to explain how they solved the problem (students often catch their mistakes while explaining and showing).

After

Bring the class together to share and discuss the task:

- Ask students to explain how they solved the problem. Record their ideas on the board, sketching any visuals

that they describe, or show their work on a document camera.

- Be careful to write the equations both horizontally and vertically so that students recognize that these are equivalent representations.
- One good visual representation is to use an empty number line. So, you can use the number line when a student suggests a strategy that involves skip counting by tens (e.g., "I started with 35, added 10 and 10 and 10 to get to 65, then counted by fives to 70, and then by ones to 72, and got 37."). Your number line on the board may look like this:

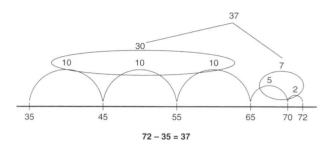

$$72 - 35 = 37$$

- If there are different answers, allow the students with different answers to explain their thinking, and the class as a whole can determine if the answer makes sense. The responsibility for deciding what is correct falls to the class, not you.
- Repeat process for the second and third problems.

ASSESSMENT

Observe

- Use a checklist to record students using strategies that involve counting by ones. You may need to meet with these students in a small group to encourage them to use skip counting as a faster, more efficient strategy.
- Look to see if students are using different strategies across the problems or using the same strategy.

Ask

- What strategy are you using?
- Can you show me with (a manipulative or hundreds chart) how you found the answer?
- Can you use skip counting to find the answer more quickly?

EXPANDED LESSON 9.3

Two More Than/Two Less Than

Mathematics Goals
- To develop the paired relationships of two more than and two less than for numbers to 12
- To be able to quickly recognize quantities in the form of domino-type dot patterns

Grade Level Guide

NCTM *Curriculum Focal Points*	*Common Core State Standards*
Representing and comparing whole numbers is a component of a kindergarten focal point.	"Count to tell the number of objects" is a standard within the domain of Counting and Cardinality in Kindergarten (CCSS, 2010, p 10). Also at the kindergarten level within the domain of Operations and Algebraic Thinking, students are asked to think about addition and subtraction as adding to and taking from.

Consider Your Students' Needs

Students must be able to count a set accurately and understand that counting tells how many. They may or may not be able to recognize patterned sets or be able to count on and count back from a given number. For those students still having difficulty matching the correct numeral and set, the written component of the activity can be omitted.

For English Language Learners
- In the "Before" phase, focus on the words "more" and "less", "more than" and "less than". Explicit attention to what a comparison statement is can help all students.
- Encourage students to do their thinking in their native language or English.

For Students with Disabilities
- Consider having ten-frames and counters available for concrete models of the dot cards.

Materials

Each student will need:
- Four dot cards, each showing 3 to 10 dots (Blackline Masters 3-8)
- 12 counters
- A crayon or pencil
- "2 More Than" recording sheet (Blackline Master 63)
- "2 Less Than" recording sheet (Blackline Master 64)

Teacher will need:
- Example of a dot pattern with six dots on it (circle stickers on a 4 × 6 index card or on a small paper plate, for example). Circle stickers work well.

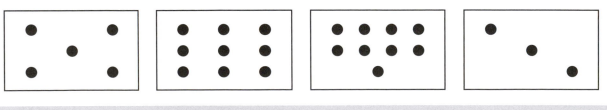

LESSON

Before

Present the focus task to the class:
- Tell students you are going to hold up a dot card. When they think they can say how many dots are on the card, they should give a "thumbs up" (silently).

- Select an easier dot card and hold it up. Wait for thumbs.
- Ask, "Can anyone tell me what how many dots this card would have if I added two more?"
- Explain that their job is to look at dot cards and create a collection of counters that is *two more than* what they see on the dot card.

- Explain to students that they will be getting a bag with supplies and to only take out the counters.
- Again, select and display one dot card. Have students work individually at their seats to count out the number of counters that would be *two more than* what is on your card.
- After adequate work time, ask one student to model on the overhead (or on the carpet, if in a circle setting).
- Discuss with the students how they can decide if the set is actually two more. Accept students' ideas and try them. Students might say: "Count each set. Set a counter aside for each dot. Make the counters into a pattern that is the same as on the dot card."

Provide clear expectations:

- Show students the first recording sheet. Point out the title "2 More Than" at the top.
- Use the example modeled above to demonstrate how to draw the same number of dots as on the dot card in the square on the recording sheet.
- Show how to draw dots in the circle to show the number of counters that they made for their two-more-than set.
- Show how to write the numerals for each amount on the lines to the side of the shapes.

During

- Send students to stations or have them work at tables or desks.

- Observe the methods that students use to count the dots on the cards and to create their sets.
- Ask questions from the "Assessment" section.
- When students complete the "2 More Than" page, give them a new set of four cards, or a set for doing "two less than." (You can base this on individual needs or on whether you are going to do "two less than" later as a whole class.)
- Challenge for capable students: Make sets of dot cards with more dots (in the teens) or have them combine two cards and find *two more than* the sum.

After

Bring the class together to share and discuss the task:

- Show students the card with six dots on it. Ask, "How many dots? How can we tell how many are two more?"
- Have different students show and explain how to think about two more than six. Begin with students who are likely to be still developing this idea. Some students may know immediately that eight is two more than six.

Repeat the "Before," "During," and "After" phases for "two less than."

ASSESSMENT

Observe

- How do students count or know how many dots are on the cards? Do they recognize patterned sets or do they count each dot? Which patterns do they know?
- How do students create their two-more-than sets? Is there an indication of the two-more-than relationship developing or being already developed? If students are working on both sides of the paper, look for similar two-less-than concepts.

- Look for ease or difficulty in recording. Do students correctly write numerals with sets?

Ask

- How are you figuring out "two more than"?
- Can you tell me how many dots are on the card if I show it for just 2 seconds? (Flash a card and ask if they know how many.)

EXPANDED LESSON 9.4

Learning about Division

Mathematics Goals
- To develop the measurement (repeated subtraction) concept of division
- To connect the measurement concept of division to multiplication and addition

Grade Level Guide

NCTM *Curriculum Focal Points*	*Common Core State Standards*
Within the heading of Number and Operations and Algebra, a focal point at third grade is to develop an understanding of division. Students explore the meaning of division of whole numbers through "successive subtraction" (NCTM, 2006, p. 15).	As part of the Standards for third-grade students, "Interpret whole-number quotients of whole numbers, e.g., interpret $56 \div 8$ as the number of objects in each share when 56 objects are partitioned equally into 8 shares, or as a number of shares when 56 objects are partitioned into equal shares of 8 objects each" (CCSS, 2010, p. 23).

Consider Your Students' Needs

Students have explored multiplication concepts, but it is not necessary that they have mastered all of their multiplication facts prior to starting division. This lesson could be used as an introduction to division. For students who have been exposed to division, the lesson can further develop early ideas and help connect the ideas to contextual situations.

For English Language Learners
- Rather than have ELLs write a story, they can illustrate the story.
- Stories about a lot of different topics can be overwhelming for students learning English. Instead, you can ask students to write stories about something specific (for example, apples).
- Be sure that students know the terms "sets" and "groups," as well as "remainder."

For Students with Disabilities
- Have students match a story problem with an equation if they are not able to write their own.

Materials
Each student will need:
- 35 counters
- Small paper cups or portion cups that will hold at least 6 counters (alternatively, students can stack counters in piles)

LESSON

Before

Begin with a simpler version of the task:

- Draw 13 counters (dots) on the board. Ask, "How many sets of 3 can we make if we have 13? How many will be left over?" Most students should be able to answer this question mentally. After receiving several answers, have a student come to the board and demonstrate how to verify the answer of four sets of 3 and 1 left. (*Note:* Depending on your students, you may want to precede the first step using a number such as 12 so that there are no remainders. Do not wait too long before remainders are addressed.)

- Ask, "What equation could we write for what we have on the board?" Accept students' ideas. Correct ideas include:
  - $3 + 3 + 3 + 3 + 1 = 13$
  - $4 \times 3 + 1 = 13$ ($3 \times 4 + 1$ technically represents three sets of 4 and 1 more.)
  - $13 \div 3 = 4$ with 1 left over

- Say, "Think of a situation in which someone might have 13 things and wants to find out how many sets of 3. Make up a story problem about your situation." Have several students share their story problems.

Present the focus task to the class:

- Distribute small paper cups or portion cups and counters to students. Pose the two problems:
  - Use 31 counters to see how many sets of 4 you can make.
  - Use 27 counters to find out how many sets of 6 you can make.
- Ask students for ideas of how they might use the cups to help them solve the problems.

Provide clear expectations:

- Write the directions on the board:
  1. Find how many sets of 4 you can make using 31 counters.
  2. Write three equations: one addition, one multiplication, and one division.
  3. Write a story problem to go with the division equation.
  4. Repeat steps 1, 2, and 3 using 27 counters to make sets of 6.

During

Initially:

- Observe that each student understands the task and is in the process of attempting to solve the first situation.
- If you find that some students, particularly those with disabilities, are struggling, you may need to start them by supporting them in the placement of 4 counters in the first cup. Then they should be able to use that model to continue.

Ongoing:

- Ask students to explain and show (on the overhead or table) why their equations go with what they did with the counters.

- Do not correct incorrect equations or story problems. You only want to be sure students are attempting to connect the activity with the symbolism and the stories.
- Challenge early finishers to see if they can do the same thing for 125 things in sets of 20. However, they will have to figure it out without using counters.

After

Bring the class together to share and discuss the task:

- Ask students to show how they know how many sets of 4 can be made with 31 counters. A picture may be drawn on the board or use counters with a projection device.
- Have several students share their equations. Ask those who have different equations to share theirs as well.
- Have students explain how their equations match what was done with the counters. If students disagree, have them respectfully explain their reasoning. Students should be comfortable with their ideas about the multiplication and addition equations. Because this is an introductory lesson on division, you should correct any misunderstandings about the division equation and what it means.
- Have several students share their story problems. Students should explain how the story situation matches the action of finding how many sets of 4 are in 31. For example: "There were 31 apples in the basket. If each apple tart requires 4 apples, how many tarts can be made?"
- If time permits, repeat with the $27 \div 6$ situation.

ASSESSMENT

Observe

- Look for evidence that students see the connection between the action of finding how many equal sets in a given quantity, and the manner in which a multiplication equation and a division equation are connected. Do not be overly concerned about the use of 4×7 instead of 7×4.
- Story problems should indicate the action of measuring equal sets of 4 rather than dividing the quantity into four sets in a process of sharing or partitioning. If students make this error, simply have them discuss

whether or not the story fits well with the action. Do not indicate that the story is incorrect. It is also possible that students will create multiplication stories with 31 being the unknown amount. Here, ask students which equation best represents the problem.

Ask

- How are multiplication, division, and addition related?
- How does your story problem connect to the division equation? Is it in any way like subtraction?

EXPANDED LESSON 9.5

Estimating Groups of Tens and Ones

Mathematics Goals

- To connect a count-by-ones understanding to a count based on the number of groups of 10 and leftovers for quantities to 100
- To measure lengths using nonstandard measures

Grade Level Guide

NCTM *Curriculum Focal Points*	*Common Core State Standards*

In grade 1, students measure by "laying multiple copies of a unit end to end and then counting the units by using groups of tens and ones." This "supports children's understanding of number lines and number relationships" (NCTM, 2006, p. 13).
 	
    In second grade one of the main focal points is "Developing an understanding of the base-ten numeration system and place-value concepts" (NCTM, 2006, p. 14).
	In first grade, as part of the Measurement and Data domain, students should measure the length of an object by laying multiple lengths of a unit end to end without gaps or overlaps.
	
	    Also in first grade, students begin to understand place value by thinking of two-digit numbers as groups of tens and ones.

Consider Your Students' Needs

Students have not yet developed a full understanding of two-digit numbers in terms of tens and ones. They are able to count a collection of objects to 100. They have talked about numbers in terms of groups of tens and have discussed number patterns on the hundreds chart.

For English Language Learners

- You may want to write the words for the objects on the recording sheet and place name tags next to the objects so that students know which object they are measuring.
- Model an example prior to doing the lesson to clarify the directions.

For Students with Disabilities

- Make sure your selection of a non-standard unit is one that students with disabilities are familiar with from other experiences. Avoid introducing a material for the first time as you are also introducing estimation with this unit.
- As the two students actually measure the length in the "Before" phase of the lesson, ask them to share aloud how they are deciding where to put the connecting cubes or other unit.

Materials

Each student will need:

- "How Long?" recording sheet (Blackline Master 65)

Each measurement station will need:

- Object that can be measured by placing measurement units end-to-end along the full length (vertical distances can be measured with connecting cubes)
- Corresponding measurement "kit" consisting of more than enough individual nonstandard units to measure the length and 10 connected units (a bar of 10 connecting cubes, a chain of 10 paper clips, or a row of 10 toothpicks point to point sandwiched between two pieces of transparent tape)

For Unit	Use Lengths
Connecting cubes	2 to 5 feet (60 cm to 180 cm)
Small paper clips	2 to 9 feet (60 cm to 270 cm)
Large paper clips	3 to 12 feet (90 cm to 4 m)
Toothpicks	5 to 12 feet (1.8 m to 4 m)

Teacher will need:

- The recording sheet for projection
- A kit of nonstandard units that can be used in the "Before" phase of the lesson

LESSON

Before

Begin with a simpler version of the task:

- Show students a length that is somewhere between 25 and 45 connecting-cube units long. For example, you might use the edge of a teacher's desk, a length of ribbon or rope, or a poster.
- Explain that you want to make an estimate of how long the item is in terms of connecting cubes. Accept estimates and record them where students can see. Expect students' guesses to be quite varied. Then suggest that it might be helpful to estimate in terms of groups of 10 units and leftovers. Show students a bar of 10 connecting cubes.
- Hold the 10 units at one end of the length to be measured and accept students' new estimates. Write the first student's estimate on the projected recording sheet. Explain that an *estimate* is what you think it might be by looking at the 10 units; it is not just a wild guess.
- Pass out the recording sheets and have students record their own estimates in the first box. Ask several students what their estimates are.
- Have two students use individual units (e.g., connecting cubes) to measure the length. It is important that they line the units end to end along the entire length so that when they have finished they will have as many actual units as required for the measure. Have two students put the units into groups of 10. Count the groups of 10, and count any leftovers separately. Record this in blanks labeled "Actual" on the projected recording sheet and have students do likewise on their papers.
- Finally, ask students how many units there are. Have the class count the entire group by ones as you set them aside or point to each. Write the number word and the number (e.g., *thirty-four 34*) on the projected recording sheet and the unit (e.g., 34 connecting cubes or 34 toothpicks). Have students write this on their recording sheets.

Present the focus task:

- At three stations, students are to see if they can make reasonable estimates of lengths in terms of groups of 10 and leftovers.
- They then check their estimates by actually measuring, making and counting groups of 10 and leftovers, and finally counting all the units.
- Explain that there are measuring kits and a length for each station. For each length, students are to:
  - Hold the 10 units at one end of the length and estimate the measure of the length in terms of 10 and

leftovers. Each student should record his or her estimate on the recording sheet.
- They are then to measure the lengths using individual units—laying them end to end with no gaps or overlaps.
- When they have placed units along the full length, they should make sets of 10, then count and record the number of groups of 10 and leftovers.
- Finally, they should count all of the units and record this as a number word and as a number. Refer to your example.

Provide clear expectations:

- Have students work in groups of two to four. Tell students that they will work together to measure each object, but each student should make their own estimate. Over the course of the three stations, each student should have the opportunity to measure an object using individual units and to measure using groups of 10 and leftovers.

During

Initially:

- Observe that students understand the task and are in the process of making a reasonable estimate before measuring each object.
- Be sure that students are making and recording estimates by comparing the length to the provided group of 10. They are not to change their estimates.

Ongoing:

- Check that students are lining individual units along the edge of the object without gaps or overlaps when measuring.
- Pay attention to how students count the total number of units. Some may already know that 4 tens and 6 leftovers is 46. However, many will count by ones. Challenge students who just count groups: "Are you sure you will get 46 if you count them all by ones?"

After

Bring the class together to share and discuss the task:

- Discuss what it means to estimate—it is not the same as a guess. Ask, "How did using a group of 10 units help you make an estimate? How does counting the groups of tens and leftovers help tell you how many units you had?" This last question is the key to this lesson. Avoid telling students how to relate the groups and leftovers to the actual number.

ASSESSMENT

Observe

- Look for students who do not make connections between the groups and leftovers and the actual counts. These students have not yet developed base-ten concepts.
- Students who confidently state the total when they have the number of groups and leftovers have indicated at least a beginning understanding of base-ten concepts.

Ask

- How did using a group of 10 units help you make an estimate?
- How does counting the groups of tens and leftovers help tell you how many units you had?

EXPANDED LESSON 9.6

Dot-Paper Fraction Equivalences

CONTENT AND TASK DECISIONS

GRADE LEVEL: 3

Mathematics Goals
- To develop a conceptual understanding of equivalent fractions; the same quantity can have different fraction names
- To look for patterns in equivalent fractions

Grade Level Guide

NCTM *Curriculum Focal Points*	*Common Core State Standards*
Developing fraction concepts is one of three focal points in grade 3: "*Number and Operations:* Developing an understanding of fractions and fraction equivalence" (NCTM, 2006, p. 15).	Fractions are one of four critical themes in grade 3. Specifically, third graders should be able to "solve problems that involve comparing fractions by using visual fraction models and strategies based on noticing equal numerators or denominators" (CCSS, 2010, p. 21).

Consider Your Students' Needs

Students should have a good understanding of what the top and bottom numbers (numerator and denominator) in a fraction represent.

For English Language Learners
- As you are telling the story, write the fractions next to the diagram and point to the representations during the story.
- Focus on the terms "numerator" and "denominator." These have Latin roots, so ELLs whose first language has a Latin root will benefit from this. Specifically, *nom* means name (the denominator is the *name* of the fraction). And *numerare* meaning "to number." In other words the numerator is the numberer. The denominator is the name of pieces. This conceptual connection is a benefit to all learners.
- In observing and assessing, encourage students to illustrate or explain or both.

For Students with Disabilities
- If students are challenged by the dot paper representations, you may need to use one-inch grid paper with color tiles to represent the fractions.
- As you are showing the fraction in the first example use a think-aloud to describe how you are thinking as you decide if the fractions are equivalent.

Materials

Each student will need:
- "Fraction Names" worksheet (Blackline Master 66)

Teacher will need:
- Transparency of or way to display centimeter dot grid (Blackline Master 37)
- Transparency of or way to display "Fraction Names" worksheet (Blackline Master 66)

LESSON

Before

Begin with a simpler version of the task:
- On the dot transparency, outline a 3×3 rectangle and shade it in as shown here.
- Tell this story: "Two students looked at this picture. Each saw a different fraction. Kyle saw $\frac{6}{9}$, but Terri said she saw $\frac{2}{3}$." Ask, "How can they see the same drawing and yet each see different fractions? Which one is right? Why?"

- Have students come to the front of the class and offer explanations for how Kyle saw the picture and how Terri saw it. When students in the class agree on and also understand a correct explanation, draw the corresponding unit fraction to aid in understanding. For example, you can explain, "Terri saw a column of three squares as $\frac{1}{3}$." Draw a column of 3 squares to the side of the rectangle. "If a column of 3 squares is $\frac{1}{3}$, then there are two columns of 3 squares shaded. Therefore, the shaded portion is $\frac{2}{3}$." Similarly, be sure that students see that one square is $\frac{1}{9}$ of the whole. "Since there are 6 squares shaded, the shaded part is $\frac{6}{9}$."

Present the focus task:

- Distribute the "Fraction Names" worksheet.
- For each shaded region on the worksheet, students are to find as many fraction names as possible.
- For each fraction name, students draw a picture of a fractional part and use words to tell how they partitioned the region. For example, if a shaded area is $\frac{4}{12}$, the student should show how the region could be partitioned into twelfths.

During

Initially:

- For students who are having difficulty getting started, draw a fractional part for them. For example, for problem 1, draw a two-square rectangle. Ask, "How many rectangles like this make up the whole? How many of the two-square rectangles are shaded? What fraction of the two-square rectangles are shaded?" Allow time for students to investigate these questions, rather than just showing them how to do it.

Ongoing:

- Students who do not seem to understand counting the fractional parts may need more development of the meaning of numerator and denominator.
- Be sure to ask questions that focus students' attention on connecting the visual to the symbols and explaining how they know if a fraction is equivalent to another fraction.
- For students who seem to have finished quickly, make sure that their explanations reflect their capabilities.

Also, consider challenging them to find even more names. In problem 2, for example, a small triangle can be used as a unit to produce $\frac{12}{24}$.

After

- Use a document camera to display students' completed Blackline Masters so that others can see. For each drawing on the worksheet, record a list of all of the fraction names that students have found for the shaded region.
- Ask students to show how they got the fractions, asking one student to explain one fraction, and a second student to explain a different fraction. For some fractions, students may have used a differently shaped unit fraction. For example, in problem 1, 4 squares of each row of 6 squares can be used to name the shaded region as $\frac{4}{6}$ or columns of the 6 columns may have been used to name $\frac{4}{6}$.
- Problem 1 can be partitioned to show $\frac{2}{3}$, $\frac{4}{6}$, $\frac{8}{12}$, and $\frac{16}{24}$. A 1×1 square could be halved to produce $\frac{32}{48}$. Also, note that three squares are $\frac{1}{10}$ of the whole. Say, "Can the shaded region be named with tenths? Yes! The shaded region contains $6\frac{2}{3}$ tenths; $6\frac{2}{3}$ in the numerator." Students often do not think of this.
- Problem 2 can be named $\frac{1}{2}$, $\frac{2}{4}$, $\frac{3}{6}$, and $\frac{6}{12}$. If a small triangle is used, it can be seen as $\frac{12}{24}$. If a trapezoid of three triangles is used, it is $\frac{4}{8}$. Students may divide it up in other ways as well.
- Problem 3 also has many equivalencies, from $\frac{1}{4}$ to $\frac{8}{32}$.
- If time permits, you may want to focus attention on all of the names for one region and discuss any patterns that students may observe.

ASSESSMENT

Observe

- Watch to see if students connect the visual with the fraction notation. For example, there may be students who do not connect the denominator (unit) with the name of the parts in the *whole*. For example, in the Problem 3 on the Blackline Master, if the full shaded region is used as the unit (fourths), some students may write $\frac{1}{3}$ (1 region to 3 regions). These students will need further foundational work with fraction concepts, in particular the meaning of denominator and numerator.
- See how many equivalencies students find. Do not expect all students to find all of the fraction names—in this way the activity is differentiated. It is, however,

critical that every student finds some equivalencies and makes the connection of why two fractions are equivalent, both in the visual and in the symbols.

Ask

- How can the same quantity (shaded area) have different fraction names?
- What patterns do you see among the equivalent fractions?
- How did you determine if two fractions name the same region?

Multiplication of Fractions Stories

CONTENT AND TASK DECISIONS

GRADE LEVEL: 5–6

Mathematics Goals

- To develop the meaning of multiplication of fractions through various area models
- To explore how different sized wholes affect area models
- To apply area models in solving real-world problems

Grade Level Guide

NCTM *Curriculum Focal Points*	*Common Core State Standards*
Multiplying fractions is part of a grade 6 focal point: "Number and Operations: Developing an understanding of and fluency with multiplication and division of fractions and decimals" (NCTM, 2006, p. 18).	Fraction computation, including multiplication, is one of three critical areas in grade 5. Specifically, fifth graders should be able to "Apply and extend previous understandings of multiplication and division to multiply and divide fractions" (CCSS, 2010, p. 36).

Consider Your Students' Needs

Students understand that multiplication can be thought of as repeated addition; that is, 3×6 means 3 sets of 6. They understand that in the context of part-whole fractions, the whole is divided into equivalent parts. They also understand the symbolic notation of fractions. Students know that the bottom number in the fraction (denominator) names the size or number of the parts they are counting. The denominator indicates how many pieces make a whole unit. They know the top number in the fraction (numerator) is the number of parts they have.

For English Language Learners

- In the car example, use real toy cars or pictures of toy cars to provide both visual support for the language and a concrete way to solve the problem.
- Focus on the terms *numerator* and *denominator*. Both of these words have partial cognates that will help ELLs of Latin languages. Specifically, *nom* means name (the denominator is the *name* of the fraction), and *numerare* meaning "to number." In other words, the numerator is the numberer (how many parts).
- Be sure the contexts in the stories are familiar to students. If they are not, change to something that is. Also,

you can modify the handout by using the same context for each story so that students don't get bogged down in different contexts.

For Students with Disabilities

- Instead of having the students draw the fractional model, give them grid paper or color tiles to support the creation of the representation.
- To help students prepare for sharing their thinking, make sure you do a "think aloud" and share your thinking when discussing the first example. Students who are struggling need explicit demonstrations of what is important to share as they talk about their approaches to the problem.

Materials

Each student will need:

- "Solving Problems Involving Fractions" worksheet (Blackline Master 67)

Teacher will need:

- Transparency of or way to display "Solving Problems Involving Fractions" worksheet (Blackline Master 67)

LESSON

Before

Begin with a simpler version of the task:

- Ask students what 3×4 means. Have them either draw a picture or say/write a word problem to show what 3×4

means. Listen to students' ideas. Capitalize on ideas that emphasize that 3×4 means 3 groups of 4.
- Pose the following word problem to students: "There are 15 cars in Michael's toy car collection. Two-thirds of the cars are red. How many red cars does Michael have?"

- Encourage students to draw pictures not only to help them think about how to solve the problem but also as a way to explain how they did the problem. Have students share their work with the class. Many students will draw 15 rectangles (cars) and then divide the 15 into three equal parts. At this point, make sure to have the students explain why they divided the 15 into three equal parts (e.g., looking for thirds because $\frac{2}{3}$ are red). Once they have three equal parts (thirds), they count two of those sets because they need $\frac{2}{3}$.
- Help students connect this situation with multiplication with whole numbers. Just as 3×4 means 3 groups of 4, $\frac{2}{3} \times 15$ means $\frac{2}{3}$ of a group of 15.

Present the focus task to the class:

- Students are to solve the three problems on the worksheet and be ready to explain their thinking. They should use both words and pictures to help them think through the problems and to show how they solved them. They should be prepared to explain their thinking.
- To differentiate for students ready for more challenging problems, pose the following task in which the pieces must be subdivided into smaller unit parts: "Zack had $\frac{2}{3}$ of the lawn that needed to be cut. If he cuts $\frac{3}{4}$ of the grass that needs to be cut, how much of the whole lawn that needs to be cut will be cut? How much will still need to be cut?"

During

Initially:

- Observe that each student understands the question and is in the process of attempting to solve the first situation.
- If students have difficulty getting started, have them represent the information in the first sentence of the task. Have them explain why their picture represents this information. Then have them read the first part of the "if" statement in the second sentence and identify what part of their original picture this amount is. Have

them color the part they just identified with a different color to make it stand out. Now have them read the question at the end of the task and think about how the part they just colored can help them answer this question.

Ongoing:

- Look for students who use different representations to think about the problems. Highlight those different ways in the "After" portion of the lesson.
- If you notice an error, rather than correct it, ask the student to explain how they solved the problem (students often catch their mistakes while explaining and showing).
- As they work, ask students to tell you what the problem is asking and how they are thinking about solving it. See "Assessment" below for details.

After

Bring the class together to share and discuss the task:

- Starting with the first problem, ask a student to come to the board to explain his or her strategy for thinking about the problem. Ask questions about why the student drew what he or she did to make sure everyone in the class follows the rationale. Encourage the class to comment or ask questions about the student's representation or thinking.
- Help students make explicit what the whole is at each stage of the problem.
- Ask if others solved the problem in a different way. If so, have the students come forward to share their solutions.
- As students share their solutions, it is important to have them compare and contrast the different solutions. Some solutions that at first appear to be different are actually equivalent. Through questioning, help students make these connections.
- Help students connect fraction multiplication with the meaning of multiplication: $\frac{1}{3} \times \frac{3}{4}$ means $\frac{1}{3}$ of a group of $\frac{3}{4}$.

ASSESSMENT

Observe

- Look for students who struggle when the whole changes in the problem. These students need more experience working with part-and-whole tasks.
- Are students correctly using the meaning of the numerator and denominator? These problems are easily solved

by thinking of the fractional parts as discrete units. For example, $\frac{2}{3}$ of $\frac{3}{4}$ is $\frac{2}{3}$ of three things called fourths.
- Are students answering the question that is being asked?

Ask

- How does your drawing show the situation in the task?
- What is the whole unit in the problem?

EXPANDED LESSON 9.8

Friendly Fractions to Decimals

CONTENT AND TASK DECISIONS	GRADE LEVEL: 4

Mathematics Goals

- To connect equivalent decimals to familiar fractions in a conceptual manner
- To reinforce the notion of the 10-to-1 relationship between adjacent digits in our numeration system

Grade Level Guide

NCTM *Curriculum Focal Points*	*Common Core State Standards*
Understanding of fractions is applied to learning about decimals in grade 4 as one of the three focal points: "*Number and Operations:* Developing an understanding of decimals, including the connections between fractions and decimals" (NCTM, 2006, p. 16).	Understanding decimals (decimal fractions) and how they relate to fractions is part of the critical area on Fractions in grade 4. Specifically, fourth graders should be able to "Understand decimal notation for fractions, and compare decimal fractions" (CCSS, 2010, p. 31).

Consider Your Students' Needs

Students are familiar with the 10-to-1 relationship between adjacent digits in our numeration system. Students must understand the part-whole meaning of fractional parts and fraction equivalence.

For English Language Learners

- Be sure instructions are clear. For example, when asking for different ways to show $\frac{1}{10}$, it will be helpful to hold up two different ways and point to each to show that they are different.
- You will be introducing the term *decimal*. The term should be discussed (with all students) in the "After" phase. *Deci-* means tens. Connect to other words they may know with this term (decagon, decade, etc.).

For Students with Disabilities

- Have some pre-shaded 10×10 grids with different fractions and ask the student to find the grid that shows $\frac{1}{2}$.

Once they identify the representation of $\frac{1}{2}$ then have them skip count to show the equivalent $\frac{50}{100}$ on the grid.

Materials

Each student will need:

- Two copies of the 10×10 grids sheets (Blackline Master 27)
- Base-ten materials (Blackline Master 14)

Teacher will need:

- Transparency of or way to display the 10×10 grids (Blackline Master 27)
- Base-ten materials (Blackline Master 14)

LESSON

Before

Begin with a simpler version of the task:

- Ask students what it means to have $\frac{1}{2}$ of something. Highlight the idea that the whole is divided into 2 *equal* parts and you have one of those parts. Showing students the 10×10 grid, ask them to shade $\frac{1}{2}$ of the grid. Ask students to share different ways to shade the grid. It might be helpful to illustrate using base-ten materials as one way to think about this task (i.e., the hundreds square is used as the whole, the tens strip is used as a tenth, and the unit square is used as a hundredth).
- Ask students to look at what they have covered and see what other names they might have for that amount (e.g., $\frac{2}{4}, \frac{4}{8}$, etc.). If someone does not offer $\frac{50}{100}$, then ask students what the fraction would be if they were using the unit square as the name of the fraction (How many hundredths?). Highlight the fact that these are all equivalent names.

Present the focus task to the class:

- Using a 10 × 10 grid, determine equivalent names for the fractions, including a fraction with the name "hundredths."
  $\frac{3}{4} \frac{2}{5} \frac{3}{8}$ *(adapt or add fractions, as appropriate, based on student needs)*

Provide clear expectations:

- Ask students to work with their own Blackline Master and base-ten blocks, but to work with a partner to share and compare their ideas. Explain that during the "After" phase, they will need to justify how they know the original fraction and the new fraction (hundredths) are equivalent.

During

Ongoing:

- Look for students who are shading their 10 × 10 grids differently. Highlight those different ways in the "After" phase of the lesson.
- If students have shaded their grid in a way that does not use long rows of ten, ask students how they could cover the area using as many strips and as few individual squares as possible.

- The $\frac{3}{8}$ task is the most challenging. A useful hint is to ask students how they would find $\frac{1}{8}$ if they had $\frac{1}{4}$.
- You may need to remind students that as they need something smaller than the smallest square on the grid, that the next smaller pieces are tenths of the little squares. Since a small square is $\frac{1}{100}$, one-tenth of it would be $\frac{1}{1000}$ and half of it would be $\frac{5}{1000}$.

After

Bring the class together to share and discuss the task:

- Introduce the decimal fraction notation at the beginning of this phase. Connect to students' experiences with tens and hundreds to now be tenths and hundredths. As students share their solutions, ask students how they can write the hundredths fraction as a decimal fraction. As students use the new notation, ask students to relate the symbols back to the diagrams.
- Students are likely to shade their grids differently. It is important to compare and contrast between different shadings so that students see that they have shaded an equivalent amount. For example, for fourths, students might shade a 5 × 5 section (half of a half). Others may shade two and a half rows of ten. Ask students to determine how these both show one-fourth.

ASSESSMENT

Observe

- Some students will be very successful with shading equal parts but will have difficulty connecting this to hundredths. As you suggest to them to use strips of 10 and individual squares, make sure they can explain why they are using these groupings rather than, say, strips of 5.
- Listen for students using the appropriate terminology (e.g., fourths, eighths, hundredths). This helps develop

the concepts of the size of the parts and will be important in the discussion in the "After" phase.

Ask

- How do you know that the fraction name and decimal name apply to the same region?
- If you are given a fraction, how do you determine how to shade a 10 × 10 grid to show that fractional amount?

EXPANDED LESSON 9.9

Division of Fractions Stories

CONTENT AND TASK DECISIONS

Mathematics Goals

- To develop the partitive meaning of division with fractions through investigating various contexts

Grade Level Guide

NCTM *Curriculum Focal Points*	*Common Core State Standards*
Understanding of division of fractions is one of the three focal points in grade 6: "*Number and Operations:* Developing an understanding of and fluency with multiplication and division of fractions and decimals" (NCTM, 2006, p. 18).	In fifth grade, students begin their understanding of division of fractions, in particular with unit fractions (continuing work in sixth grade). In grade 5, students will, "Apply and extend previous understandings of division to divide unit fractions by whole numbers and whole numbers by unit fractions" (CCSS, 2010, p. 36). In grade 6, students will "Interpret and compute quotients of fractions, and solve word problems involving division of fractions by fractions, e.g., by using visual fraction models and equations to represent the problem" (CCSS, 2010, p. 42).

Consider Your Students' Needs

Students have solved both partition and measurement problems with whole numbers. They understand the symbolic notation of fractions (i.e., they know what the numerator in the fraction means—the number of parts— and what the denominator in the fraction means—the kind of parts we are counting). The students can add fractions and find equivalent fractions.

For English Language Learners

- Use visuals for the opening story problem (real gum or counters to represent gum) and model it with people in the class.
- Provide an opportunity for students to work with a partner who will be able to help with vocabulary.
- Encourage students to use both their native language and English as they work in groups.

For Students with Disabilities

- After debriefing the problem with the gum, use a think-aloud to highlight some of the thinking strategies that come into the decision making as you solve the problem. Jot down some of these ideas so that students can use them as a reference.
- Try suggesting that students who are struggling using a single representation such as a bar diagram, possibly using cash register tape.

Materials

- Teacher will want to have a way to project the stories and the solutions.

LESSON

Before

Begin with a simpler version of the task:

- Ask students how they would solve the following story problem if they did not know their multiplication facts: "Marie bought 24 pieces of bubble gum to share among her 3 friends and herself. How many pieces of gum will each person get?"

- Have them draw a picture or think about how they would act out the story to determine the answer. Listen to students' ideas. Capitalize on ideas that emphasize the sharing action in the problem.

Present the focus task to the class:

- Students are to solve the following problems:

- Cassie has $5\frac{1}{4}$ yards of ribbon to make three bows for birthday packages. How much ribbon should she use for each bow if she wants to use the same length of ribbon for each?
- Mark has $1\frac{1}{4}$ hours to finish his three household chores. If he divides his time evenly, how much time can he spend on each?
- Students should draw pictures and have a written explanation for their solutions. They should also be prepared to explain their thinking. Before you come together as a class, have students explain their ideas to a partner.

Provide clear expectations:

- Have students work independently and then share their work with a partner.

During

Initially:

- Be sure that students are drawing pictures to help them think about how to do the problems and explain their thinking.

Ongoing:

- Look for students who use different representations to think about the problems. Highlight those different ways in the "After" phase of the lesson.
- To differentiate for advanced learners, pose another problem to them in which the parts must be split into smaller parts (like the second problem in the task). For example, "Ryan has $6\frac{2}{3}$ yards of rope to hang 4 bird feeders. How much rope will he use for each feeder if he wants to use the same length of rope for each?"
- Monitor partner discussions as students explain their thinking in order to address any misconceptions or difficulties during the whole class discussion.

After

Bring the class together to share and discuss the task:

- For each problem, first get answers from the class. If more than one answer is offered, simply record them and offer no evaluation.
- Have students come to the board to explain their strategies for thinking about the problem. You may need to ask questions about drawings or explanations to make sure everyone in the class follows the rationale. Encourage the class to comment or ask questions about the student's representation or thinking. Ask if others used a different representation or solved the problem in a different way. If so, have the students come forward to share their solutions. If there are different answers, the class should evaluate the solution strategies and decide which answer is correct and why.
- Discuss the different representations students use (e.g., some students use circles or rectangles, whereas others may use a number line) and how the action in the story is one of sharing.
- For problems that require the parts to be split into smaller parts, students will likely use different approaches. For example, for the second problem in the given task, some students will first divide the hour into thirds and then the quarter hour into twelfths, whereas other students will divide the hour into twelfths and share the twelfths between the 3 chores. It is important to have students compare and contrast the different approaches. Some solutions that at first appear to be different are actually equivalent in many ways. Through questioning, help students make these connections.
- Help students notice that while they are answering these questions, they are also asking, "How much is in the whole?" or "How much for one?" This mode of thinking will help students when the divisor is a fraction.

ASSESSMENT

Observe

- Are students using their understanding of the meaning of fractions to help them draw a representation or solve the problem in another way? Using the meaning of the fraction is imperative when the problem requires splitting the part into smaller parts.
- Look for students who struggle with identifying the whole. These students need more experience working with part-and-whole tasks.

Ask

- What is the problem asking you to partition?
- How many parts/groups will you have?
- What is the size of each part?

How Many In Between?

CONTENT AND TASK DECISIONS
GRADE LEVEL: 4–6

Mathematics Goals
- To compare fractions and decimals
- To develop the concept of density of the rational numbers (there is always another fraction/decimal fraction that can be found between any two given fractions/decimals)
- To reinforce the idea that fractions and decimal numbers are different symbolic notations for the same quantities

Grade Level Guide

NCTM *Curriculum Focal Points*	*Common Core State Standards*
Connecting fractions to decimals and comparing decimals (and fractions) are part of a focal point in grade 4: "*Number and Operations:* Developing an understanding of decimals, including the connections between fractions and decimals" (NCTM, 2006, p. 16).	Understanding fractions is a major emphasis in grade 4. Included in this work on fractions is connecting to decimals. Students will be able to, "Understand decimal notation for fractions, and compare decimal fractions" (CCSS, 2010, p. 31). In sixth grade, students study rational numbers in more depth: "Apply and extend previous understandings of numbers to the system of rational numbers" (CCSS, 2010, p. 43).

Consider Your Students' Needs

Students are skilled at finding equivalent fractions and at converting fractions to decimals.

For English Language Learners
- The word "between" needs attention in the "Before" phase. In particular that "between" doesn't mean the value has to be exactly in the middle. This can be modeled with people in front of the room and the word can be written and described on the board.
- Students from other countries often do more mental math, and this should be valued. If you are not clear on how someone found an "in between" fraction or decimal, ask if they will explain or write how they thought about it. Having the student share a clever mental strategy is also a good idea.

For Students with Disabilities
- You may need to scaffold this task for students who are struggling by selecting the first two fractions for them to work on rather than using what the class suggests. In that way you can select fractions that have denominators that are easily compared, such as thirds and twelfths. Once students explore an approach to finding fractions between those limits, then they can move to more challenging combinations.

Materials
- Number line or other linear representation (e.g., Cuisenaire Rods) to help students visualize relative size of the numbers

LESSON

Before

Begin with a simpler version of the task:
- Ask students to list four fractions between $\frac{1}{9}$ and $\frac{8}{9}$. This should be an easy task and should not require much, if any, discussion. Now ask students to find four fractions between $\frac{1}{2}$ and $\frac{9}{10}$. Have students share the fractions that they have identified and the strategies they used to find

them. Resist telling students any method to use. The fractions $\frac{6}{10}$, $\frac{7}{10}$, and $\frac{8}{10}$ are easy to find; a fourth fraction may be a challenge if students are looking for fractions with common denominators. However, $\frac{2}{3}$, $\frac{3}{4}$, $\frac{5}{6}$, $\frac{7}{8}$, and $\frac{8}{9}$ are among the many other possible solutions. Listen to and encourage the class to discuss students' ideas about approaches to finding the fourth fraction.

Present the focus task to the class:

- As a class, select two fractions that students believe are "really close" on the number line. The challenge is to find 10 fractions that are between the two fractions. [Note: This is an easy lesson to differentiate by tiering—provide different starting fractions that vary in difficulty for different groups of students.]
- Students can use any method they wish to find their "in between" fractions, but they have to be able to explain their methods in the "After" phase.

Provide clear expectations:

- After the class has chosen the two fractions, the students work individually.

During

Ongoing:

- Look for students who are identifying fractions using various strategies. Possible strategies include:
  - Trying different fractions without a system (often leading to fractions not in the desired interval)
  - Getting a large common denominator and then using consecutive numerators
  - Converting the given fractions to decimals and using decimal representations to find a value in between
- Resist telling students how to find the fractions—they will have to rely on their own understanding of fractions to come up with a solution.
- Think about what information you can glean from students' strategies about their understanding of fractions.

After

Bring the class together to share and discuss the task:

- Have students share the fractions they have identified and the strategies they used to find them. Listen to, but do not judge, students' ideas. Instead, encourage the class to discuss students' ideas about approaches to finding the fractions.
- If students convert the fractions to decimals, see if they can convert one or more of the decimal numbers to fractions. Use this strategy to highlight that these are different symbolic notations for the same quantities. If you suspect that students are not convinced that the fraction and decimal number represent equivalent quantities, give them a copy of the 10×10 grids and ask them to represent the fraction quantity on one grid and the decimal quantity on another grid and compare the amounts.
- Ask students if they think they could find 10 more fractions between two of the closest fractions they found in this activity. Encourage students to discuss their conjectures. If there is any doubt, have the class work together to find 10 more fractions.
- At the conclusion of this lesson, explain that what they have been exploring is the concept of the *density of the rational numbers*. Students may be able to come up with their own definition of what it means to say that the rational numbers are *dense*.

ASSESSMENT

Observe

- Do students have a systematic way to determine fractions between the given fractions or are they haphazardly identifying possibilities?
- If students convert the fractions to decimals, do they only identify decimals in between the two given quantities? Can they also solve the problem using fractions? If they struggle with using fractions, this may indicate a weak understanding of equivalent fractions.
- How do students respond to finding more fractions between two of the closest fractions identified in the activity? Are they hesitant or do they seem to understand the concept of density?

Ask

- How can you find a fraction whose value is between any two other fractions?
- How can converting a fraction to a decimal help?
- How many fractions can we find between the two fractions we used? (This it what it means to say that rational numbers are "dense.")

EXPANDED LESSON 9.11

Comparing Ratios

Mathematics Goals
- To develop conceptual strategies for comparing ratios in various contexts
- To develop proportional reasoning (multiplicative as opposed to additive)

Grade Level Guide

NCTM *Curriculum Focal Points*	*Common Core State Standards*
Ratios appear as part of a focal point in grade 6: "*Number and Operations:* Connecting ratio and rate to multiplication and division" (NCTM, 2006, p. 18) and is imbedded in the algebraic thinking in grade 6 as well. Applying ratio understanding to proportions is a focal point in grade 7: "*Number and Operations* and *Algebra* and *Geometry:* Developing an understanding of and applying proportionality, including similarity" (NCTM, 2006, p. 19).	Ratios and rates serves as one of four critical areas in grade 6: "connecting ratio and rate to whole number multiplication and division and using concepts of ratio and rate to solve problems" (CCSS, 2010, p. 39). Specifically, the goal for sixth graders is to "expand the scope of problems for which they can use multiplication and division to solve problems, and they connect ratios and fractions. Students solve a wide variety of problems involving ratios and rates" (CCSS, 2010, p. 39).

Consider Your Students' Needs

Students understand equivalent fractions. They are also familiar with the term *unit fraction* (e.g., $\frac{1}{3}$, $\frac{1}{4}$, $\frac{1}{9}$). Students have had experiences with ratios, but some may still not be able to distinguish between additive and multiplicative relationships. Some students may have also used symbolic or mechanical methods for solving proportions in a prior year, but the assumption is that these methods are not well understood.

For English Language Learners
- For the warm-up, show an illustration of a running track (for example, the one at your school or one from the Internet).
- Reinforce the terms *ratio* and *rate* throughout the lesson. Encourage all students to use the appropriate language in their small groups and in their presentations.
- When solving tasks 2–4, be sure the context is understood through use of visuals or realia (real objects). Alternatively, problem 3 can be the one context used, and three examples given (that mirror 2–4). This is a way to engage in the content but limit the linguistic demands.

- Students should be encouraged to discuss the problem in their native language, as well as in English.

For Students with Disabilities
- Support students by explicitly sharing that they should look for a strategy to find how much time it takes for Terry to run one lap. Describe this as a unit rate. Have students find the unit rate for other problems.
- You may want to consider modifying problem 2 to having Jill walk 3 steps every 12 seconds to give students who struggle a bit more practice with finding the unit rate with more compatible numbers. Then you can change the original problem with Jill walking 3 steps every 10 seconds.

Materials
Each student will need:
- "It's a Matter of Rates" worksheet (Blackline Master 68)
- Ratio tables (optional)

Teacher will need:
- Transparency of or way to display "It's a Matter of Rates" (Blackline Master 68)

LESSON

Before

Present the focus task to the class:

[Note: This is a longer "Before" phase that includes the solving of one problem before doing the others—it could be that the "Before" takes a full lesson and the next two phases are the focus of day 2.]

- Read the first problem on the "It's a Matter of Rates" worksheet to students. Ask them to guess which runner is faster. Get a show of hands for Terry and then for Susan.

- Next have students think for a moment about how they determine which runner is actually faster. Students should share their ideas with a partner.

- Accept student ideas without evaluating them at this time. If a ratio table has not been introduced, share it as one tool you have used for thinking about this type of problem. Ask students to work with a partner on one of the strategies they have heard.

- Ask students to prepare illustrations and explanations of their solution to Terry's and Susan's rate. Discuss the different approaches and ask questions that help students see how one solution connects to another solution.

- Focus discussion on generalizing the strategies that worked—for example, that people found something the same about the two (either the laps or the time) so that they could compare.

- Assign the other three problems for students to solve. Notice that problem 2 has a context similar to problem 1, but the others are quite different examples of ratio or rate.

During

Ongoing:

- For students who are having difficulty, look at one ratio in a problem and ask what the unit rate is. For example, "How fast can Terry run in one minute? How often does Jack take a step up the hill?" In the first three problems, one or both of the ratios can be converted to a unit rate.

- For students who are ready for a challenge, differentiate by changing the numbers so that neither rate is easily simplified to a unit rate.

- Do not give students an algorithm. Instead, encourage them to make sense of the numbers in the given context.

After

Bring the class together to share and discuss the task:

- For each problem, ask students to share their strategies. Do not evaluate students' approaches, but allow the class to discuss and question the different strategies and make connections among them. Through questioning, help the students compare and contrast the different approaches.

- If students use unit rates in their strategies, help the class relate unit rates to the concept of unit fractions.

- Change the numbers in one or more problems so that unit rates are not easy to use. For example, suppose that Terry runs 5 laps in 12 minutes and Susan runs 2 laps in 5 minutes. How students respond to this problem will give you insight into choosing problems for the next lesson.

- As an extension, have students create their own problems using proportional reasoning with two ratios that are not easily compared or easily simplified to unit rates.

ASSESSMENT

Observe

- Look for students who focus on additive relationships. These students are not seeing the multiplicative relationship of proportionality.

- Which students are using a unit rate approach? Which are not? Are students using different forms of the ratios to create two fractions with the same numerators? With the same denominators?

- Watch for students who are using a mechanical method (such as the cross-product algorithm). These methods do not develop proportional reasoning and should not be encouraged (or introduced) until students have had many experiences with intuitive and conceptual methods. If students are using such methods, ask for them to explain why it works or ask if they can find the solution another way.

Ask

- What strategies are you using for comparing ratios?
- How are unit ratios like/different from unit fractions?
- How does a ratio table help with comparing two ratios?
- Can you have a common numerator to compare two ratios?

EXPANDED LESSON 9.12

One Up and One Down

Mathematics Goals

- To discover and explore number patterns within the context of addition
- To understand how complementary changes in two addends leave the sum unchanged

Grade Level Guide

NCTM *Curriculum Focal Point*	*Common Core State Standards*
In a focal point connection under "Algebra" at both kindergarten and grade 1, students work with number patterns to explore relationships that will eventually result in the creation of generalizable rules.	In the domain of Operations and Algebraic Thinking, kindergarteners add by using a variety of ways to represent the problems. In first grade, students add using the relationship between addition and subtraction and are expected to understand the meaning of the equal sign.

Consider Your Students' Needs

Students need not know their addition combinations to engage in this lesson. However, they should have been exposed to the plus and equal sign and understand how an addition equation is a representation of two parts of a whole.

For English Language Learners

- Be sure that students know the words "up" and "down," which can be acted out (asking students to stand up and sit down (emphasizing the words up and down).
- As needed, provide translations for the numbers.

For Students with Disabilities

- Use a mathematics balance (a plastic "number line" on a fulcrum). This can be used to dramatically model the movement of one hanging weight and the effect it has on the balance of the equation. If you do not have such a balance, use a two sided mat with an equal sign in the middle to have students demonstrate making equations that show that what is on the left side of the mat is the same as (or equal to) what is on the right side of the mat.

Materials

Each student will need:

- Counters
- Calculators (optional)

LESSON

Before

Present the focus task to the class:

- Explain this problem: "The other day, a friend of mine was thinking about adding 7 + 7." Write 7 + 7 on the board. "She wondered what would happen if she made the first 7 one more and the second 7 one less." With students' help, write this new sum, 8 + 6, on the board. Have students complete each equation.
- Ask, "Why do you think the answers are the same?" Have students offer their ideas. Ask, "Do you think this same plan will work if we started with 5 + 5 or 8 + 8?" Discuss this briefly.
- To differentiate the task, some students could use counters to try to figure out why 7 + 7 and 8 + 6 have the same answers. Then try another sum, like 5 + 5, and see if it works for that sum also.
- For more advanced students, the task is to use counters and try to figure out why 7 + 7 and 8 + 6 have the same answers. Will it work for any double (like 5 + 5, 6 + 6, 8 + 8, and so on)? What if the two numbers you begin with are not the same?
- Students should use pictures, numbers, and words to show their thinking. If someone picks up the papers, they should be able to understand what students' ideas are.

Provide clear expectations:

- You may want to have students work in pairs. Work could be shown on large chart paper to be shared with the class.

During

Initially:

- Observe that students have access to the materials they need to solve the problem. Observe that each student understands the question and is in the process of attempting to solve the first situation.

Ongoing:

- Some students may use their counters and complete each sum independently without relating one to the other. Ask these students to show you 7 + 7 with counters. Be sure that there are two separate piles of seven and not a single pile of 14. Ask, "How could you change these piles to show 8 + 6?" Observe how students make the changes so that later you can invite students to show their different ways.
- Encourage students to get their ideas on paper for the 7 + 7 case before they explore further.
- How much you push students to explore further depends on the abilities and maturity of the students. In the lower grades, you might remind them to try another double such as 5 + 5 and see if the same thing works there. Older students can be challenged with more open-ended explorations, such as: "Does it always work? Do you have to start with a double? What if you change the numbers by 2 or some other number? What about really big numbers like 87 + 87?" (For large numbers, students should be encouraged to use calculators, even if they cannot compute the sums by hand.)
- For those students who may find this exploration rather easy, challenge them to see how this might work for subtraction.

After

Bring the class together to share and discuss the task:

- Select students to share their ideas. Perhaps call first on students who have struggled and need to be encouraged. Although it is good for students to see the more sophisticated ideas, it is important to also focus on emerging ideas as well. For each student who shares, encourage students to ask questions or to offer additional ideas.
- Some students may have difficulty articulating their ideas. Suggest that they use counters on the overhead or magnetic counters on the board so that they can show students their thinking.
- Ask students how this idea could help them if they forgot how much 5 + 7 was. (5 + 7 will be the same as 6 + 6. Similarly, 6 + 8 is double 7, and so on.)

ASSESSMENT

Observe

- Especially for very young learners, be aware of students who do not have a clear connection between a model for addition—especially a part-part-whole model—and the symbolic equation that represents this. Many students learn only to use counters to get answers but do not see the counters as a way to show what the equation means.
- Students who shove counters together and begin counting at once to solve an addition equation are the most likely to have difficulty with this activity.
- A few students will see this activity as rather simple. These students have a good understanding of what addition means.

Ask

- How does changing one number (or pile of counters) up one and the other pile down one affect the sum? Why is that?
- Did you see a number pattern with your problems?
- What do you think would happen if we change the numbers by adding two to each?

Geometric Growing Patterns: Predict How Many

CONTENT AND TASK DECISIONS

Mathematics Goals

- To explore growing patterns using three representations: pictures or drawings, table of values, and a rule
- To identify the relationships between the step number and the value at that step in a growing pattern (determine the rule) as a foundation for the concept of function

Grade Level Guide

NCTM *Curriculum Focal Points*	Common Core State Standards
Exploring growing patterns, in particular being about to determine a rule for non-numeric growing patterns is a grade 4 connection.	The Mathematical Practices, in particular, *Look for and make use of structure* is central to this lesson as "students look closely to discern a pattern or structure" (CCSS, 2010, p. 8). In fourth grade, students "Generate and analyze patterns" (p. 29), and in fifth grade students extend this work to "analyze patterns and relationships" (p. 35).

Consider Your Students' Needs

Students have had some experience with growing patterns. They have extended growing patterns with appropriate materials and explained why their extensions followed the patterns. Students have created tables to record the numeric component of patterns (the number of objects at each step). They have found and described recursive relationships (i.e., how the pattern changes from one step to the next). They may not have not begun to use variables in their explanations.

For English Language Learners

- In the "Before" phase, reinforce the language needed for the lesson: pattern, rule, symbols, step number, step value (number of sticks). In addition, the context may need vocabulary support (windows, arrays).
- Many of these terms mean something different in everyday language, so take time to compare the mathematical meaning to the everyday meaning.
- Because this is a lot of terminology and there is different meaning to the terms in everyday language, working on vocabulary up front will benefit ELLs and others as well. (They will then use these words as they engage in

the lesson.) Consider a game format such as pictionary or concentration. Or use note cards and have students draw the everyday meaning and the math meaning on opposite sides of the card.
- Reinforce these terms throughout the lesson.

For Student with Disabilities

- Consider having toothpicks or rods available for modeling the steps in the window problem. Then move to two-color counters to create the arrays in the dot array pattern.

Materials

Each student will need:

- "Predict How Many" (Windows) worksheet (Blackline Master 69)
- "Predict How Many (Dot Arrays) worksheet (Blackline Master 70)

Teacher will need:

- Transparencies or copies to project of "Predict How Many" worksheets (Blackline Masters 69–70)

LESSON

Before

Present the focus task to the class:

- Distribute the "Windows" pattern worksheet and display it on the overhead. Explain that the table shows how many sticks are needed to make all of the windows for that step. Have students look at the next two steps and fill in the next two entries of the table.
- Ask, "If we wanted to find how many sticks it would take to have 20 windows—the twentieth step—what patterns can we use to help us so that we would not have to draw all of the steps?" Suggest that students look for ways to count the sticks in groupings and try to connect the groupings to the step numbers. Have students work for a while in pairs and then solicit ideas from the class. Here are some possible ideas that students may suggest:

  1. "The tops and bottoms have the same number of sticks as the step number. There is one more vertical stick than the step number." [Step (top) + Step (bottom) + (Step + 1) (vertical sides)]
  2. "There is a square of four sticks, then each new step adds three more. That is, four plus three times one less than the step number." [$4 + 3 \times (\text{Step} - 1)$]
  3. "One stick at the start, then there are as many sets of three as the step number." [$1 + 3 \times \text{Step}$]
  4. Looking only at the table and not the drawing: "Start with 4 then add 3, one less time than the step number." This gives the same result as idea number 2. Help students make the connection from the table to the drawing (and to the rule).

- For each suggestion that you get, write the idea in a manner similar to the expressions shown here. Notice in these expressions that "step" is actually a variable and could be replaced by n or S or any other letter. It is not necessary that students come up with all of these ideas. Erase the ideas that have been suggested.
- Have students use an idea that they like and explain their rule on the "Windows" worksheet. Then have them use the rule to finish the table.
- Have students continue independently with the second worksheet, "Dot Arrays." Students should extend the pattern and make table entries accordingly.

- Students should describe in words the pattern they see in the picture. They should use the picture and/or table to determine the value for the twentieth step.

Provide clear expectations:

- Students may work with partners to share ideas, but each student needs to complete the worksheets.

During

Initially:

- Be sure students understand what they did with the "Windows" worksheet before they continue with "Dot Arrays."

Ongoing:

- If students are having difficulty finding a relationship, suggest that they look for ways to count the dots without having to count each one. If they use the same method of counting for each step, they should begin to see how their counting method relates to the step numbers. Have them write a numeric expression for each step that matches their counting procedure. For example, step 2 is 2×3, step 4 is 3×4, and so on.
- Once students think they have identified a relationship, make sure they test their conjecture with other parts of the table and picture.

After

Bring the class together to share and discuss the task:

- Ask what entry students found for step 20. List all results on the board without comment. The correct result is 420, but do not evaluate any responses.
- Ask students to come to the board to explain their strategies for identifying and extending the pattern. Encourage the class to comment or ask questions about methods of counting the dots or thinking about the rule for step 20.
- For students who use only the table to find a pattern, have the class see how their idea can be related to the drawings of the dots.

ASSESSMENT

Observe

- Are students able to see the connections between the pictorial representation of the pattern and the table of values?
- Look for students who are simply generating all the entries in the table to determine the twentieth entry. These students need to be encouraged to look for patterns in the manner that they count the dots.

Ask

- Describe the pattern you see in the drawing.
- Describe the pattern you see in the table.
- Describe how you can find the number in the twentieth step in the table, in the diagram, and using the equation.
- How can you use the pattern in the drawing or table to write a rule for the situation?

EXPANDED LESSON 9.14

Create a Journey Story

Mathematics Goals

- To interpret line graphs
- To write scenarios that are representative of given graphs
- To explain why certain graphs represent impossible situations

Grade Level Guide

NCTM *Curriculum Focal Points*	Common Core State Standards
Being able to connect representations (like stories and graphs), and including patterns, models, and relationships as contexts is a grade 5 connection.	The Mathematical Practices, in particular, *Reason abstractly and quantitatively*, is central to this lesson as students analyze the graph and determine a context that could fit the graph. This type of task is appropriate for fifth graders, who must "analyze patterns and relationships," including analyzing graphs (CCSS, 2010, p. 35).

Consider Your Students' Needs

Students may have explored their rate of walking with a calculator-based ranger (motion detector) to learn how walking rates are modeled in a graph. For instance, they understand that the faster they walk, the steeper the line that is generated in the display. Students have experienced graphing ordered pairs in a coordinate plane. (The motion-detector experience is not a prerequisite for this lesson.)

For English Language Learners

- Since this lesson is about creating stories, allow students to write their stories in their native language. You can use software for translations, if needed.
- Consider language proficiency when pairing students so that those with limited English might be able to work with someone who can assist in translation.

- Use sentence starters or fill-in-the-blank sentences to assist those that know little English so that they can create stories by filling in the important conceptual information.

For Students with Disabilities

- Create a set of story scenarios for several of the graphs. Have students who are struggling match the story to the appropriate graph.

Materials

Each student will need:

- "Create a Journey Story" worksheet (Blackline Master 71)

Teacher will need:

- Transparency or copy to project of "Create a Journey Story" worksheet (Blackline Master 71)

LESSON

Before

Begin with a simpler version of the task:

- Ask students to sketch a graph of the distance a car travels in the following story: "A car is traveling along a road at a steady speed and comes to a stop sign. It stops for the sign and then accelerates to the same speed as before."
- Point out that the horizontal axis should represent *time* and the vertical axis should represent *distance*.
- Have students share their sketches. Resist evaluating the sketches. Encourage students to comment on and question classmates' ideas. Draw attention to different

periods of time on the horizontal axis and how the distance changes within that period. A reasonable sketch might look like one of these:

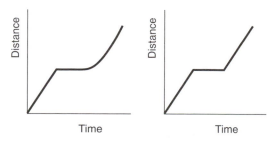

- The graph on the left has a curve following the stopped (horizontal) segment, indicating speeding up from stopped to the former speed. The one on the right does not account for the speeding up, but is still an appropriate representation of the situation.

Present the focus task to the class:

- The "Create a Journey Story" worksheet shows time–distance graphs created by a student. Each is supposed to represent the journey of a single vehicle or person. For each of the graphs, make up a plausible journey story or explain why it is not possible to do so.
- For those graphs that can represent a journey, students should make up a simple yet plausible journey story. The story may involve walking, running, or driving a car.
- Point out that some of the graphs cannot represent any credible journey. For those graphs, they are to explain why.

During

Initially:

- If a student is having trouble getting started, cover up all but the first part of the graph he or she is working on. Ask the student to think about what that part of the graph tells him or her about the distance traveled or the time elapsed. Help the student translate that information into a story context. Repeat with the next part of the graph.

Ongoing:

- As individual students write their stories, ask them to explain to you what is happening in their stories at various points in the graph.
- To differentiate, ask more advanced students to mark and label units along both axes of a graph to match the journey story. For students having difficulty, you might mark the axes and ask questions such as, "How much time did it take for the person or car to go 2 miles?"
- For students ready for a challenge, differentiate by asking them to graph the *speed* of the car in the "Before" section of the lesson over the same interval of time.

After

Bring the class together to share and discuss the task:

- Have students share one of their stories without telling which graph the story is supposed to match. Have the class discuss which graph best fits the story.
- Ask students to explain why the impossible graphs are impossible. (Graph D is impossible because it shows different positions at the same time. Graph F is impossible because in the vertical segment the position changes but no time elapses.)
- Discuss the steepness (slope) of lines in different segments of the graph. Ask what it means if the graph is steeper in one portion than in another.
- After identifying stories for each graph, compare stories for the same graph. Have students discuss the similarities and the differences.

ASSESSMENT

Observe

- Look for students who create journey stories that mimic the shape of the graph by the movement of the journey but that do not reflect the relationship of distance versus time. For example, for graph A, such a student might describe walking on a straight path and then veering off the path to the left. This story does not interpret the graph as a relationship between distance and time but rather as a map.
- Are students able to articulate through their stories the reason for different slopes in different parts of the graph? That is, steeper lines indicate faster speeds.

Downward sloping lines indicate moving backward or toward the starting point. (A person/car could turn around and move forward or go backward without turning around. The graph would be the same.)

Ask

- Why is this graph impossible?
- What does a horizontal line segment in the graph mean?
- What does the steepness (slope) mean in this segment of the graph?
- What does a downward sloping line segment mean?

EXPANDED LESSON 9.15

Crooked Paths

CONTENT AND TASK DECISIONS

Mathematics Goals

- To help students understand that length is an attribute that need not be in a straight line (for example, the distance around an object or a nonstraight path has length just as does a straight object)
- To use a nonstandard measurement tool (e.g., string, blocks) to measure lengths

Grade Level Guide

NCTM *Curriculum Focal Points*	*Common Core State Standards*
Students in prekindergarten think about which objects have the attribute of length and can compare objects' lengths. In kindergarten, students use length to compare objects. First graders measure using multiple copies of units end to end.	*Kindergarten students begin to describe attributes of objects that can be measured with length.* In grade 1, one of four focal areas is students measuring lengths indirectly and by iterating (or using groups of the same unit).

Consider Your Students' Needs

Students have made comparisons of straight objects or paths and have learned the meaning of *longer* and *shorter* in that context. Students have not used units or rulers to measure lengths.

For English Language Learners

- Students may need language support for the terms *longer*, *shorter*, *straight*, and *crooked*. You can have students model what these terms mean and/or use objects to illustrate their meaning. Also, reinforce the meaning of *estimate*.
- Use pair-share and/or encourage use of native language in the "After" phase when students are explaining their thinking about the longer paths.

For Students with Disabilities

- Tape the end of the string to the beginning of the path, then mark the end of the measurement on the string

with a marker. Use another string for the other path in the same way. Then compare the lengths.
- Students may have trouble with thinking about the estimates of length when one path is "crooked." You might want to show an example of two paths on the floor (one crooked and one straight) and have students walk each to see which takes longer to walk. Then they can think about estimating the paths made in the learning stations.

Materials

- Masking tape
- Rope, string, or yarn that is at least 10 feet long for each station
- One "Crooked Paths" recording sheet for every pair of students (Blackline Master 72)

LESSON

Before

This will be a station activity. Set up three identical stations around the room. Each station consists of two crooked paths made of masking tape. Try to make them about the same in each station. Path A is a zigzag of four straight-line segments that total about 9 feet. Path B is more S-shaped and is about 7 feet long. Make path B "look" longer by spreading it out more.

Begin with a simpler version of the task:

- Show the class pairs of straight objects, such as a pencil and a crayon, or two lines drawn on the board. For each pair, ask, "Which is longer? Which is shorter? How can we tell?"
- On the board, draw a half-circle and beneath it a line segment about as long as the diameter. Ask, "How can we tell which of these is longer?" Solicit ideas. Be sure students hear the idea that the curve is longer than the line segment and that some students provide good reasons. For example, say, "If you had to walk on these, it would take longer to walk the curved path."

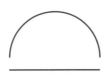

Present the focus task to the class:

- Gather students around one station. Say, "One path might be longer or they might be the same. Your task is to decide."
- Show students the worksheets and explain how to use them. Explain that they are to circle the path that is longer or circle both paths if they think they are the same. Then they are to draw a picture to show how they decided. Have students work in pairs.
- Ask students which path they think is longer or whether they think they are the same. Say, "Before you begin work, put an X on the picture of the path that you think is longer. This is your estimate." Have a few students share their estimates and their reasoning.
- Show students that there is string for comparing lengths, but they can use linked paper clips, blocks, or whatever materials they want to help them decide.

Provide clear expectations:

- Students will work with partners at the stations.

During

- Monitor station activity but do not interfere. Be sure students are completing worksheets to the best of their abilities.
- If a pair seems unable to make a decision, ask, "If a toy car was going to go along these paths, which path would it travel longer on?" Or, "Could you use some blocks from over in the block corner to help?"
- Challenge task for students who need a challenge: Make a long row of blocks in a straight line that is just as long as the curvy path.

After

Bring the class together to share and discuss the task:

- Remind students of the task of comparing the two paths. Have students refer to their worksheets as they talk about what they did.
- Ask, "How many thought the zigzag path was longer?" Count and record on the board next to a zigzag. "How many thought the curvy path was longer?" Count and record. "How many thought they were about the same?" Count and record. Ask students if the estimates they made were the same as the result that they figured out. Were they surprised? Why?
- Select pairs to explain what they did. Get as many different ideas and methods as possible.
- If students disagree about which path is longer, have them explain their reasoning in a way that might convince those who disagree. Give students the opportunity to change their minds, but ask, "What made you change your minds?"

ASSESSMENT

Observe

- Look for students who understand how length can exist on a curved path (correctly compare or make appropriate attempt). This can be a checklist item based on the discussion or observations.
- For students who used units, did they use like-sized units or make appropriate use of materials?

Ask

- Which path is longer? How do you know?
- How can path A be longer if it takes less room to make on the floor than path B?

Fixed Areas

CONTENT AND TASK DECISIONS	GRADE LEVEL: 3–4

Mathematics Goals

- To contrast the concepts of area and perimeter
- To develop an understanding of the relationship between area and perimeter of different shapes when the area is fixed
- To compare and contrast the units used to measure perimeter and those used to measure area

Grade Level Guide

NCTM *Curriculum Focal Points*	*Common Core State Standards*
Perimeter is a grade 3 connection within measurement. Area is a grade 4 focal point in Measurement: "Developing an understanding of area and determining the areas of two-dimensional shapes" (NCTM, 2006, p. 16).	Area is one of four critical themes in grade 3: "developing understanding of the structure of rectangular arrays and of area." Specifically, students will be able to "recognize perimeter as an attribute of plane figures and distinguish between linear and area measures" (CCSS, 2010, p. 22).

Consider Your Students' Needs

Students have worked with the ideas of area and perimeter. Some, if not the majority of, students can find the area and perimeter of given figures and may even be able to state the formulas for finding the perimeter and area of a rectangle. However, they may become confused as to which formula to use.

For English Language Learners

- Build background for the terms *rectangle*, *length*, *width*, *area*, and *perimeter*. Ask students if they have heard of these words and use their ideas to talk about their mathematical meaning.
- Use visuals (tiles) as you model the mathematical terms.

For Students with Special Needs

- Students who struggle may need to use a computer-based program to model different areas or a geoboard.
- Sometimes the large number of color tiles used for an area of 24 or 26 can be distracting. Students may focus more on the construction than the mathematical concept. Consider using a smaller total, like 16.
- If you are using color tiles to model smaller areas, create a special set with the word "Area" written with a permanent marker on each. The use of these tiles to create the shapes with an area will reinforce the difference between area and perimeter. Also note for students who confuse these two measures that the word "Rim" is in the word perimeter—this mnemonic can jog the memory of students who struggle.

Materials

Each student will need:

- 36 square tiles, such as color tiles
- Two or three sheets of "Rectangles Made with 36 Tiles" grid paper (Blackline Master 73)
- "Fixed Area" recording sheet (Blackline Master 74)

Teacher will need:

- Color tiles
- "Rectangles Made with 36 Tiles" grid paper (Blackline Master 73)
- "Fixed Area" recording sheet (Blackline Master 74)

LESSON

Before

Begin with a simpler version of the task:

- Have students build a rectangle using 12 tiles at their desks. Explain that the rectangle should be filled in, not just a border. After eliciting some ideas, ask a student to come to the document camera and make a rectangle as described.
- Model sketching the rectangle on a grid. Record the dimensions of the rectangle in the recording chart—for example, "2 by 6."
- Ask, "What do we mean by *perimeter*? How do we measure perimeter?" After helping students define *perimeter* and describe how it is measured, ask students for the perimeter of this rectangle. Ask a student to come to the document camera to measure the perimeter of the rectangle. (Use either the rectangle made from tiles or the one sketched on grid paper.) Emphasize that the units used to measure perimeter are one-dimensional, or linear, and that perimeter is just the distance around an object. Record the perimeter in the chart.
- Ask, "What do we mean by *area*? How do we measure area?" After helping students define *area* and describe how it is measured, ask for the area of this rectangle. Here you want to make explicit that the units used to measure area are two-dimensional and, therefore, cover a region. After counting the tiles, record the area in square units on the chart.
- Have students make a different rectangle using 12 tiles at their desks and record the perimeter and area as before. Students will need to decide what "different" means. Is a 2×6 rectangle different from a 6×2 rectangle? Although these are congruent, students may wish to consider these as being different, which is okay for this activity.

Present the focus task to the class:

- See how many different rectangles can be made with 36 tiles.
- Determine and record the perimeter and area for each rectangle.

Provide clear expectations:

- Write the following directions on the board:
  1. Find a rectangle using *all* 36 tiles.
  2. Sketch the rectangle on the grid paper.
  3. Measure and record the perimeter and area of the rectangle on the recording chart.
  4. Find a new rectangle using *all* 36 tiles and repeat steps 2–4.
- Place students in pairs to work collaboratively, but require that each student draw his or her own sketches and use his or her own recording sheet.

During

Initially:

- Question students to be sure they understand the task and the meaning of *area* and *perimeter*. Look for students who are confusing these terms.
- Be sure students are both drawing the rectangles and recording them appropriately in the chart.

Ongoing:

- Observe and ask the assessment questions, posing one or two to a student and moving to another student (see the "Assessment" section of this lesson).

After

Bring the class together to share and discuss the task:

- Ask students what they have found out about perimeter and area. Ask, "Did the perimeter stay the same? Is that what you expected? When is the perimeter big and when is it small?"
- Ask students how they can be sure they have all of the possible rectangles.
- Ask students to describe what happens to the perimeter as the length and width change. ("The perimeter gets shorter as the rectangle gets fatter." "The square has the shortest perimeter.") Provide time to pair-share ideas.

ASSESSMENT

Observe

- Are students confusing perimeter and area?
- As students form new rectangles, are they aware that the area is not changing because they are using the same number of tiles each time? These students may not know what area is, or they may be confusing it with perimeter.
- Are students looking for patterns in how to find the perimeter?

- Are students stating important concepts or patterns to their partners?

Ask

- What is the area of the rectangle you just made?
- What is the perimeter of the rectangle you just made?
- How is area different from perimeter?
- How do you measure area? Perimeter? How are the units different? How are the units similar?

EXPANDED LESSON 9.17

Shape Sorts

CONTENT AND TASK DECISIONS

Mathematics Goals

- To develop an awareness of the wide variety of ways that two-dimensional shapes can be alike
- To establish classifications of shapes by various properties, including both traditional categorizations and informal, student-generated categories
- To introduce the names of common shapes or important properties (when and if the opportunity arises within the activity)

Grade Level Guide

NCTM *Curriculum Focal Points*	*Common Core State Standards*
Kindergarteners use ideas about shapes to describe geometric ideas. In first grade students recognize that shapes have properties that help describe how they are alike and different from other shapes. This work continues in grade 2 and is a full focal point in grade 3 as students are asked to describe the properties of two-dimensional shapes.	Kindergarteners identify, describe, analyze, and compare shapes. They can use informal language to describe the shapes to point out their common attributes and differences. First, second, and third graders use reasoning to distinguish between defining attributes and they can draw shapes that have specific defining attributes.

Consider Your Students' Needs

Students need no prerequisite knowledge for this lesson. The activity will naturally adjust itself to the ideas held by the students. The level of vocabulary and the types of observations that students make will depend on prior geometric experiences of the students and their verbal skills.

For English Language Learners

- As students describe what they notice about a shape, or are identifying how their shape is like another, ask that they point at the aspect of the shape(s) they are describing so that everyone can understand.
- Record a list of the ideas students share to describe their shapes and draw a sketch next to it as a reminder.

For Students with Disabilities

- In the first part of the lesson, as student brainstorm different possible ideas that describe their shapes, record

some of these on the board so that students can use these examples later as a guide for their own "target shape rule."
- Make sure the rule for a given target shape is written down near the target shape so that students with disabilities can refer to it during the session.

Materials

Each group of three to five students will need:

- Collection of two-dimensional shapes (Blackline Masters 41 to 47 provide a collection of 49 shapes. Duplicate each set on card stock and cut out the shapes. You may want to laminate the card stock before you cut out the shapes. Only use one color cardstock so that the attribute of color does not become a focus for some students.)

LESSON

Before

Begin with a simpler version of the task:

- Gather students in a circle where all can see and have access to one set of shapes.
- Have each student select a shape. Ask students to think of things that they can say about their shape. Go around

the group and ask students to hold up their shape and tell one or two of their ideas.
- Return all shapes to the pile and select one shape. Place this "target" shape for all to see. Each student is to find a shape that is like the target shape in some way. Again, have students share their ideas. You may want to repeat this with another shape.

Present the focus task to the class:

- Each group of students is to select one shape from the collection to be the target shape just as you did. Then they announce their "rule" to the group. Then other students are to find as many other shapes that are like the target shape as they can. However, all the shapes they find must be like the target shape *in the same way*. For example, if the student uses "has straight sides" as a rule, each student in turn adds other shapes to the "has straight sides" group. They cannot also use another descriptor of the target shape such as "has a square corner" to add to the group. That would be two different ways or two rules.
- Explain that when you visit each group, you want to see a collection of shapes that go together according to the same rule. You will see if you can guess their rule by looking at the shapes they have put together.
- When you have checked their first rule, you will select a new target shape for them. They should make a new collection of shapes using a different rule. When they have finished, each student should draw a new shape on paper that would fit the rule. All of the drawings should then be alike in the same way. (For kindergarten and first-grade students, you will probably explain this part as you visit their group.)

Provide clear expectations:

- Students are to work in groups of three to five members.
- Students should take turns choosing descriptive properties (attributes) for the target shape.

During

- Listen carefully for the types of ideas that students are using. Are they using "non-geometric" language such as "pointy," "looks like a house," or "has a straight bottom," or are they beginning to talk about more geometric properties such as "square corners," "sides that go the same way" (parallel), or "dented in" (concave)? If they are using shape names, are they using them correctly?
- Introduce and reinforce correct terminology for shapes, however, do not make terminology and definitions a focus of the activity. Allow students to use their own ideas.
- To differentiate, you may want to challenge students by quickly creating a small group of shapes that go together according to a secret rule. See if they can figure out what the rule is and find other shapes that go with your collection.

After

Bring the class together to share and discuss the task:

- Collect students' drawings, keeping the groups intact. Gather students together so that all will be able to see the drawings. (This could be done the day after the "During" portion of the lesson.)
- Display the drawings from one group. Have students from other groups see if they can guess the rule for the drawings. If the drawings are not adequate to identify the rule, have those who made the drawings find a few shapes from the collection of shapes that also fit the rule.
- To expand students' ideas or interject new ideas, you may want to create a set of shapes using a secret rule, as described previously. Base your rule on a property of the shapes that the students have not yet thought of.

ASSESSMENT

Observe

- Do not think of this activity as something that students should master. This lesson can be repeated numerous times over the course of the year. As students have more and more experiences with shapes, they will be able to create different, more sophisticated sorting rules.
- Watch for students who talk about shapes in terms of relative attributes such as "bottom," "pointing up," or "has a side near the windows." These same students will not recognize a square as such if it has been turned to look like a diamond. When this happens, pick up the shape, turn it slowly, and ask the student if it is still pointing up (or whatever other attribute they are dis-

cussing). Point out that the shape doesn't change, only the way it is positioned.

- If you have introduced vocabulary that is important, you can informally assess students' knowledge of that vocabulary during this activity. Every type of shape that a primary-grade student needs to know is included in the set. There are examples of right angles, parallel lines, concave and convex shapes, shapes with line symmetry, and shapes with rotational symmetry.

Ask

- How are these shapes alike?
- What other shapes are like the ones in this group?
- What is a shape that does NOT belong? Why?

Diagonals of Quadrilaterals

CONTENT AND TASK DECISIONS

Mathematics Goals

- To investigate the properties of the diagonals of quadrilaterals
- To clarify the meaning of the terms *quadrilateral*, *diagonal*, *perpendicular*, and *bisect*, as well as the names of specific types of quadrilaterals

Grade Level Guide

NCTM *Curriculum Focal Points*	*Common Core State Standards*
Students in third grade describe and analyze properties of two-dimensional shapes to classify and connect attributes to definitions of shapes. They are able to build and draw shapes to better understand the properties of two-dimensional space.	Fifth-grade students are able to use the properties of two-dimensional shapes to group them into categories. In the sixth grade, students reason about relationships among shapes. They decompose shapes and relate quadrilaterals to rectangles in a variety of ways. Seventh graders draw, construct, and describe geometrical figures and describe the relationships between them.

Consider Your Students' Needs

Students should be able to identify different types of quadrilaterals (rectangle, parallelogram, trapezoid, kite, rhombus) and talk about their properties in terms of the lengths of sides and the angles formed by the sides. They should also understand the terms *quadrilateral*, *diagonal*, *congruent*, *perpendicular*, and *bisect*.

For English Language Learners

- While all students will need special attention to these terms, using cognates and visuals will be essential for ELLs. For example, *quad-* in quadrilateral (*quadra* means square in Spanish) and *bi-* as in bilingual or biannual, with *sect* meaning section. However, do not take so much time on language that students are not able to focus on and engage in the higher level thinking of the lesson.
- Add visuals for each term in the table on Blackline Master 75 (or have students do this).

For Students with Disabilities

- It might be helpful to brainstorm a list of the possible quadrilaterals and have students work from each to explore the diagonals.

- For students who struggle you may want to have cards with a pictorial representation of each quadrilateral and its name. Having them available will support students in completing the Properties of Quadrilateral Diagonals chart. You may need to have enough cards so students can write on them and draw in the diagonals. Then they can model the drawings they made of the diagonals with matching tagboard strips and fasteners.

Materials

Each student will need:

- Three strips of cardstock or tagboard about 2 cm wide (two strips should be about 30 cm long and one about 20 cm long). Punch a hole near each end. Divide the distance between the holes by 8 and use this distance to evenly space 7 holes between the ends. (One set per pair of students)
- Brass fasteners
- "Properties of Quadrilateral Diagonals" recording sheet (Blackline Master 75)
- 1-cm square dot-grid paper (Blackline Master 37)

Teacher will need:

- Transparency of or way to display Blackline Master 75 and at least two transparencies of Blackline Master 37 or copies for use with a projection device.

LESSON

Before

Begin with a simpler version of the task:

- On the board, write the terms *diagonal*, *congruent*, *bisect*, and *perpendicular*.

- Using the two diagonal strips that are equal in length, show students how to join them in the middle of each with the brass fastener. Join the diagonals so that they bisect each other at a right angle. Lay the diagonals on the overhead and ask students to tell what they can about how the two are related. Refer to the terms on the board. As students share their observations, record the properties on the first line of the transparency by checking the "Yes" column under Congruent Diagonals, checking the "Both" column under Diagonals Bisected, and checking the "Perpendicular" column under Intersections of Diagonals. Clarify the meaning of terminology as necessary. Now ask students to think about what quadrilateral would be formed if the ends of the diagonals were connected. On the overhead, mark the vertices through the holes at the end of each diagonal on the dot-grid paper. Use a straightedge to connect the vertices and, thus, form a square.

- On the dot-grid transparency, show students how they can draw two intersecting lines with the same properties (congruent, bisecting each other, and perpendicular). Then connect the endpoints of these lines to form the quadrilateral. Have students draw a pair of intersecting congruent lines on their own paper. Have them use lines that are either shorter or longer than the two on the transparency. When they connect the endpoints, all students should get squares regardless of the lengths of their diagonals.
- Together generate a list of possible types of quadrilaterals that might be formed. You may wish to put this list on the board.

Present the focus task to the class:

- Students are to use the three strips of tagboard to determine the properties of diagonals that will produce different types of quadrilaterals.
- Before giving students the task, remind them that they can use the third, shorter diagonal with one of the longer diagonals to form a quadrilateral with noncongruent diagonals.
- Make clear to students that they are to work in pairs to identify the properties of the diagonals and the quadrilateral formed by the diagonals. They are to record their findings on their own worksheets and also draw a corresponding pair of diagonals and the quadrilateral on their dot grid. They should put the name of the quadrilateral on each drawing.

Provide clear expectations:

- Students will work with partners, but each student needs to complete his or her own worksheets.

During

Initially:

- If students are having difficulty getting started, suggest that they try creating diagonals with one set of properties from the worksheet.

Ongoing:

- Observe how students are determining the properties of diagonals that produce different quadrilaterals. Do they start with the diagonal relationships to see what shapes can be made? Or do they start with examples of the shapes and determine the diagonal relationships? Either approach is fine.
- Do they have a systematic way of generating different quadrilaterals? For example, do they use the same two diagonals, keep one property constant (e.g., diagonals are perpendicular), and then look for ways to vary the other property (e.g., diagonals bisect or do not bisect each other)?
- For students who are ready for a challenge, have them determine the properties that will produce a non-isosceles trapezoid.

After

Bring the class together to share and discuss the task:

- As students share their findings, have them draw the diagonals and quadrilateral on your dot-grid transparency (Blackline Master 37).
- Referring to the descriptions (properties) of the diagonals, ask students if *all* quadrilaterals of a given type have the same diagonal properties. For example, will all rhombuses have these same diagonal properties? Use the transparency of the dot-grid paper to have students make drawings to test various hypotheses regarding the quadrilateral type and the properties of the diagonals.
- Ask students to look at the quadrilaterals that have a diagonal property in common (e.g., all quadrilaterals whose diagonals bisect each other) and to make conjectures about other properties in the quadrilaterals that happen as a result of the common diagonal property.

ASSESSMENT

Observe

- Are they testing their hypotheses with different sizes of quadrilaterals using the grid paper? Or are they convinced without using the grid paper? If so, how are they convinced? Are they even questioning what might happen with different examples of the same quadrilateral? The answers to these questions will provide evidence that students are or are not beginning to think at van Hiele level 2.

Ask

- What is a *diagonal*?
- What does *perpendicular* mean?
- What does *bisect* mean?
- What do you know about the diagonals of (name a specific quadrilateral)?
- When naming a quadrilateral, does the length of the diagonals matter if the properties remain the same?
- Does the size of the quadrilateral change the properties of the diagonals of a specific quadrilateral?

Field Experience Guide: Resources for Teachers of Elementary and Middle School Mathematics © Pearson Education, Inc., 2013

Triangle Midsegments

CONTENT AND TASK DECISIONS

Mathematics Goals

- To investigate the relationship between a triangle's midsegment and its base
- To develop the rationale for why particular relationships exist in a triangle
- To develop logical reasoning in a geometric context

Grade Level Guide

NCTM *Curriculum Focal Points*	*Common Core State Standards*
Students in grade 7 explore proportionality by investigating similar objects. By using scale factors they compare lengths in two figures. In eighth grade, students prove that similar triangles exist because the "particular configurations of lines give rise to similar triangles because of the congruent angles created when a transversal cuts parallel lines" (NCTM, 2006, p. 19).	In the seventh grade. one of the standards under Geometry states that students should be able to draw and describe geometrical figures. including the relationships between the figures. Students in the eighth grade should use information arguments to establish facts about the angle measures of triangles and about the measures of angles that are created when parallel lines are cut by a transversal. Also, in one of the Standards for Mathematical Practices, *Using appropriate tools strategically*, they suggest that dynamic geometry environments can provide students ways to investigate geometrical relationships.

Consider Your Students' Needs

Most students are beginning to function at van Hiele level 2, where they are ready to grapple with "why" and "what-if" questions. Students are aware of the properties of angles formed by cutting parallel lines with a transverse line. They also have experience working with similar triangles. To do the lesson with a dynamic geometry software program, students should be relatively competent with the program tools and be able to independently draw different geometric objects (e.g., triangles, lines, line segments), label vertices, find midpoints, and measure lengths and angles.

For English Language Learners

- Before the lesson begins, use student-friendly words and visuals to communicate the goal of the lesson—to see whether the midsegment is somehow related to the base.
- Discuss with students what "conjecture" means and what "justification" means.
- Encourage students to use both words and pictures in the development of their conjectures.

For Student with Disabilities

- During the phase of the lesson where conjectures are made and supported with reasoning you may want to support students with disabilities by creating a table. Here you can ask them first to measure and record the angles ADE, ABC, AED, and ACB. Also have them measure the line segments AD, AE, AB, and AC (they already have BD and DE). Then they can use this information to support ideas about relationships.

Materials

This lesson can be done either with computers or on paper. As described, the lesson only assumes a demonstration computer with display screen. Although desirable, a computer is not required. The computer used in the lesson requires a dynamic geometry program, such as *The Geometer's Sketchpad* or *Wingeom* (free software).

Each student will need:

- Ruler that measures in centimeters

LESSON

Before

Present the focus task to the class:

- Have each student draw a line segment measuring 16 cm near the long edge of a blank sheet of paper.

Demonstrate using the computer. Label the segment BC.

- Have students randomly select another point somewhere on their papers but at least several centimeters above BC. Illustrate on the computer that you want all students to have very different points. Some might be in the upper left, in the upper right, near the center, and so on. Have them label this point A and then draw segments AB and AC to create triangle ABC. Do the same on the computer.

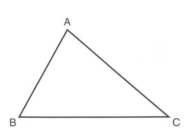

- Next, students find the midpoints D and E of AB and AC, respectively, and draw the midsegment DE. Do the same on the computer. You can introduce the term *midsegment* as the line joining the midpoints of two sides of a triangle.
- Have students measure their midsegments and report what they find. Amazingly, all students should report a measure of 8 cm. On the computer, measure BC and DE. Move point A all over the screen. The two measures will stay the same, with the length of DE being half of BC. Even if B or C is moved, the ratio of BC to DE will remain 2 to 1.
- Ask students for any conjectures they may have about why this relationship exists. Discuss each idea briefly but without any evaluation.
- On the computer, draw a line through A parallel to BC. Have students draw a similar line on their paper. Label points F and G on the line as shown here.

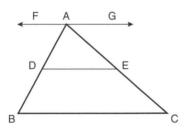

- Ask students what else they know about the figure now that line FG has been added. List all ideas on the board.

- Ask the students what conjecture can be made about the midsegment of any triangle. What reason can be given for why the conjecture might be true?
- Students are to write out a conjecture about the midsegment of a triangle. In pairs, students are to continue to explore their sketch, looking for reasons why this particular relationship between the midsegment of a triangle and its base exists. They should record all of their ideas and justifications and be ready to share them with the class. If they wish to explore an idea on the computer sketch, they should be allowed to do so.

Provide clear expectations:

- Students are to work in pairs. Each student should record his or her own reasoning concerning the conjectures.

During

- Resist giving too much guidance at first. See what students can do on their own. Notice what they focus on in forming conjectures.
- For students having difficulty, suggest that they focus on angles ADE and ABC, as well as angles AED and ACB. (These pairs of angles are congruent.)
- Suggest that they list all pairs of angles that they know are congruent. Why are they congruent?
- If necessary, ask students to compare triangle ABC with triangle ADE. What do they notice? They should note that the triangles are similar. Why are they similar?

After

Bring the class together to share and discuss the task:

- Have students discuss their initial arguments for why the midsegment relationship holds. They can use the demonstration computer to share their ideas.
- Using their ideas, help students build arguments so that they can see how one idea in their reasoning flows to the next in a logical sequence.

ASSESSMENT

Observe

- Look for students who struggle seeing the connections or relationships between properties. These students may not be functioning at level 2 of the van Hiele levels of geometric thought.
- Do students see the difference between simply observing a relationship and considering the reasons the relationship exists?

Ask

- Why is your conjecture about the midsegment of triangles true?
- Why doesn't the size of your triangle affect the ratio of the midsegment to the base?
- Would the conjecture hold true if you used a different side of the triangle for the base? Why?
- Why are triangles ABC and ADE similar?

EXPANDED LESSON 9.20

Using Data to Answer a Question

CONTENT AND TASK DECISIONS

Mathematics Goals

- To determine a question that can be answered through gathering data
- To determine how to gather the data
- To use data to create graphs
- To use graphs to answer questions concerning a population

Grade Level Guide

NCTM *Curriculum Focal Points*	*Common Core State Standards*
Students in kindergarten collect data and use counting to answer questions. By first grade, students are representing data in picture graphs and bar graphs. This is extended in third grade when students construct and analyze a variety of graphs and data representations.	First graders organize, represent, and interpret data. They are able to ask and answer questions by comparing data. By second grade, students are able to draw picture graphs and bar graphs (using a single unit scale) to represent data. They are also able to use the information in a bar graph to answer problems.

Consider Your Students' Needs

This lesson assumes that students have had experiences with several different types of graphs, including Venn diagrams and some form of bar graph, and that they are able to use tallies or numbers for gathering data. You may also want to allow students to do this phase of the lesson using appropriate graphing programs on the computer. Involve students in selecting questions that are of interest to them and culturally relevant.

For English Language Learners

- Include written prompts and pair-share for the discussions at the start of this lesson as a way to increase the participation of ELLs.
- Model the process of gathering data using students from the class. You can model "how to" and "how not to" as a way to help all students (particularly ELLs) comprehend the process.
- In selecting how the data will be displayed, show illustrations of different options and have them labeled with the appropriate terminology.

For Students with Disabilities

- Provide a table with the possible answers for students with disabilities if they are collecting data from another class. This will support them in organizing the tallies.
- When students are creating a bar graph, have them make an X in the grid prior to coloring. This will help them focus on the quantity to ensure accuracy.
- When analyzing the data, pose some questions that will help students compare data points in a "think aloud" mode. Some students with disabilities may need to hear the way you compare data to help them draw conclusions and answer the question.

Materials

- Large pieces of paper, such as chart paper
- Grid paper, such as a 1-cm grid (see Blackline Master 35)
- Chart grid paper (optional)
- Markers/crayons
- Connecting cubes or other manipulatives for graphing data
- Computers (visit http://nlvm.usu.edu for free graph-making programs)

LESSON

This lesson may require several days to complete. It employs the four-step process of doing statistics: (1) What question do we want to answer? (2) How will we collect the data? (3) What type of analysis (e.g., a graph) should we use to view our data? (4) What do the data tell us about our question? In this lesson, the process is split into two tasks with the fourth phase addressed in the "After" portion of the second task.

LESSON PART I

Before

Present the first task to the class:

- Engage the students in a discussion of what question they would like to answer. How you guide this discussion will vary with the age of your students and perhaps their recent experiences, such as a field trip, a unit of study in science, or a book that has been read to the class. Consider such ideas as favorites (books, food, etc.), nature or science (weather, what lives in our yards), comparisons (something about your class as compared with another class, children compared to adults), measures (heights, arm spans), how many (pets, hours watching TV, minutes spent brushing teeth), and so on.

- Once a question or questions are determined, talk about how information (data) can be collected. If a survey is required, you will probably need to help students formulate one to three questions that have simple responses—not full sentences or explanations. What is important is that students are personally invested in the decisions. Remember to limit options to a reasonable amount when deciding upon choices for answers (such as in a question about favorites).

- Discuss *how* they can gather data to answer the question. This is not easy, as students will need to think about ways to get data from all classmates without duplicating, for example. Set students to gathering the data. If the collection involves getting data from home or from another class, you will need to help students be very organized about doing this so that real data are available when you need it.

Provide clear expectations:

- Students may be working in groups to answer different questions, or this may be a whole class project. During the second task, students will work best in groups of two or three. This may mean that there will be multiple groups working on the same question and/or with the same data.

- Materials should be available for students to select what they desire for their group when they are organizing and displaying their data.

- Students may use computer graphing to display their data.

During

- Monitor the data collection to be sure it is being gathered appropriately and recorded in a way that the students will know what the data mean.

After

Bring the class together to share and discuss the task:

- When the data have been collected, briefly discuss what data the class, groups, or individuals have gathered.

- Ask students what they notice about their data. They might be able to say some comparison statements. Can they answer the question(s) they posed? What new questions might emerge?

- Suggest to students that they might be able to learn more about their question if they display their data in some kind of graph. At this point, a new problem develops, as presented in the second task.

LESSON PART II

Before

- Decide on a type of graph to make with the data that will help answer your question. Make the graph.

- Engage the class in thinking about the various types of graphs that they know how to make and ask for ideas about matching a type of graph with the question to be answered and the data gathered. You may need to remind students about techniques they have seen or that are available on the computer.

- Show students the types of materials available to them, including the computer. They are to select a type of graph, then use the data they have collected to create a presentation of the data in a way that they believe answers the question.

During

Initially:

- Be sure students are productively working. Move around to the groups to answer any questions.

Ongoing:

- Have students use the grid paper to create bar graphs. Try to make sure the graphs represent the data and will not distort conclusions.

- Encourage students to add titles (linked to the question answered) and labels to their posters or presentations to help explain the data shown in the graph.

After

- Have groups display their graphs. Take turns having students explain their graphs and what their graph tells us related to the original questions.

- Discuss which graphs best answered the question and why, or what advantages one graph (e.g., circle) has over another (e.g., bar).

- Ask students if they can answer other questions using the data.

- Finally, ask students what new questions might be asked, having learned what they did from this question.

ASSESSMENT

Observe

- Are students using a table, checklist, or tally to gather their data? Do they have a process in place to ensure they gather data from each person only once?

- Are students considering appropriate types of graphs? Do they understand how the type of data limits what makes sense for a graph?

- Are students able to actually create the graph?

- Do students know how to interpret the data in the graph? Can they make conjectures?

Ask

- What do we need to consider when planning a survey or question?
- What do you need to do to gather data correctly?

- How did you decide on the type of graph to make?
- How did you create your graph?
- What does (indicate specific data point) mean on the graph?
- What does the data tell us about the question posed?

Design a Fair Game

CONTENT AND TASK DECISIONS

Mathematics Goals

- To explore informally the probability of an event with equally likely outcomes through an experiment
- To consider what equally likely events (fair games) look like
- To explore the concept of variation and the Law of Large Numbers

Grade Level Guide

NCTM *Curriculum Focal Points*	*Common Core State Standards*
Probability, in particular being able to explore equally likely outcomes and establish theoretical probabilities, is one of the four grade 7 connections.	Seventh graders are expected to be able to, "Investigate chance processes and develop, use, and evaluate probability models" (CCSS, 2010, p. 50). In particular, students "begin informal work with random sampling to generate data sets and learn about the importance of representative samples for drawing inferences" (CCSS, 2010, p. 46).

Consider Your Students' Needs

Although students need not have a firm understanding of probability, they should have been exposed to the basic idea that the outcome of an experiment can lie at different points along the probability continuum from impossible (0) to certain (1).

For English Language Learners

- The instructions are complicated in this lesson, so providing them in writing and/or adding illustrations will help ELLs understand the focus task.
- The mathematical terms *fair*, *equally likely*, *probability*, and *variability* are key words to develop in the lesson, with variability being a word better addressed in the

"After" phase when students are describing what happened in their games.

For Students with Disabilities

- Students who struggle may be challenged to create their own game. Instead have cards for games that use different combinations of tiles. Have students try the games, sorting the cards into "fair games" and "unfair games."

Materials

Each pair of students will need:

- Small paper bag (opaque)
- Color tiles, connecting cubes, or any like-shaped object that comes in 4 colors
- Note card (one per pair)

LESSON

Before

Begin with a simpler version of the task:

- Discuss children's favorite games. Ask, "Have you ever wondered how games are created? Today we are going to make up our own games and decide if they are fair games." Explain that the game will consist of putting tiles (or whatever is to be used) in a bag and taking turns drawing out a tile. Each player will be given a color (or

two). The person whose color is drawn gets a point. After ten draws, the game is over.

- Say, "Suppose we wanted to put in two colors of tiles, red and blue. We want four tiles in the bag. How many of each tile should we put in?" Play the game quickly between two halves of the class. Be sure to return the tile to the bag after each draw. Ask if they think this is a good game or not. Is it fair? Why?

- Now suggest putting in five red tiles and seven blue tiles. Play the game quickly between two halves of the class. Be sure to return the tile to the bag after each draw. Ask if they think this is a fair game. Why or why not?

Present the focus task to the class:

- In partners, have students design a game of their own. In the design of the game, each player gets points for two colors. The number of each color has to be different (so if there are 5 red, there cannot be 5 of the other colors). Of the two colors for each player, one of the colors is worth 2 points and one is worth only 1 point. The tiles are drawn one at a time and returned to the bag.

Provide clear expectations:

- Students work with partners.
- Students must prepare the game, placing the appropriate colored tiles/cubes in the bag and writing on a note card which colors are worth 2 points and 1 point for Player 1 and Player 2.

During

Initially:

- Be sure that students understand the directions and are applying them correctly in designing their game.

Ongoing:

- Watch for when students are getting close to having their games prepared. Give a time limit for preparing a bag for play. The team must also prepare the note card telling the players which colors score what points.
- Have each pair of students trade bags and note cards with another pair of students.
- Play the game to 10 points. Repeat 3 times. Ask, "Is the game fair? Why/why not?"
- Then have the students empty their bags (prepared by another group) and see if they think the game was designed to be fair. Tell students to be ready to report to the group whether their game was fair or not.
- Listen to the ideas that students use in deciding if the game is fair or not. With only 10 points in a game, the winner may continue to be the same person, even if the game is designed fairly. This notion of variation (and the need for large samples—Law of Large Numbers) is a core concept in probability. Listening to these discussions will give you insights into students' understanding of variability and fairness.

After

Bring the class together to share and discuss the task:

- Have groups share their reports on whether the game they played was fair and their justification. Ask students who won the three games.
- Ask students why a game might be fair and yet the same person wins all the games. "You thought the game was fair, but Sandra won every time. Why do you think that happened? If you play a lot of times, who do you think will win the most times?"
- Engage the class in this discussion of game designs, probability, and short- and long-term results.

ASSESSMENT

Observe

- Pay attention to students who seem to believe more in chance or luck than in observable probabilities. This is a main idea that you want to develop at this point in their understanding of probability.
- Try to decide how well your students are able to determine the probabilities of the outcomes in these games. Students who correctly analyze these games—who can tell if a game is fair or not and who can design fair and unfair games—are ready to progress further.

Ask

- What are the possible outcomes—what could you draw out of the bag?
- Is it as likely that you will draw a red tile as a green one (or whatever colors you are using)? Why?
- If a game is fair, does that mean if you won the last game, I will win the next one? Why or why not?

Bar Graphs to Circle Graphs

CONTENT AND TASK DECISIONS

Mathematics Goals

- To introduce the use of a circle graph (pie chart) to display data
- To explore the concept of percent

Grade Level Guide

NCTM *Curriculum Focal Points*	*Common Core State Standards*
In grades 4 and 5, students construct and analyze a variety of graphs to solve problems. Also in the fifth grade students begin to apply their understanding of whole numbers and fractions to construct and analyze graphs. This background prepares students for seventh grade, when students are expected to apply percentages to make and interpret circle graphs.	In grades 4 and 5, student construct a variety of graphs to answer questions and solve problems.

Consider Your Students' Needs

Students have previously made a variety of graphs, such as bar graphs, line plots, and tally charts, but have limited or no experience with circle graphs. They have not been introduced formally to the idea of percentage. If students have explored the connections between decimals and fractions, this lesson can be used to both expand that connection and also introduce the concept of percent.

For English Language Learners

- In thinking of topics for which students will gather data, be sure to consider topics that are culturally relevant. (Eye color would not be in a largely Hispanic population, for example.)
- When explaining the problem, use language/categories that would be familiar to the ELL.
- Provide illustrations of bar graphs and circle graphs as a reference for students.

For Students with Disabilities

- Some students with disabilities may have a difficult time analyzing or "seeing" the circle graph when they are

standing in the circle. You may need to have a visual of a circle graph, such as the one in Figure 21.8 in the text, to show the overhead view of what is taking place.

Materials

Each student will need:

- Rational Number Wheel (Blackline Master 28)
- 2-cm grid paper (Blackline Master 34)
- Access to scissors, tape, and crayons

Teacher will need:

- Rational Number Wheel (Blackline Master 28) cut out for use
- Transparency of or way to display 2-cm grid paper (Blackline Master 34)
- Five pieces of yarn or string, each about 10 to 12 feet long
- Heavy weight such as a brick or large book (the ends of the string will be anchored to this weight as the center of a class-sized circle graph)

LESSON

This lesson may take two days. Prior to this lesson, students must have gathered data to answer a question of their own. This can be a common data set for the class or individual students, or groups can gather their own data

sets from different questions. Use questions that lend themselves to being grouped in three to five categories. The following are offered as examples:

- What are the favorite _____ (e.g., TV shows) of students in the fourth grade? (Gather data by listing four shows and "other.")
- What are the populations of the top 50 cities in our state? (Get data from the Internet. Group the data into three categories.)
- How many students buy lunch at our school on each day of the school week? (Get data from the cafeteria staff.)

Before

Begin with a simpler version of the task:

- Ask a question in which each student will have one of three to five choices. For example: What are the colors of our eyes? Write the choices on the board (brown, blue, green, other).
- Create a bar graph on the 2-cm grid, coloring in one square for each student as he or she tells you the color of his or her eyes.
- Have the students form a human bar graph by aligning themselves in rows for each color. Next, help the students rearrange their rows into a circle formed of all the students in the class. In the center of the circle place the weight with the strings attached. Extend a string to be held by students between each different color of eyes (between the brown and green, the green and blue, and so on). To explore the idea of percents, place a Rational Number Wheel at the center where the strings come together. With the strings fairly straight you can estimate the percentage of students in each category by counting the number of hash marks in-between the two strings on the Rational Number Wheel.

Present the focus task to the class:

- Decide on an appropriate way to graph the data gathered prior to this lesson to answer the students' question(s).
- Students are to make one or more graphs to illustrate the data they collected to answer their question. Allow students to use whatever graphing technique(s) they choose.

Provide clear expectations:

- You may want to do the "Before" portion of the lesson somewhere other than the classroom so that there is room to form a circle of all your students.

During

Initially:

- This is an example of a lesson in which students are introduced to a new convention. The circle graph does not arise out of a problem or task. Rather, you are showing students how such a graph is made.
- Since you are introducing a convention—how to make a circle graph—you are mainly looking for students who are having difficulty understanding how the graph is made. Students who need help making their graphs can get help from peers or from you.

Ongoing:

- Discuss with individual students or groups how their graphs will help others answer their question. Keep their focus on good ways to answer the question.

After

Bring the class together to share and discuss the task:

- Have several students or groups display their graphs and have the class decide if the graphs help answer the question the data were collected to answer.
- If students have not made a bar graph of their data, have them do so. Each bar should be colored differently or marked with pencil to distinguish the bars. Have students cut the bars from the graph and tape them end to end to form a long strip. The two ends of the strip are then taped together to form a loop. This loop is similar to the circle students made by rearranging their rows at the start of the lesson.
- Have students place the loop on the paper with the Rational Number Wheel and form the loop into a circle. The center of the circle should be the center of the wheel. Next they draw straight lines from the center of the wheel to the divisions between the different bars, as they did earlier with the strings in their human graph. If the loop is smaller than the wheel, extend the lines to the edge of the wheel. Demonstrate all of this on the overhead projector using the transparent wheel and one of the students' bar graph loops. Show how the first line drawn should align with one of the major subdivisions on the wheel.
- Project the wheel (using projector). Examine the wheel and note that it has ten large subdivisions, each with ten smaller divisions, for a total of 100 sections. Each is *1 percent of the whole.* Explain that 1 percent is the same as $\frac{1}{100}$.
- With this information, students can now label their own circle graphs as another representation of the data they collected. Have a discussion about which graph, the bar graph or the circle graph, is best for answering their question.

ASSESSMENT

Observe

- Once the circle graphs have been made, see how well students seem to understand how the circle graph represents the data.

Ask

- How are the bar graph and circle graph the same? How are they different?

- Which graph (bar or circle) is easier to use to answer our question(s)? Why?
- If we asked 100 people our question, about how many do you think would answer the way you did (if the circle graph is based on survey data)?

Testing Bag Designs

CONTENT AND TASK DECISIONS

GRADE LEVEL: 5–7

Mathematics Goals

- To develop the concept that some events are more or less likely than others
- To explain that for repeated trials of a simple experiment, the outcomes of prior trials have no impact on the next (i.e., the "hand that draws the tile" has no memory)
- To describe the phenomena that the results for a small number of trials may be quite different from those experienced in the long run.

Grade Level Guide

NCTM *Curriculum Focal Points*	Common Core State Standards
Probability, in particular being able to explore equally likely outcomes and establish theoretical probabilities, is one of the four grade 7 connections.	Seventh graders are expected to be able to, "Investigate chance processes and develop, use, and evaluate probability models" (CCSS, 2010, p. 50). In particular, students "begin informal work with random sampling to generate data sets and learn about the importance of representative samples for drawing inferences" (CCSS, 2010, p. 46).

Consider Your Students' Needs

Students should have been introduced to the idea of a probability continuum. They should have some experience with simple probability.

For English Language Learners

- Reinforce language of impossible, not likely, equally likely, likely, and certain. Record a probability line (like the one on the "Design a Bag" Blackline Master) and note these terms on it.
- Model what is meant by trial and experiment.
- Provide translation support for the questions in the assessment, or at least provide them in writing to students.

For Students with Disabilities

- To support students who are struggling you may want to adapt the "Design a Bag" Blackline Master to contain only 10 squares. Then students can model directly on the sheet with color tiles or cubes as they think about 20% (or another percentage).

Materials

Each pair of students will need:

- "Design a Bag" Activity (Blackline Master 60).
- Paper lunch bag
- Color tiles or cubes

LESSON

Before

Present the focus task to the class:

- Students are to design a bag designed to create the chance of drawing a designated color about 20 percent of the time. (The mark on the probability line is an indicator of the targeted percent.) Ask students to think about how many red tiles and how many yellow tiles they would need if they were going to draw yellow 20% of the time?

- Ask students to think about this value as a fraction. Consider fraction equivalencies such as those with a denominator of 10 (how many yellow tiles out of 10 tiles?)
- Have students pair-share their reasoning for the number of each color they plan to put in their bag.
- Select one pair's bag design that students seem to agree represents 20% (0.2 mark) and instruct them to fill their own bags as suggested.

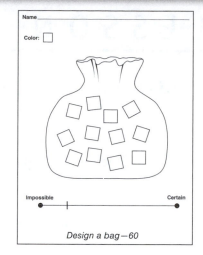

Name _____

Color: ☐

Impossible ●——————|——————● Certain

Design a bag—60

- Ask what they think will happen if they draw a tile from their bag ten times (replacing it each time before the next draw). How many of the designated color do they think they will get? Encourage a discussion of their thinking.
- Once students fill the bag according to the design, they shake the bag and draw one tile. If a tile of the designated color is drawn, a tally mark is recorded for Yes. If a tile of any other color is drawn, a tally mark is recorded for No. The tile should be replaced in the bag and the bag shaken. This process is repeated 20 times. Students should be ready to discuss their results.

Provide clear expectations:

- Students will work with partners.

During

Initially:

- Make sure that students are replacing each tile and shaking the bag before drawing another tile.

Ongoing:

- Are students appropriately recording as they draw tiles?
- Ask students questions about what is occurring with their trials. For example, what do students think when they retrieve the same color tile repeatedly?

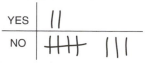

After

Bring the class together to share and discuss the task:

- Discuss with the class how their respective experiments turned out. Did they turn out the way students expected? With the small number of trials, there will be groups that get rather unexpected results.
- Use results from students' small number of trials to discuss ideas such as how drawing a red tile seven straight times affects the chance of drawing a red tile the next time.
- Make a large recording table of the data combining all of the groups. Stop and discuss the data at several points as students give you their results. There should be many more No's than Yes's. Here the discussion can help students see that if the experiment is repeated numerous times, the chances are about as predicted. If students have discussed percents, stopping after data have been collected from 10 students (100 trials) or from 20 students (200 trials) might be useful because the total numbers lend themselves to simple percentage calculations.

ASSESSMENT

Observe

- The small-group testing of a design suggests to students that chance is not an absolute predictor in the short run. How do students react to results that are unexpected?
- The group graph may help students understand the difficult concept that chance tends to approach what is expected in the long run. However, this idea involves comparing ratios in the small number of trials with ratios in the large number of trials. For example, the result for 15 trials may be 36 yeses out of 150 total. It will be difficult for students to compare this with 3 yeses out of 10 trials or 43 yeses out of 200.

Ask

- Are the results from your 10 trials similar to the results of the whole class? Which do you think is more representative of the situation? Why?
- If you draw a red tile three times in a row, will that change your chances of drawing a red tile on your next draw? Why or why not?
- If 20 percent of your tiles/cubes are red, does the color of the other tiles have an impact on your experiment?
- Looking at a specific "Design a Bag" worksheet, which color has the highest probability of being drawn? Which has the least probability?
- If in my bag I have only 1 green tile and 5 blue tiles, and I draw a tile and replace it 10 times, is it possible to draw green more times than blue?

EXPANDED LESSON 9.24

Toying with Measures of Central Tendency

CONTENT AND TASK DECISIONS

Mathematics Goals

- To develop an understanding of how characteristics of a data set (e.g., distribution of data, outliers) affect the mean, median, and mode

Grade Level Guide

NCTM *Curriculum Focal Points*	*Common Core State Standards*
In eighth grade, students use the mean, median, and mode to summarize data sets. They explore how changes in data values effect changes in the mean, median, and mode.	Students in the sixth grade describe data using measures of center (mean and median). They understand how the mean is a balance point.

Consider Your Students' Needs

Students know how to find the mean, median, and mode of a data set.

For English Language Learners

- If these terms are not already known, *mean, median,* and *mode* will need explicit attention prior to the lesson, which may include visuals and translations.
- All students, but particularly ELLs, will benefit from a focus on what prediction and estimation mean as they participate in the "Before" phase of the lesson.

For Students with Disabilities

- Students with disabilities may find that working with a partner on the Toying with Measures recording sheet will help them support their thinking.

- Using a set of play dollar bills to represent the total toy purchases and six "piles" to put the money in, students can see how the mean can play out as a balance point in more concrete ways.

Materials

Each student will need:

- "Toying with Measures" worksheet (Blackline Master 77)

Teacher will need:

- Transparency of or way to display "Toy Purchases" (Blackline Master 76)

LESSON

Before

Begin with a simpler version of the task:

- Give the students the following data set: 3, 3, 3, 3, 3. Ask them to determine the mean, median, and mode. After verifying that the mean, median, and mode for this set is 3, ask the students to predict what, if any, changes in these statistics would occur if the number 15 was added to the set. Elicit students' ideas and rationales, asking others to comment on or question the ideas.
- Students should be able to compute the new statistics mentally. Clearly, the median and mode for this new data set remain unchanged. The mean changes from 3

to 5. For each of these statistics, discuss why changes occurred or did not occur.

Present the focus task to the class:

- On the display of "Toy Purchases," show students the six toys that they have purchased and their prices. Have students calculate the mean, median, and mode for this data set and share those values to ensure that all students have found the correct values.
- The task is to make a series of changes to this original data set of six prices (see the five suggestions below). For each change, first predict—*without computation*—the mean, median, and mode for the new data set and

give a reason for the predictions. Second, for each change compute the actual statistics for the changed set and compare these to the predictions. Each of the following changes to the data set are made to the original set of six toy prices:

1. You decide to buy a seventh toy that costs $20.
2. You return the $1 toy to the store (leaving only five toys).
3. By buying six toys, the store gives you a free toy.
4. You decide to buy a second clown for $12.
5. Make a change you think will be interesting.

- Present the recording sheet "Toying with Measures" to the class. Students first record their predictions of the new mean, median, and mode along with their reason for the prediction for each of the five changes. Be sure students understand that each change is to the original set of six toys. The fifth change is one that they think might make an interesting change in the statistics.

- After sharing predictions and reasons with a partner, students should calculate the statistics and compare those with their predictions. If a prediction is very different from the calculation, they should try to find an error in their reasoning.

Provide clear expectations:

- Students work in pairs, but each student needs to complete the "Toying with Measures" worksheet.

During

Initially:

- Be sure students understand that each change is to the original set of six toys.

Ongoing:

- Listen to individual students' predictions and justifications for those predictions. Is there evidence in students' explanations of their understanding the meaning of the different statistics?

- How are students incorporating the free toy into the set? Do they believe it will affect the mean, median, and mode? (The free toy adds a seventh data point of $0. The mean and median will change.)

- Be sure students do not change their predictions after doing the calculations. They want to talk about the differences in their prediction and the actual results.

- For a challenge, ask the following question: "Suppose that one new toy is added that increases the mean from $6 to $7. How much does the new toy cost?"

After

Bring the class together to share and discuss the task:

- Have students share their predictions and reasoning and discuss how their predictions compared with the actual statistics.

- Discuss what effect outliers (data that are much greater or smaller than the rest of the data in the set) seem to have on the mean, median, and mode and which statistic(s) are affected more by an outlier.

- Based on their findings, which measure of central tendency do they think would be a better representation of a data set that contains one or more outliers? Students should realize that the mean is significantly affected by extreme values, especially for small sets of data.

- Discuss the fact that these have been very small data sets. How would similar changes affect the mean and median if there were about 100 items in the data set?

ASSESSMENT

Observe

- How are students using current values for mean, median, and mode to make predictions? Are their predictions reasonable?

- Do students seem dependent on procedures to determine mean, median, and mode?

Ask

- Which statistic is affected most by an outlier? Why?
- Which statistic is unaffected or barely affected by an outlier? Why?
- Can you determine the change in the mean (mode or median) without completely redoing the process of finding the mean (mode or median) for the data set? How?

10 Mathematics Activities

In order to offer students opportunities to develop mathematical proficiency, as described in the Common Core State Standards for Mathematical Practice, the tasks students are given must offer opportunities for making sense of mathematics, justifying, generalizing, giving examples, using different approaches, using mathematical models, using tools, and so on. As described in Part I, and in Chapter 9, such tasks should be used every day—it is through daily instruction with lessons designed to incorporate the Mathematical Practices that students will become mathematically proficient.

The activities provided here have the potential for students to engage in the Mathematical Practices—but you must develop the *before*, *during* and *after* lesson to ensure this is the case. What questions will you ask? How will you ensure everyone can engage in the task and be challenged by it? How will students demonstrate their understanding? One of the great challenges in teaching is setting up a task in a way that will engage students in higher-level thinking, rather than to simplify it into something easy that takes away real opportunities to engage in doing mathematics.

	Title of Mathematics Activity	Content Focus (related chapter in *Elementary and Middle School Mathematics*)	Grade Level Recommendation (based on *Common Core State Standards*)
10.1	The Find!	To develop efficient counting strategies, such as counting by twos or fives (Ch. 8)	Grades pre-K–1
10.2	Move It, Move It	To develop the Make 10 and Up Over 10 strategies for adding one-digit numbers (Ch. 9, 10)	Grades 1–2
10.3	Odd or Even?	To determine whether a sum of two numbers has an odd or even sum; to explain properties of odd and even numbers (Ch. 9, 12, 14)	Grades 2–3
10.4	Factor Quest	To create rectangular arrays of a number in order to determine all of its factors (Ch. 9)	Grade 4
10.5	The Other Part of 100	To find the value that, when added to a given two-digit number, equals 100 (Ch. 11)	Grade 2
10.6	Interference	To determine the least common multiple of two numbers (in a context) (Ch. 13)	Grade 6
10.7	Target Number	To flexibly use whole number operations to reach a desired total; to explain the impact of an operation (Ch. 9, 12, 13)	Grades 6–8
10.8	Building Bridges	To analyze patterns in geometric growing patterns; to describe in words the general rule for a geometric growing pattern (Ch. 14)	Grades 5–6
10.9	Compensation Decision	To compare linear and exponential growth in a context (Ch. 14)	Grade 8

	Title of Mathematics Activity	Content Focus (related chapter in *Elementary and Middle School Mathematics*)	Grade Level Recommendation (based on *Common Core State Standards*)
10.10	Solving the Mystery	To use variables to illustrate equivalences in symbolic expressions and equations (Ch. 14)	Grade 6–7
10.11	Fraction Find	To be able to find fractions between any two given fractions (density of rational numbers) (Ch. 15)	Grades 4–5
10.12	Illustrating Ratios	To create and analyze a ratio table and related graph; to use tables and graphs to analyze a proportional situation (Ch. 18)	Grades 6–7
10.13	Cover All	To explain strategies for finding how many square tiles cover a rectangle region; to explain how to use repeated addition and/or multiplication to find areas of rectangles (Ch. 19)	Grade 3
10.14	Find the Zero	To find sums of integers; to describe and illustrate integer addition and connect equations to other representations (Ch. 23)	Grades 5–6

10.1 The Find!

Grades: Pre-K–1

Math: Students will develop efficient counting strategies, such as counting by twos or fives.

Task: I was looking in the closet and found this box of (some countable objects such as beans, connecting cubes, etc.). How many do you think there are? Can you help me count them?

Expectation: Students will be given a set of counters (20 to 30 for kindergartners, up to 100 for first graders). In pairs or individually, learners will be asked to state how many there are and how they know. They should draw how they grouped and counted their objects on the recording sheet. Students will be asked to explain how to communicate that number to others (orally, written, symbolically).

The Find!

Name: _____

Use this space to show how many counters you have in your box. You can use pictures, words, or numerals.

10.2 Move It, Move It

Grades: 1–2

Math: Students will develop the Make 10 and Up Over 10 strategies for adding one-digit numbers.

Task: How can I change the sum to make it easier to add?

Expectation: Students can work individually or in pairs. Give students a mat with two ten-frames and beans or round chips to cover the frames (see Blackline Master 11). Give students a deck of cards with values between 0 and 9. Two cards are turned up. Using beans or chips, students cover each frame to represent the problem (9 + 6 would mean covering 9 places on one frame and 6 on the other). This is recorded in column 1. Then students "move it"— fill one of the two ten-frames by moving beans or chips to fill one of them. Be sure students explain what they did and connect to the new equation. For example, 9 + 6 may have become 10 + 5 by moving one counter to the first ten-frame. Emphasize strategies that are working for that student (5 as an Anchor, Make 10, and/or Up Over 10).

Move It, Move It

Name: _____

In the ten-frames provided, show the original problem, how you changed it, and what the sum is.

Starting Problem	After I "Moved It"

Equation: _____

New equation: _____

Answer: _____

Starting Problem	After I "Moved It"

Equation: _____

New equation: _____

Answer: _____

Odd or Even?

Name: _____

Is the sum of two consecutive numbers odd or even? How do you know? Complete the table below.

First addend	Second addend	Sum

Are the sums odd or even? Do you think the sums will always be that way? Write an explanation for how you know.

Field Experience Guide: Resources for Teachers of Elementary and Middle School Mathematics © Pearson Education, Inc., 2013

10.4 Factor Quest

Grade: 4

Math: Students will create rectangular arrays of a number in order to determine all of its factors.

Task: How many different rectangular arrangements of a given number of tiles can you make?

Expectation: Using several numbers that have a relatively large number of factors (e.g., 24, 36), students will attempt to build rectangular arrays that have the given number (e.g., an 8 by 3 array for 24). You can also have different groups/pairs of students with different numbers and have them share their resulting rectangles with the class. Students should write multiplication sentences for each rectangle they make and then list the factors of the selected number. Students can use color tiles or grid paper to model or illustrate the rectangles. Questions you may ask include: Is a 4 by 9 and 9 by 4 the same rectangle? What is the relationship between the rectangles you are building and the factors of the number? How many factors does [your number] have? What numbers will have very few arrays? Will there always be an even number of factors?

Factor Quest

Name: _____

Use the grid here to record rectangles that have an area of _____. Label each arrangement with a multiplication sentence.

1. Factors for _____: _____

2. What is the relationship between the rectangles and the factors?

Field Experience Guide: Resources for Teachers of Elementary and Middle School Mathematics © Pearson Education, Inc., 2013

10.5 The Other Part of 100

Grade: 2

Math: Students will find the value that, when added to a given two-digit number, equals 100.

Task: Can you make 100?

Expectation: This activity encourages students to apply their knowledge of tens and ones in order to make 100. Place students in partners and have them take turns creating the first number and finding the number that would make 100. Give students little ten-frame cards to build their numbers. For example, a student may use four full cards and a six card to make 46. Their partner then either mentally, or using cards, figures out that the amount to make 100 is 54. Encourage students to tell their strategies to their partners as they work and to think of ways they can check to see if their answer is correct. One hundred is an important benchmark; being able to add up to 100 and then add on will become very important in adding three-digit numbers. In this investigation, it will be important to see if students are counting by tens and by ones to figure out the missing value.

Two students work together with a set of little ten-frame cards. One student makes a two-digit number. Then both students work mentally to determine what goes with the ten-frame amount to make 100. They write their solutions on paper and then check by making the other part with the cards to see if the total is 100. Students take turns making the original number. Figure 11.14 in *Elementary and Middle School Mathematics* shows three different thought processes that students might use.

The Other Part of 100

Name: _____

In partners you are building two-digit numbers and finding the "match" to make 100. You can solve these mentally, or use the hundreds chart or ten-frames. Take turns making the original number. Only record the turns where you are finding the "other part."

My Partner's Starting Number	Other Part of 100	How I Thought about It
1.		
2.		
3.		
4.		
5.		
6.		
7.		
8.		

A new person joins your group and wants to learn how to find the Other Part of 100. Explain a strategy that would help her find the other part:

Here is Maurice's chart—Can you figure out what he is doing wrong and help correct the mistake?

My Partner's Starting Number	Other Part of 100	How I Thought about It
1. 34	76	I made sure that the tens added to ten and the ones added to ten.
2. 29	81	
3. 63	47	

My explanation to help Maurice:

10.6 Interference

Grade: 6

Math: Students will determine the least common multiple of two numbers (in a context).

Task: Two artificial satellites are in orbits that pass directly over your school. When they are both directly over your school, they cause interference with your school's telecommunication reception. One satellite makes one revolution around the earth every 25 hours; the other makes one revolution around the earth every 20 hours. At 8:00 A.M. on December 3 they were both directly over your school. When (date and time) will both be directly over your school again?

Expectation: Students will work in pairs to discuss the problem but must submit an individual write-up. Students will explain their solution process. Students may create tables, draw pictures, or use a calculator to help them in their solution process.

You might need to consider discussing the meaning of orbit. Encourage the construction of a table to examine the relationships. Students may struggle with the "passage of time" (i.e., 24 hours in a day). Stimulate discussion around the idea that the time elapsed from the start time to each time a satellite is over the school is a multiple of the number of hours of the orbit. A possible writing assessment could be a letter to the school board explaining when they can anticipate telecommunication interference.

Interference

Two artificial satellites are in orbits that pass directly over your school. When they are both directly over your school, they cause interference with your school's telecommunication reception. One satellite makes one revolution around the earth every 20 hours; the other makes one revolution around the earth every 25 hours. At 8:00 a.m. on December 3 they were both directly over your school. When (date and time) will both be directly over your school again?

Explain your answer in the space below.

If you were planning the revolution times of two satellites, what would be two compatible options so that they would not interfere very often? Explain.

10.7 Target Number

Grades: 6–8 (this is easily modified for younger students by lowering the number of dice used and the operations involved)

Math: Students will flexibly use whole-number operations to reach a desired total. Students will be able to explain the impact of an operation.

Task: Roll seven number cubes (two the same color, the rest a different color). For the two number cubes of the same color, multiply the value on one of them by ten, then add that amount to the other number cube. This becomes your target number. For example, if the dice show 2 and 6, the target number could be 62 or 26. The values on the remaining five number cubes are then to be combined using each once and any mathematical operation known to you (including using some as exponents) to come as close as possible to the target number.

Expectation: Students can work in small groups and each try to see who can come the closest. Students will justify their expressions and write them. For each combination, students should record the expression and check for accuracy in both computation and order of operations notation. For a student's result to be considered correct, it must be recorded accurately. Students in the group can check the written answer using calculators. Each target number can be approached from a variety of interesting and mathematically legitimate ways. In fact, there may be several different expressions for the same target number. The opportunity for students to hear others give their expressions and to compare them to their own provides ample opportunity to deepen their number and operation senses.

Target Number

Name: _____

Work in groups of three or four. Use seven number cubes. Mark two of them (or ensure they are the same color). Roll those two. Multiply the value showing on one of them by ten and add it to the value showing on the other. This becomes your target number. Record this number on the chart below. Roll the other five number cubes. Use the values on the five cubes, each only once, to write an expression that when solved is a number as close as possible to the target number (you might even hit the target number!). Record your expression in the chart below. If you find a second expression that is as close or closer, or someone in your group does, record it as your second expression.

Target Number	My Expression	My Result	Second Expression	Second Result

10.8 Building Bridges

Grades: 5–6

Math: Students will analyze patterns in geometric growing patterns. Students will describe in words the general rule for a geometric growing pattern.

Task: Determine the amount of material you need to construct a bridge. If we define a bridge span as shown in step 1, then how many uprights and how many cross pieces do we need to build an X (any number) span bridge?

Expectation: Working individually, students will construct bridges of different span lengths for each type of bridge presented. Students will determine a relationship to figure out how many pieces they need to build any bridge length. Students will record their solutions on a recording sheet. It may be helpful for students to record their data in a four-column table, with the step number in the left column, number of uprights, number of cross pieces, and number of total pieces. It will be important for the teacher to ask questions that help students connect what is happening in the model and what is recorded on the table. This activity is easily adaptable to easier growing patterns or more difficult growing patterns. In addition, although this task calls for the use of Cuisenaire rods, similar tasks can be created using any material (e.g., connecting cubes, pattern blocks, color tiles). In fact, after completing experiences like this one, students can design their own growing patterns.

Building Bridges

Name: _____

Using Cuisenaire rods, construct step 1 and step 2 of a bridge like this one:

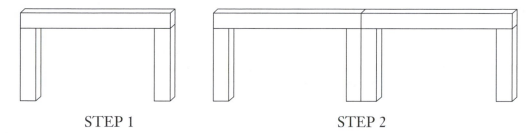

STEP 1   STEP 2

Choose one color (length) for the upright pieces. Choose a different color (length) to be used for the cross piece.

Now, using this type of span, build a 3-step bridge.

1. How many uprights did you need?
2. How many cross pieces did you need?
3. How long (in centimeters) is your bridge?
4. How many pieces did you need altogether?

Build a 5-step bridge.

1. How many uprights did you need?
2. How many cross pieces did you need?
3. How long (in centimeters) is your bridge?
4. How many pieces did you need altogether?

Without building a 9-step bridge, predict the following.

1. How many uprights would you need? How do you know?
2. How many cross pieces would you need? How do you know?
3. How long (in centimeters) will your bridge be? How do you know?
4. How many pieces would you need altogether?

Write a rule (in words) for figuring out the total number of each type of rod you would need to build a bridge if you knew how many steps the bridge had.

_____

_____

_____

_____

10.9 Compensation Decision

Grade: 8

Math: Students will compare linear and exponential growth in a context.

Task: Jocelyn wanted to make some extra money. Her father offered to pay her for odd jobs around the home for a month and gave her a choice of two options. The first option was that her father would pay her $12.00 each week. The second option was that her father would pay her in the following manner for a week: on Monday he would give his daughter $0.01, on Tuesday $0.02, on Wednesday $0.04, and so on through Sunday. What would you tell Jocelyn to do to earn the greatest amount?

Expectation: Students will create tables and graphs for each of these compensation packages. They can use the tables and/or the graph to determine an equation. They will analyze their representations to justify which compensation plan is better. Discussion should focus students' attention to where they can find this information across the representations. Have groups present how they solved their problem. Ask students to consider adaptations to this problem; for example, what if the options expanded for 2 months? What if one amount were to change?

Compensation Decision

Name: _____

Jocelyn wanted to make some extra money. Her father offered to pay her for odd jobs around the home for a month and gave her a choice of two options. The first option was that her father would pay her $12.00 each week. The second option was that her father would pay her in the following manner for a week: on Monday he would give his daughter $0.01, on Tuesday $0.02, on Wednesday $0.04, and so on through Sunday. What would you tell Jocelyn to do to earn the greatest amount?

Use this space to solve this problem. You can make a table or a list to help you. Be sure to explain how you know that your solution is the one that will earn Jocelyn the greatest amount!

10.10 Solving the Mystery

Grades: 6–7

Math: Students will use variables to illustrate equivalences in symbolic expressions and equations.

Task: Your older sister attempts to impress you with an old number trick. It goes like this: Think of a number, double it, and add nine. Then add your original number to it and divide by three. Now add four and subtract your original number. The result, she says, is seven. How does this work? Can you prove that this is not magic, but algebra in action?

Expectation: Present the trick to the students initially as an opportunity to do some mental mathematics. Ask them whether they think it will work all the time. Can they prove it? Students should be using variables as a tool for exploring this number trick. If they start by trying out various numbers, it will help them to see that they can plug in a variable instead of a number to see why it works. Algebra is a formal symbolic language for mathematics. Students in this task have an opportunity to discover the power of algebra as a communication tool. Being able to express the relationship either in symbols or in pictures lays a nice foundation for future algebraic concepts.

Ask students to explain how they used variables to discover how the trick works. Challenge them to make up a number trick on their own.

Solving the Mystery

Name: _____

Your older sister attempts to impress you with an old number trick. It goes like this:

1. Choose a number.
2. Double it.
3. Add nine.
4. Add your original number.
5. Divide by three.
6. Add four.
7. Subtract your original number.
8. Your result is seven.

Did it work? Does it work every time? How do you know? Prove that this is not magic, but algebra in action.

10.11 Fraction Find

Grades: 4–5

Math: Given two fractions, students will be able to find fractions that are between them. Students will justify that given any two fractions, there is always another one in between (density of rational numbers).

Task: Find a fraction that is between $\frac{5}{8}$ and $\frac{3}{4}$. How do you know you are right? How many different ways of explaining this can you find?

Expectation: Students are to discover that there are many fractions between these two fractions and in fact, given any two fractions, they can find one in between. This task may need to be scaffolded. You might begin with a warm-up that has a context and uses easier fractions. For example, if a person was walking around a track and had passed the $\frac{1}{2}$-mile mark but had not yet reached the $\frac{3}{4}$-mile mark, at what distance could they possibly be? Explain to students that they should all be able to find one rational number between $\frac{5}{8}$ and $\frac{3}{4}$, but challenge them to find more than one. Encourage the use of manipulatives and pictures. During the sharing of results, students should notice that there are many answers. Ask students to decide how many fractions are between $\frac{5}{8}$ and $\frac{3}{4}$.

Fraction Find

Name: _____

Find a fraction that is between $\frac{5}{8}$ and $\frac{3}{4}$. How do you know you are right? Illustrate or explain how you found the fraction here.

How many different fractions can you find that are between $\frac{5}{8}$ and $\frac{3}{4}$?

Record all the fractions that you and your partner find below, with an illustration or explanation of how you found it.

10.12 Illustrating Ratios

Grades: 6–7

Math: Students will create and analyze a ratio table and related graph. Students will use tables and graphs to analyze a proportional situation.

Task: Monique works for a company that makes Doohickeys. Her company has one machine that can make a certain number of Doohickeys per minute. Monique observed the machine and collected data to see how many Doohickeys were made in 1 minute. An order for 72 Doohickeys came in from AB textbook publishers. She needs to predict how long it will take to make the 72 Doohickeys. From the data provided, can you help her make her prediction? How long will it take to make 100 Doohickeys?

Expectation: Students will complete the ratio table and graph the data. Question prompts should be created to help students see patterns in the table, in the graph, and between the two. They will also use these data to make a prediction. They will write a letter to the AB textbook publisher explaining how long it will take to complete their order and how they know it will take that long. There is an opportunity to ask many "what if" questions here to deepen students' understanding of ratios (e.g., what if the Doohickey machine were faster? How would the table change? How would the graph change?). For students with less experience using ratios, you can either adapt the numbers in the table so that Doohickeys are a multiple of minutes, or do a warm-up with easier numbers.

Illustrating Ratios

Name: _____

Monique works for a company that makes Doohickeys. Her company has one machine that can make a certain number of Doohickeys per minute. Monique observed the machine and collected data to see how many Doohickeys were made in 1 minute, as shown in the following table. An order for 72 Doohickeys came in from AB textbook publishers. She needs to predict how long it will take to make the 72 Doohickeys. From the data provided, can you help her make her prediction? How long would it take to make 100 Doohickeys?

Minutes	4		16	22	28	34
Doohickeys		27	36			

Graph your results here. Label the axes.

How long will it take to make 72 Doohickeys? How do you know?

How long will it take to make 100 Doohickeys? How do you know?

Write a letter to AB textbook publishers explaining how long it will take to make their 72 Doohickeys and how you know. Use proper letter writing style.

10.13 Cover All

Grade: 3

Math: Students will explain strategies for finding how many square tiles cover a rectangle region. Students will explain how to use repeated addition and/or multiplication to find areas of rectangles.

Task: How many square tiles (1 inch by 1 inch) are needed to cover the rectangle on this page?

Expectation: Students may want to cut out their tile, and even use more than one tile. This is a good way to support their initial exploration, but limit the number of tiles so that they begin to see other ways to find area (other than covering the entire surface). As with any measurement task, it is a good practice to ask students first to estimate how many they think will cover the surface. Students may work in pairs to discuss the problem, but each must submit an individual write-up. Students may verify their estimates using real tiles. Students will explain their solution process. If possible, students can extend this activity to finding areas of other rectangles or rectangular shapes in the classroom.

Cover All

Name:_____

For a mosaic project in art, you and your friend are trying to determine how many tiles of this size will cover the area below. How many tiles do you think will cover the page? How do you know? Explain your answer in the space below.

Explain how you figured out the number of tiles.

_____

_____

_____

_____

_____

_____

10.14 Find the Zero

Grades: 5–6

Math: Students will find sums of integers. Students will describe and illustrate integer addition and connect equations to other representations.

Task: How can you solve integer addition problems using the Finding the Zero strategy? What does this look like in an equation? A picture? An example?

Expectation: Before beginning the activity, ask students to tell you the sums of several opposites (e.g., $4 + {}^-4$). Then, ask students to look at a sum that is not opposites (e.g., $7 + {}^-4$) and ask if they can "find a zero" by partitioning one of the numbers (e.g., $(3 + 4) + {}^-4$) and solve. Students, in particular students with disabilities, may benefit from creating a "zero box" below each problem as they solve it, as illustrated below.

$12 + {}^-5 =$
Zero Box: $\boxed{5 + {}^-5}$
$(7 + 5) + {}^-5 = 7 + (5 + {}^-5) = 7 + 0 = 7$

Introduce the activity by modeling how to solve an equation, draw an illustration, and give an example. Have several students share different contexts for explaining the one example. Encourage students to select a context that makes sense to them. If students struggle coming up with their own example or story, one way to scaffold the task is to ask the following three prompts: Where did you start? How far did you go? Where are you now? (Swanson, 2010). So, for example, a student might write: "I was 3 feet under water, then dove down 5 feet. Where am I now?" As students are working, ask them to show you the connections among the three representations.

Find the Zero

Name: _____

In this activity, you can use the Find the Zero strategy to add integers. In each sum, illustrate your strategy and provide a visual and explanation using an example of your choice (temperature, golf scores, height, money, etc.).

Example of Find the Zero strategy: $12 + {}^-5 =$
Expanded equation "showing" the zero: $(7 + 5) + {}^-5 = 7 + (5 + {}^-5) = 7 + 0 = 7$

My Equation and Solution	My Picture/Illustration	My Explanation and Example

11 Balanced Assessment Tasks

In this section are three performance assessments. As with the lessons and activities in Chapters 9 and 10, these are opportunities in which students can continue to develop their Mathematical Proficiencies. Because these are assessments, including rubrics, you can also assess the extent to which a student is demonstrating their mathematical proficiency.

These tasks and rubrics are offered as an example of how problem-based tasks can be used to determine student understanding. The tasks themselves have been field tested with students in public schools whose responses have been examined to develop the included rubrics. These rubrics are holistic in nature and are intended to help you recognize the importance of identifying the core mathematics content and looking for evidence of understanding by describing elements of performance. Each task also has a completed sample solution to help you see the type of response you might expect.

	Title of Balanced Assessment Task	Content Focus	Grade Level Recommendation (based on *Common Core State Standards*)
11.1	Magic Age Rings	To apply rules to numbers (Ch. 9, 12)	Grades 2–4
11.2	Grocery Store	To reason algebraically (Ch. 14)	Grades 6–8
11.3	Bolts and Nuts!	To analyze change in a practical situation (Ch. 18)	Grades 5–7

Source: Adapted from *Balanced Assessment for the Mathematics Curriculum, Elementary Grades Assessment Packages 1 and 2*, © 1999 by the Regents of the University of California. Published by Pearson Education, Inc., publishing as Dale Seymour Publications, an imprint of the Pearson Learning Group. Used by permission.

11.1 Magic Age Rings

Grades: 2-4

Math: To apply rules (e.g., add 5) to numbers. Write number sentences to represent pattern. Combine various arithmetic operations to solve complex problems.

Task: This task asks students to imagine they are wearing magic rings that change their age. A blue ring doubles one's age, a green ring adds five years, and a yellow ring takes two years away from one's age. Students calculate the effects of wearing different rings and answer questions about this imaginary situation. You may wish to extend this task by posing some of these challenges to your students:

- Make up your own question about these magic rings. Work out the answer. Ask someone else to answer your question.
- Are there any ages that are impossible to produce with the rings?
- Invent different types of rings that also change your age. What would be the most useful set of rings to have if you want to increase your age?

Investigate what happens when you put two rings in a different order (blue first, then green, or green first, then blue). For which combinations of rings does order matter? Are there combinations in which order doesn't make any difference? Why is this?

Expectation: Most fourth graders should be able to tackle the mathematics of this task. It assumes that students have had prior opportunities to explore the ways addition, subtraction, multiplication, and division relate to each other. The task also assumes that students have some understanding of the significance of order of operations and that they know the meaning of doubling a quantity. Students may discuss the task in pairs, but each student should complete an individual written response.

Magic Age Rings

Name: _____

You are ten years old and as a birthday present you have been given three boxes of magic rings.

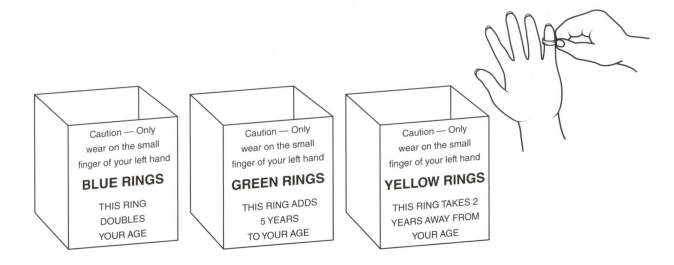

Caution — Only wear on the small finger of your left hand
BLUE RINGS
THIS RING DOUBLES YOUR AGE

Caution — Only wear on the small finger of your left hand
GREEN RINGS
THIS RING ADDS 5 YEARS TO YOUR AGE

Caution — Only wear on the small finger of your left hand
YELLOW RINGS
THIS RING TAKES 2 YEARS AWAY FROM YOUR AGE

With great care you slip one of the green rings onto the little finger of your left hand. At once you start to grow and, within seconds, the magic has worked—you are 15 years old. Discuss this with your partner. What does it mean to "double" your age?

1. Complete the table.

Imagine that you are . . .	Rings you wear	Age you become	Number sentences to explain this
10 years old	Green	15	10 + 5 = 15
10 years old	Blue		
10 years old	Yellow		
10 years old	Green and then blue	30	10 + 5 = 15 15 + 15 = 30
10 years old	Green and then yellow	13	10 + 5 = 15 15 − 2 = 13
10 years old	Green and another green		
10 years old	Yellow and then blue		
10 years old	Yellow and another yellow		

2. Use your imagination. Choose to be any age and wear any combination of rings. Complete the table.

Imagine that you are . . .	Rings you wear	Age you become	Number sentences to explain this

3. Latosha is 11 years old. She puts on three blue rings. How old is she now? Explain your answer.

4. Margaux is 10 years old, but she wants to be 18. What rings should she put on to change her age to 18 years? Explain your answer.

5. Lloyd is 9 years old. He has a blue ring and a green ring. He wants to wear both rings. Will it make any difference to his age which ring he puts on first? Explain your answer.

6. Jessica is wearing a yellow ring and she tells you she is 13 years old. She takes off the yellow ring and she is back to her real age. What is her real age? Explain your answer.

7. Rashad is wearing three rings and is 12 years old. First he takes off a yellow ring, then a blue ring, and finally a green ring. He is back to his real age. How old is he? Explain your answer.

Magic Age Rings: Sample Solution

1.

Imagine that you are . . .	Rings you wear	Age you become	Number sentences to explain this
10 years old	Green	15	$10 + 5 = 15$
10 years old	Blue	**20**	**$10 + 10 = 20$**
10 years old	Yellow	**8**	**$10 - 2 = 8$**
10 years old	Green and then blue	30	$10 + 5 = 15$ $15 + 15 = 30$
10 years old	Green and then yellow	13	$10 + 5 = 15$ $15 - 2 = 13$
10 years old	Green and another green	**20**	**$10 + 15 = 15$** **$15 + 5 = 20$**
10 years old	Yellow and then blue	**16**	**$10 - 2 = 8$** **$8 + 8 = 16$**
10 years old	Yellow and another yellow	6	**$10 - 2 = 8$** **$8 - 2 = 6$**

*Other number sentences may also be correct. For example, doubling may be shown as "× 2."

2. There is no reason students should not complete this table with examples that use three or more rings—for example, "Blue, then green, then yellow."

3. Latosha will be 88 years old. $11 \times 2 = 22, 22 \times 2 = 44, 44 \times 2 = 88$

4. Margaux could put on a blue ring and then a yellow ring. $10 \times 2 = 20, 20 - 2 = 18$. Or she could put on two green rings and then a yellow ring. $10 + 5 = 15, 15 + 5 = 20, 20 - 2 = 18$. There are other solutions.

5. It does make a difference which ring Lloyd puts on first. If he puts on the blue ring first, his age becomes 23 years. $9 \times 2 = 18, 18 + 5 = 23$. But if he puts on the green ring first, he becomes 28 years old. $9 + 5 = 14, 14 \times 2 = 28$

6. Jessica's real age is 15 years. A yellow ring takes 2 years off your age. So removing a yellow ring will do the opposite. It will make Jessica two years older. $13 + 2 = 15$

7. Rashad's real age is 2 years. $12 + 2 = 14, 14 \div 2 = 7, 7 - 5 = 2$. This last question is difficult as it really demands some understanding of inverse operations.

Rubric

Characterizing Performance

This section offers a characterization of student responses and provides indications of the ways the students were successful or unsuccessful in engaging with and completing the task. The descriptions are keyed to the Core Elements of Performance. Our global descriptions of student work range from "The student needs significant instruction" to "The student's work meets the essential demands of the task."

The characterization of student responses for this task is based on these Core Elements of Performance:

1. Apply simple functions in a problem-solving situation.
2. Use combinations of various arithmetic operations to solve problems.
3. Demonstrate understanding of what effect reversing the order of operations has on a problem.
4. Use doubling and an understanding of inverse operations to solve complex problems.
5. Explain how answers are decided.

Descriptions of Student Work

The student needs significant instruction. These papers show evidence of some limited success in one or two of the core elements of performance, most commonly in the first and second.

The student needs some instruction. These papers provide evidence of ability in the first two core elements, both in the tables and in some of the problems. There may be some limited evidence of performance in the last three core elements: this evidence, however, is weak and inconsistent. This level of work will show the ability to apply simple functions and to combine various arithmetic operations not just in the table but also in some of the problems 3 through 7. Generally, there will not be evidence of an ability to work with inverse operations, or to double numbers correctly or consistently. The paper will not provide evidence of understanding the importance of order of operations. Explanations will be limited and/or weak.

The student's work needs to be revised. There will be evidence of ability to perform in at least four out of five of the core elements of performance. There may be some inconsistency in one or two core elements (for example, the response may correctly show doubling in the table, but incorrectly solve problem 3, or correctly solve problem 5, but make a mistake in order of operations in the table). The answers may be all correct, but missing any explanation.

The student's work meets the essential demands of the task. There will be no mistakes (or only very minor mistakes) in the tables. Problems 3 through 7 will fully demonstrate ability in all five core elements of performance. There may be an error in one of the elements of performance; however, that element will be correctly demonstrated elsewhere (for example, many otherwise very strong students will make a mistake on problem 7).

11.2 Grocery Store

Grades: 6–8

Math: Students will be reasoning algebraically. Students will generalize patterns and write them symbolically.

Task: This task asks students to consider the planning of a layout for a new grocery store. Students answer questions using scale models of shopping carts to solve problems related to the store's floor plan.

Expectation: It is assumed that students have had experience with ratio and proportion and with generalizing linear situations symbolically. Students may discuss the task in pairs, but then complete an individual written response.

This task places numerous demands on students. They must successfully move back and forth between the real world and scale model and use proportional reasoning, but they must also know when not to rely on proportional reasoning alone. For example, students are often tempted to measure the 12 nested carts and use this information to answer question 3 (length of 20 nested carts) and question 4 (number of carts that fit in a 10-meter space) by reasoning proportionally. The results they obtain will be off, but not by much. However, this type of reasoning shows a lack of attention to the first cart, which is a constant term—a central idea in linear functions, and an idea students must account for in question 4 in order to produce a generalization that accurately represents the relationships in the situation.

Nevertheless, a purely proportional approach that ignores the constant term would not prove detrimental in the real world of shopping carts, especially when dealing with large numbers. As you increase the number of shopping carts, the relative effect of the greater length of the first cart (when compared to the stick-out length of each cart) decreases.

The task also involves concepts of measurement. The questions do not indicate to students the level of accuracy required. Some students use rough measurements of the scale model while others strive for as much accuracy as possible. All reasonable responses are accepted.

Grocery Store

Name: _____

Rasheed is planning the layout for a new grocery store. He found the diagram below in a supply catalog. It shows a drawing of a single shopping cart and a drawing of 12 shopping carts that are "nested" together. (The drawings are $\frac{1}{24}$th of the real size.)

length

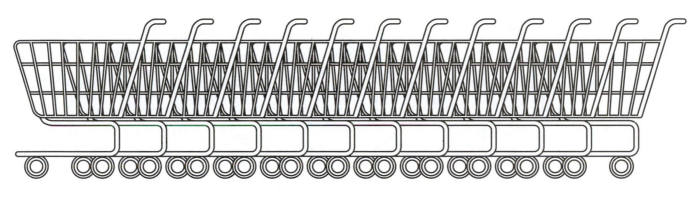

Rasheed has several questions:

1. What is the length of a real shopping cart?

2. When the real carts are nested, how much does each cart stick out beyond the next one in the line?

3. What would be the total length of a row of 20 real nested carts?

4. What rule or formula could I use to find the length of a row of real nested carts for any (*n*) number of carts?

5. How many real nested carts could fit in a space 10 meters long?

Write a letter to Rasheed that answers his questions.

- For each question, explain your answer so that he can understand it and use it to make decisions about the store.
- To explain question 4, you may want to draw and label a diagram that tells what each part of your formula represents.

Grocery Store: Sample Solution

The following is a sample solution using centimeters. Students may also use inch measurements, although this will require conversion to metric for the last question.

Dear Rasheed,

Here are answers to your questions. I hope they will help you in planning your store. Good luck!

My answer to question 1: The length of a real shopping cart is 96 cm, or .96 m. The scale model of a single shopping cart measures 4 cm. Since the scale is 1 to 24, multiply by 24 to get the real length: 4 cm × 24 = 96 cm.

My answer to question 2: Each cart sticks out beyond the next one in line approximately 26.4 cm or about .26 m. In the scale model of the nested carts, I measured the distance between the handles on the first and second shopping carts and got about 1.1 cm (although it looks like it's a little more than that). You could measure in other ways too—by the grills, between the last two carts, and so on. Anyway, it comes out roughly the same. Then I multiplied by 24 to get the real length: 1.1 cm × 24 = 26.4 cm.

My answer to question 3: The total length of 20 nested carts is approximately 5.98 m. In any row of nested carts, the first cart will take up 96 cm. Each additional cart will add 26.4 cm to the total length. Since you need the length of 20 carts, I added the length of one cart and 19 stick outs to get 96 cm + (19 × 26.4) = 597.6 cm, or about 5.98 m.

My answer to question 4: If L is the total length in centimeters of n nested carts, then the total length of n nested carts is $L = 96 + 26.4(n - 1)$, which can be written as $L = 26.4n + 69.6$. I got this formula in a way similar to finding the answer to your last question. The 96 is for the length of the first cart. After the first cart, there are $n - 1$ carts sticking out. So I multiplied the number of "stick outs" ($n - 1$) by the length of each "stick out" (26.4) and added it all to the length of the first cart (96) giving me $L = 96 + 26.4(n - 1)$. Remember that this formula gives length in centimeters.

My answer to question 5: About 35 carts could fit in a space 10 meters long. I got this answer by using the above formula and letting $L = 10$ m. Since the formula finds length in centimeters, I let $L = 1000$ cm. Plugging this in, I got $1000 - 26.4n + 69.6$. I solved for n: $n = 35.24$. Since you can't have parts of shopping carts, I rounded this number down to 35.

I hope that these answers help you to make decisions about your store.

Sincerely,
A. Student

Rubric

Characterizing Performance

This section offers a characterization of student responses and provides indications of the ways the students were successful or unsuccessful in engaging with and completing the task. The descriptions are keyed to the Core Elements of Performance. Our global descriptions of student work range from "The student needs significant instruction" to "The student's work meets the essential demands of the task."

The characterization of student responses for this task is based on these Core Elements of Performance:

1. Reason using ratio and proportion and successfully move back and forth between a real-world situation and a scale model to determine the lengths of shopping carts
2. Use algebraic reasoning to solve for an unknown and to generalize a linear relationship symbolically
3. Communicate mathematical reasoning

Descriptions of Student Work

The student needs significant instruction. Student may answer some questions correctly (either in the letter to Rasheed or beside the question) but does not successfully find an unknown (as in questions 3 and 5) or formulate a symbolic generalization (as in question 4).

The student needs some instruction. Student successfully finds an unknown (questions 3 and 5) but does not demonstrate an understanding of how to arrive at a general formula.

The student's work needs to be revised. Student successfully finds the unknown (questions 3 and 5) and shows an understanding of how to generalize the situation, but fails to arrive at a completely correct formula.

The student's work meets the essential demands of the task. Student successfully finds the unknown and arrives at a correct generalization of the situation. Minor errors that do not distort the reasonableness of solutions are permitted.

11.3 Bolts and Nuts!

Grades: 5–7

Math: Students analyze change in a practical situation. Students make ratio calculations to determine the relationship between two variables.

Task: Students estimate, measure, and calculate the number of turns made to the nut and the distance it moves. Calculations bring in simple ideas of ratio, which pupils of this age will normally find quite challenging.

Expectation: Students should be familiar with measurements in millimeters and meters. Students may discuss the task in pairs, but each student should complete an individual written response. Encourage students to model the problem and/or to create a table to help analyze the situation.

Bolts and Nuts!

Name: _____

Work with a partner on this problem.
You should have a nut, a bolt, a ruler, and a calculator.

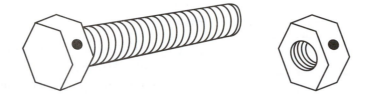

Fix the nut onto the bolt.
Turn the nut so that it moves along the bolt.

1. How many complete turns will move the nut 25 mm along the bolt?

   First make a guess.
   Your guess: _____ turns move the nut 25 mm.
   Your partner's guess: _____ turns move the nut 25 mm.

   Talk to your partner about how you will answer this question. You will need to measure 25 mm
   with the ruler. There are some marks on the nut and bolt that may help you count the turns.

   Your answer: _____ turns move the nut 25 mm.
   Your partner's answer: _____ turns move the nut 25 mm.

   Do you agree? If not, who has the right answer?

Now try to answer the following questions *without touching the nut and bolt.*

2. How many times would you have to turn the nut to move it 50 mm? _____

3. Complete this table.

Distance the Nut Moves	Number of Turns	
25 mm		←Write in your answer from the previous page
50 mm		←Write in your answer from the last question.
100 mm		←Figure this out.
200 mm		←Figure this out.
1 m		←Figure this out.

To answer these you will need to imagine a bolt that is longer than the one you are using. The 1-meter bolt would be giant-sized because 1 meter = 1000 mm.

4. How far would the nut move if you turned it 50 complete turns? Explain how you figured this out:

_____

_____

_____

Bolts and Nuts! Sample Solution

1. It takes 20 turns to move the nut 25 mm.
2. You'd have to turn the nut about 40 times to move it 50 mm.
3.

Distance the Nut Moves	Number of Turns
25 mm	About 20
50 mm	About 40
100 mm	About 80
200 mm	About 160
1 m	About 800

4. If 1 meter or 1000 mm takes about 800 turns, then 125 mm takes about 100 turns. Therefore, 50 turns would move the nut about 62 mm.

Rubric

Characterizing Performance

This section offers a characterization of student responses and provides indications of the ways in which the students were successful or unsuccessful in engaging with and completing the task. The descriptions are keyed to the Core Elements of Performance. Our global descriptions of student work range from "The student needs significant instruction" to "The student's work meets the essential demands of the task."

The characterization of student responses for this task is based on these Core Elements of Performance:

1. Take pairs of measurements in a practical situation
2. Make simple ratio calculations

Descriptions of Student Work

The student needs significant instruction. The table shows, at most, an attempt to make the estimates or measurements.

The student needs some instruction. An attempt has been made to make the estimates and measurements. The table has been at least partially completed, but there is a poor understanding of proportion.

The student's work needs to be revised. Measurements have been correctly made within the generous margin of error (± 4 turns). The table has been partially completed with most figures in proportion.

The student's work meets the essential demands of the task. Measurements have been correctly made within the generous margin of error (±4 turns). The student may have indicated somewhere on the response that figures are "rough," "approximate," or "estimated." The student can handle simple ratio calculations as indicated either by the table completed with all figures in proportion, or by a consistent answer to the final question.

Part *III*

Blackline Masters

The reproducible Blackline Masters featured in this section can be used for making instructional materials to support activities. They are also available on MyEducationLab (www.myeducationlab.com).

Suggestions for Use and Construction of Materials

Cardstock Materials

A good way to have many materials made quickly and easily for students is to have them duplicated on cardstock, laminated, and then cut into smaller pieces if desired. Once cut, materials are best kept in clear freezer bags with zip-type closures. Punch a hole near the top of the bag so that you do not store air.

The following list is a suggestion for materials that can be made from cardstock using the masters in this section. Quantity suggestions are also given.

Dot Cards 3–8

One complete set of cards will serve four to six children. Duplicate each set in a different color so that mixed sets can be separated easily. Laminate and then cut with a paper cutter.

Five-Frames and Ten-Frames 9–10

Five-frames and ten-frames are best duplicated on light-colored card stock. Do not laminate; if you do, the mats will curl and counters will slide around.

10 × 10 Multiplication Array 12

Make one per student in any color. Lamination is suggested. Provide each student with an L-shaped piece of cardstock to frame the array.

Base-Ten Materials 14

Run copies on white cardstock. One sheet will make 4 hundreds and 10 tens or 4 hundreds and 100 ones. Cut into pieces with a paper cutter. It is recommended that you *not* laminate the base-ten pieces. A kit consisting of 10 hundreds, 30 tens, and 30 ones is adequate for each student or pair of students.

Little Ten-Frames 15–16

There are two masters for these materials. One has full ten-frames and the other has one to nine dots, including two with five dots. Copy the 1-to-9 master on one color of card stock and the full ten-frames on another and then laminate. Cut into little ten-frames. Each set consists of 20 pieces: 10 full ten-frames and 10 of the 1-to-9 pieces, including 2 fives. Make a set for each student.

Place-Value Mat (with Ten-Frames) 17

Mats can be duplicated on any pastel cardstock. It is recommended that you not laminate these because they tend to curl and counters slide around. Make one for every student.

Circular Fraction Pieces 24–26

Make three copies of each page of the master. To have a separate master for each size, cut the disks apart and tape onto blank pages with three of the same type on a page. Duplicate each master on a different color cardstock. Laminate and then cut the circles out. A kit for one or two students should have two circles of each size piece.

Rational Number Wheel 28

These disks should be made on cardstock. Duplicate the master on two contrasting colors. Laminate and cut the circles and also the slot on the dotted line. Make a set for each student.

Tangrams and Mosaic Puzzle 51

Copy the tangrams and the mosaic puzzle on cardstock. For younger children, the cardstock should mounted on poster board to make the pieces thicker and easier to put together in puzzles. Prepare one set per student.

Woozle Cards 59

Copy the Woozle Card master on white cardstock. You need two copies per set. Before laminating, color one set one color and the other a different color. An easy way to color the cards is to make one pass around the inside of each Woozle, leaving the rest of the creature white. If you color the entire Woozle, the dots may not show up. Make one set for every four students.

Many masters lend themselves to demonstration purposes. The 10 × 10 array, the blank hundreds board, and the large geoboard are examples. The five-frame and ten-frame work well with counters. The place-value mat can be used with strips and squares or with counters and cups directly on the document camera or opaque projector. The missing-part blank and the record blanks for the four algorithms are pages that you may wish to write on as a demonstration.

The 10,000 grid is the easiest way there is to show 10,000 or to model four-place decimal numbers.

The degrees and wedges page is the very best way to illustrate what a degree is and also to help explain protractors.

All of the line and dot grids are useful for modeling. You may find it a good idea to have several copies of each easily available.

2 more plus 2	**2 more** plus 2	**1 more** plus 1
2 less minus 2	**1 less** minus 1	**1 more** plus 1
2 less minus 2	**1 less** minus 1	**zero**

More-or-less cards —1

0	1	2	3
4	5	6	7
8	9	10	

Number cards — 2

Field Experience Guide: Resources for Teachers of Elementary and Middle School Mathematics © Pearson Education, Inc., 2013

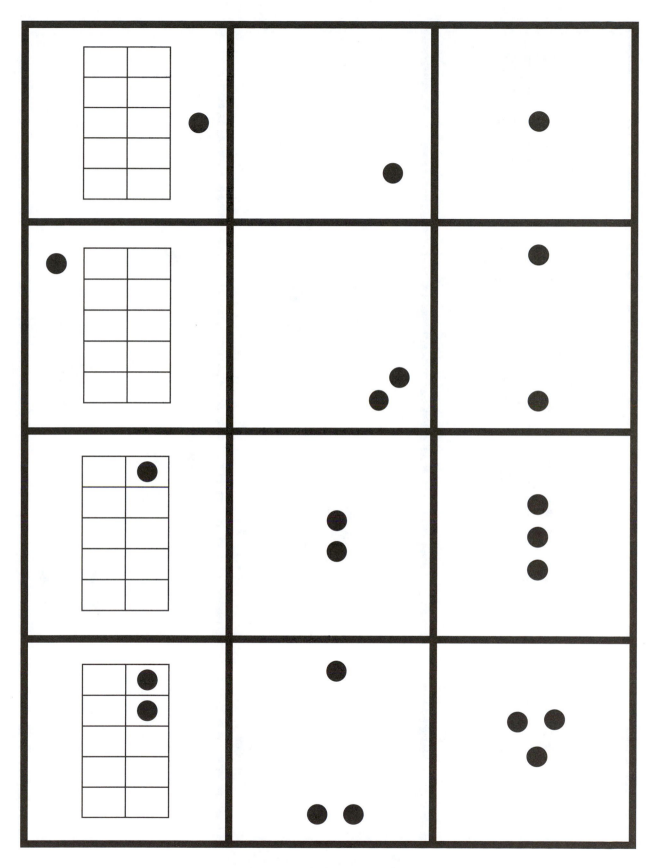

Dot cards — 3

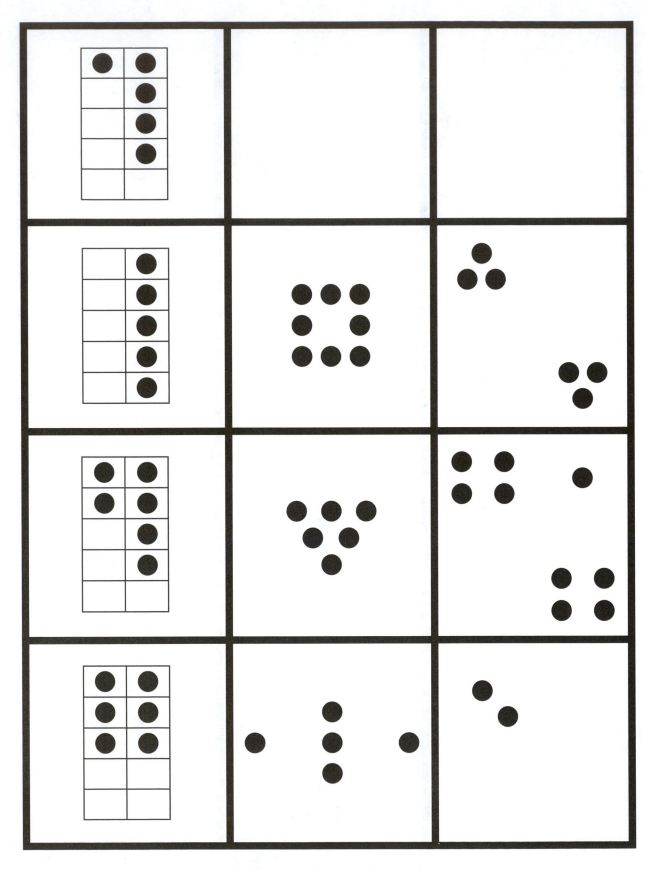

Dot cards — 4

Field Experience Guide: Resources for Teachers of Elementary and Middle School Mathematics © Pearson Education, Inc., 2013

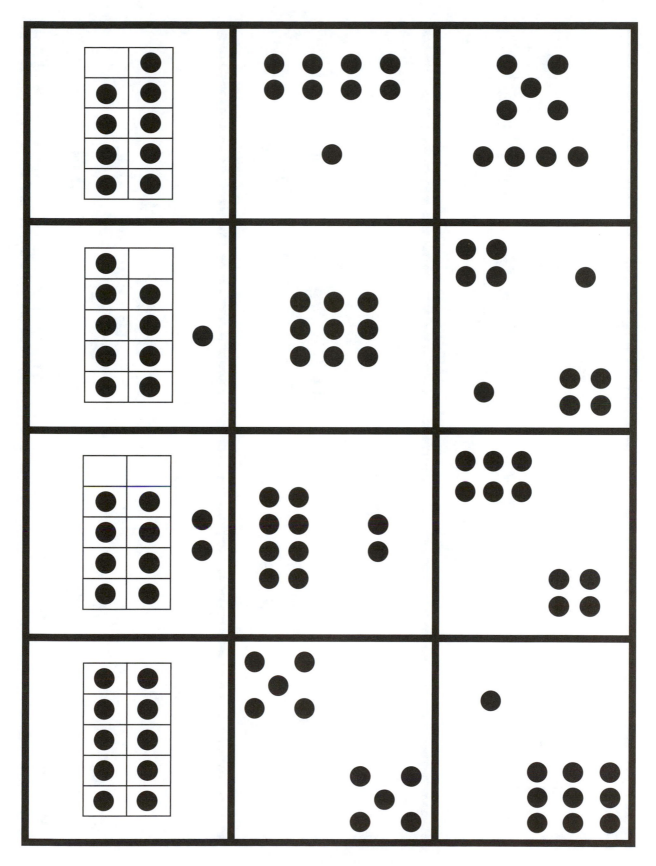

Dot cards —5

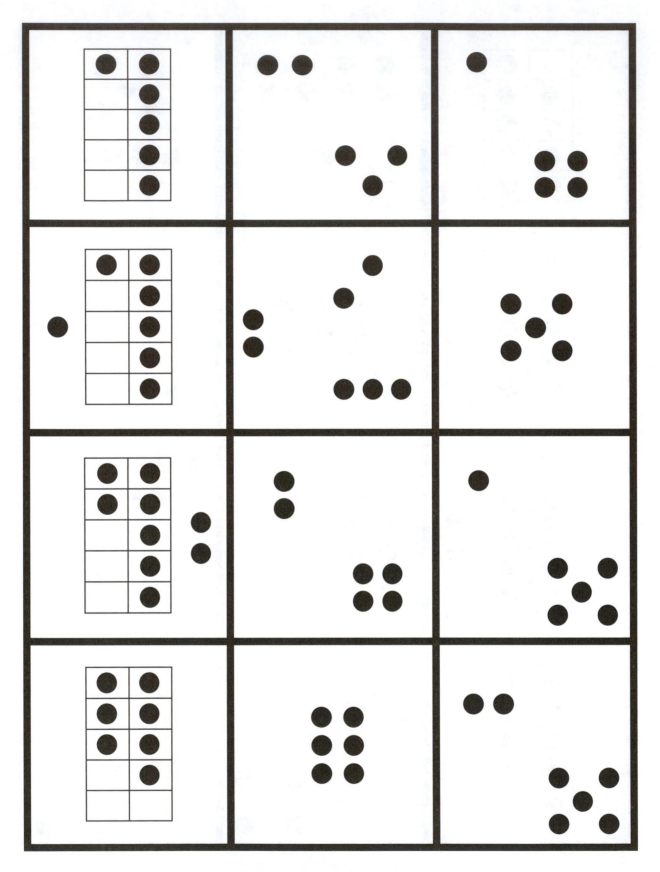

Dot cards —6

Field Experience Guide: Resources for Teachers of Elementary and Middle School Mathematics © Pearson Education, Inc., 2013

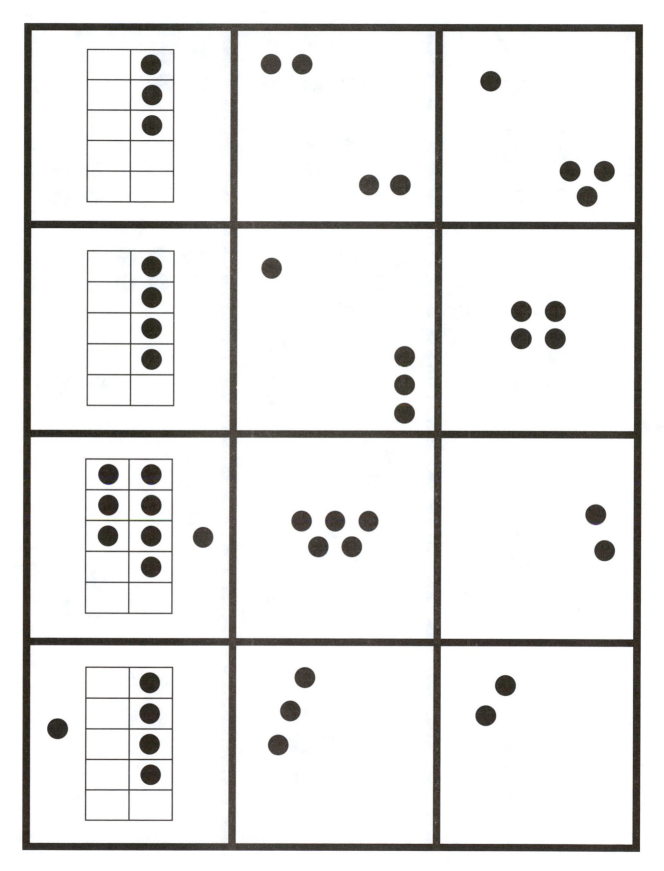

Dot cards —7

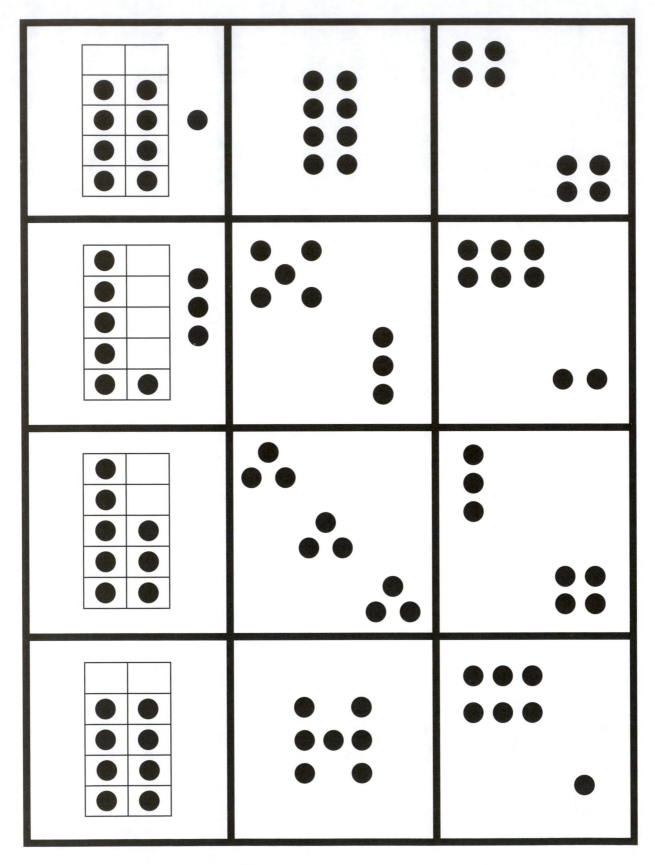

Dot cards —8

Field Experience Guide: Resources for Teachers of Elementary and Middle School Mathematics © Pearson Education, Inc., 2013

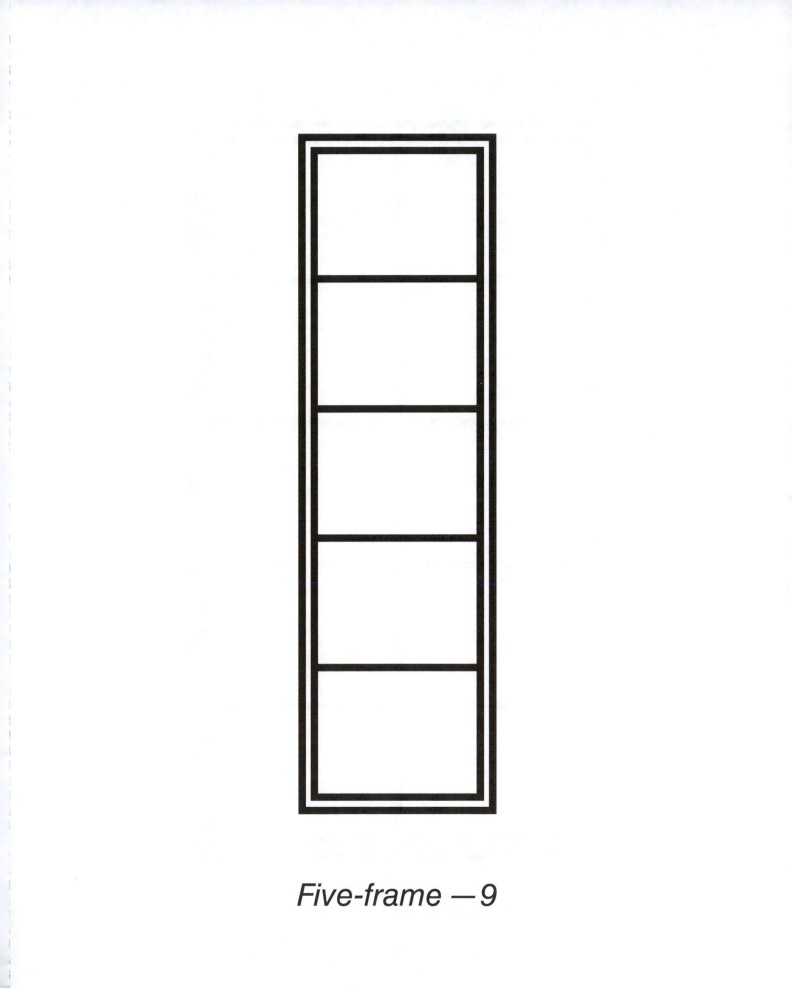

Five-frame — 9

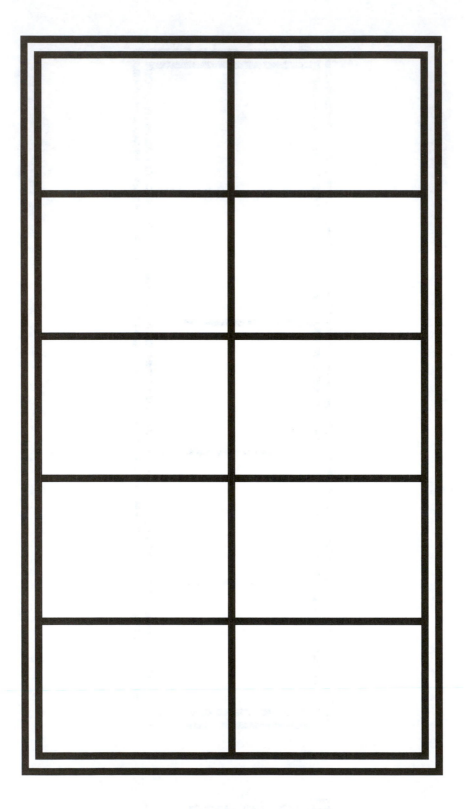

Ten-frame —10

Field Experience Guide: Resources for Teachers of Elementary and Middle School Mathematics © Pearson Education, Inc., 2013

Double ten-frame —11

10 × 10 multiplication array —12

Field Experience Guide: Resources for Teachers of Elementary and Middle School Mathematics © Pearson Education, Inc., 2013

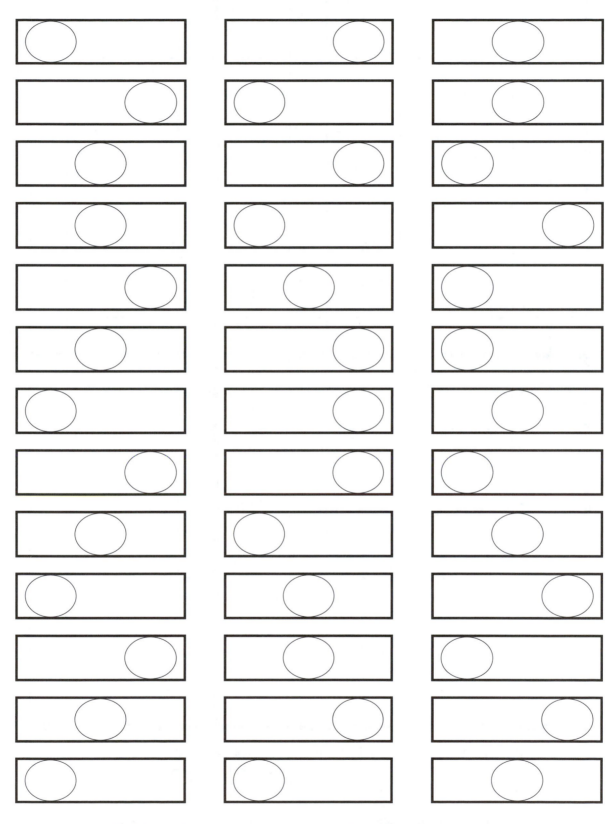

Missing-part worksheet —13

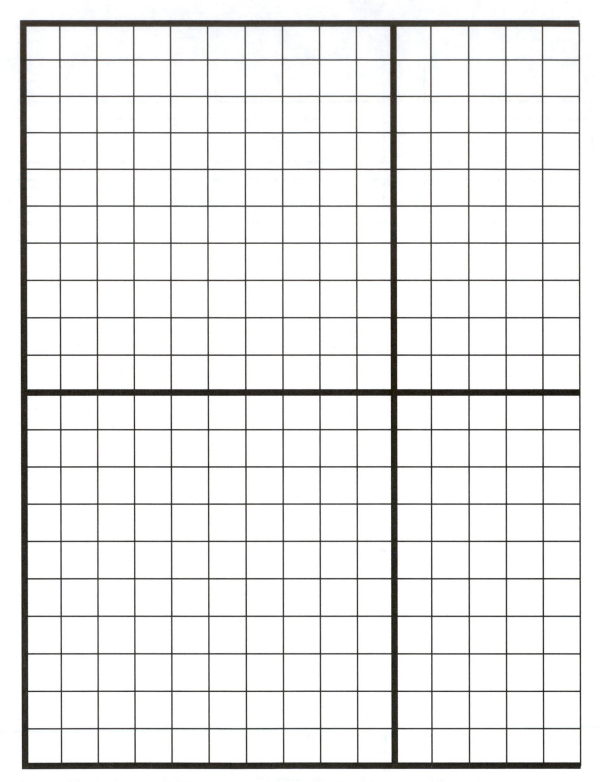

1. Make two copies of this page. Cut out the grid from each copy.
2. Overlap the two grids, and tape onto a blank sheet to form a 20-by-25-cm grid with 4 complete hundreds squares and 2 rows of 5 tens each.
3. Use this as a master to make copies on card stock.

Base-ten materials —14

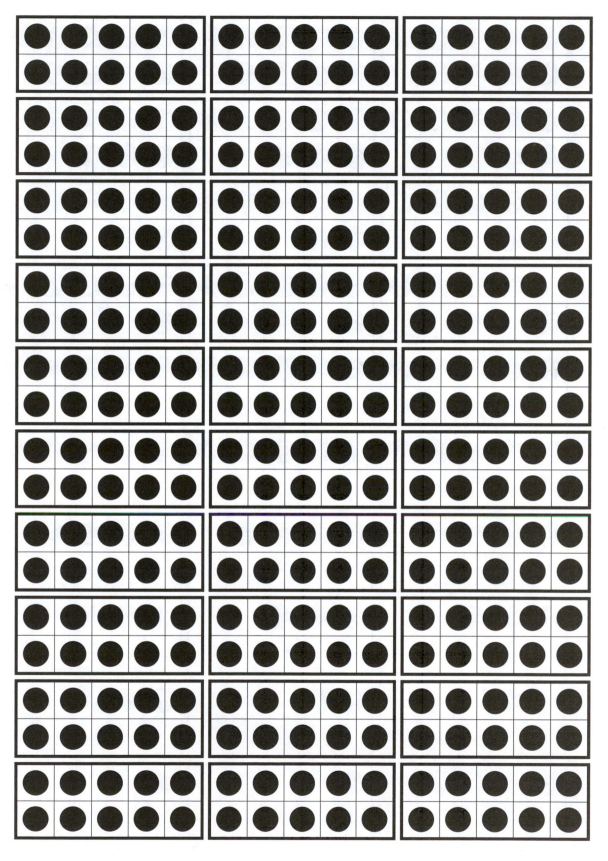

Little ten-frames—15

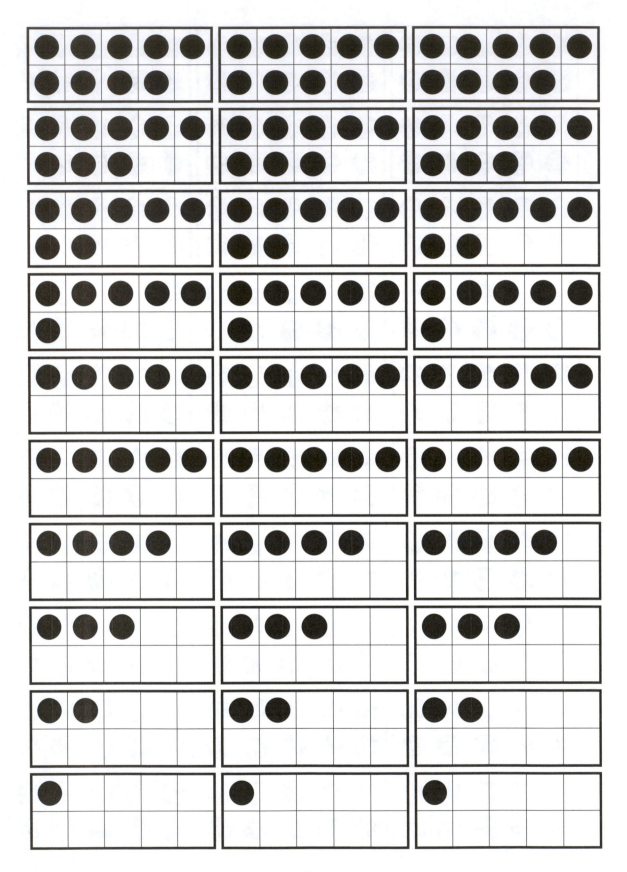

Little ten-frames—16

Field Experience Guide: Resources for Teachers of Elementary and Middle School Mathematics © Pearson Education, Inc., 2013

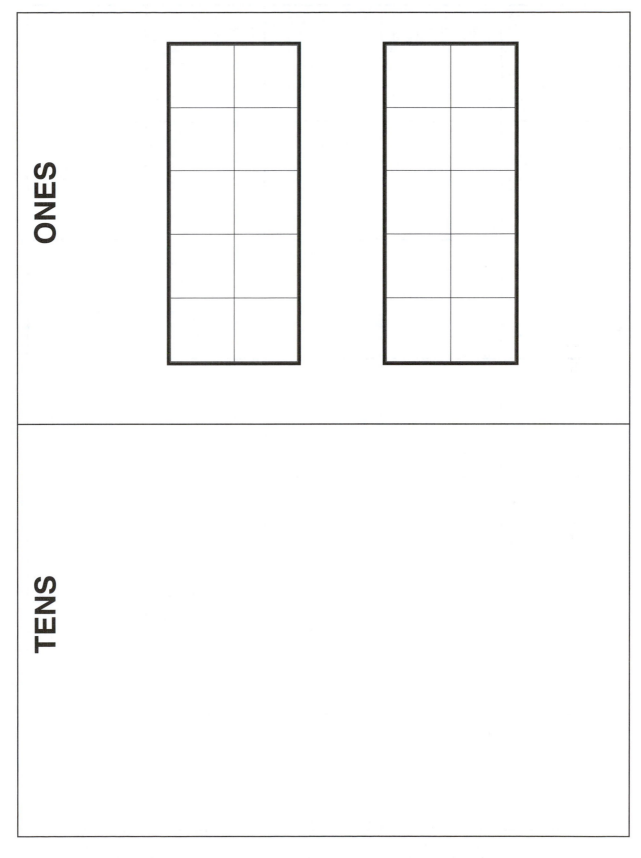

Place-value mat (with ten-frames)—17

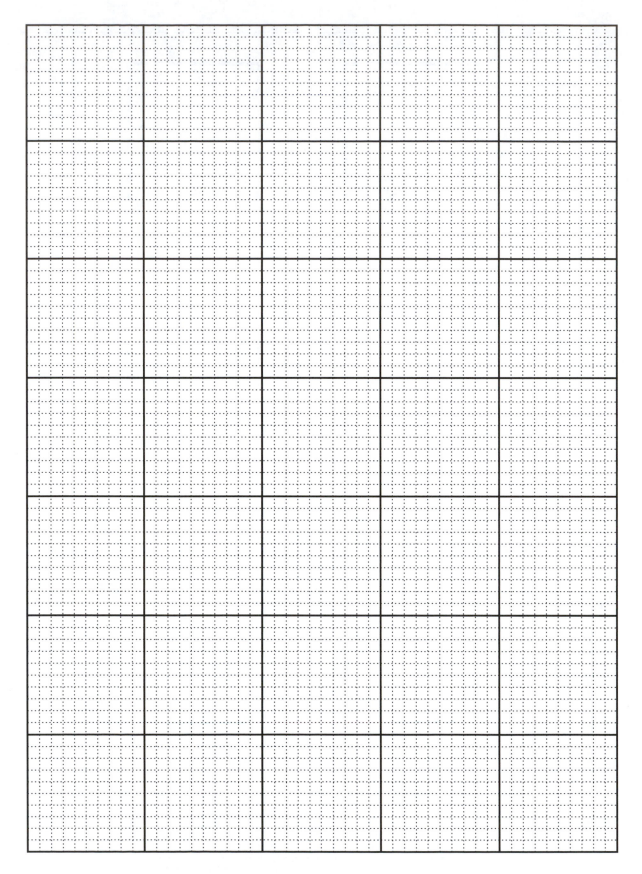

Base-ten grid paper—18

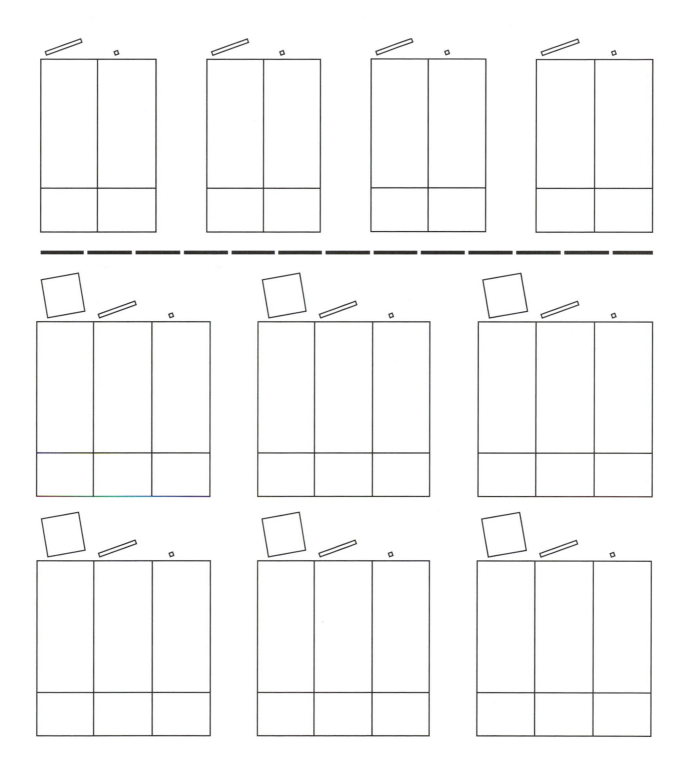

Addition and subtraction recording charts —19

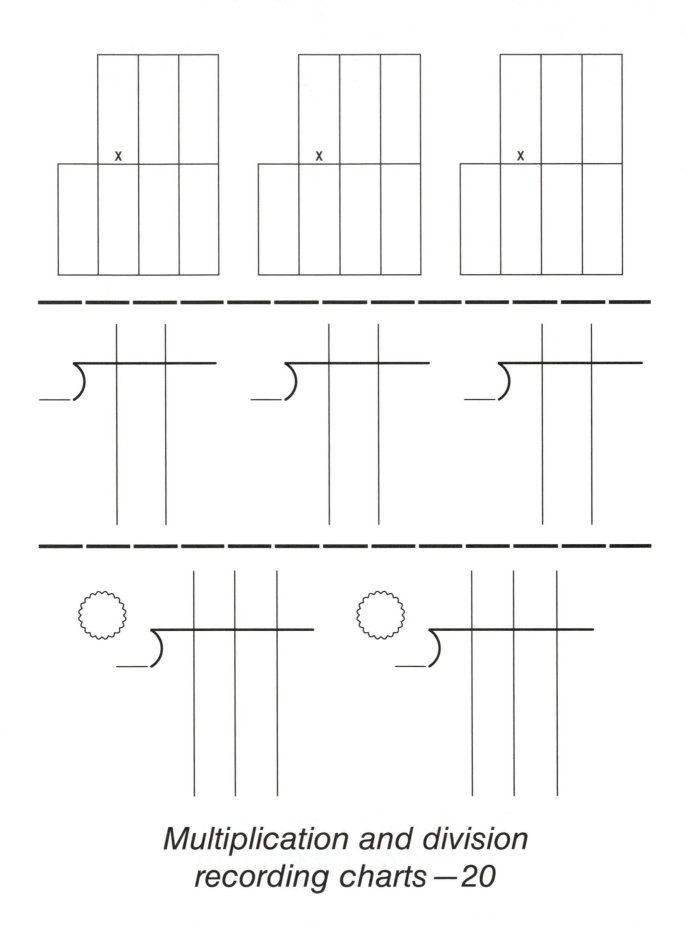

*Multiplication and division
recording charts—20*

Field Experience Guide: Resources for Teachers of Elementary and Middle School Mathematics © Pearson Education, Inc., 2013

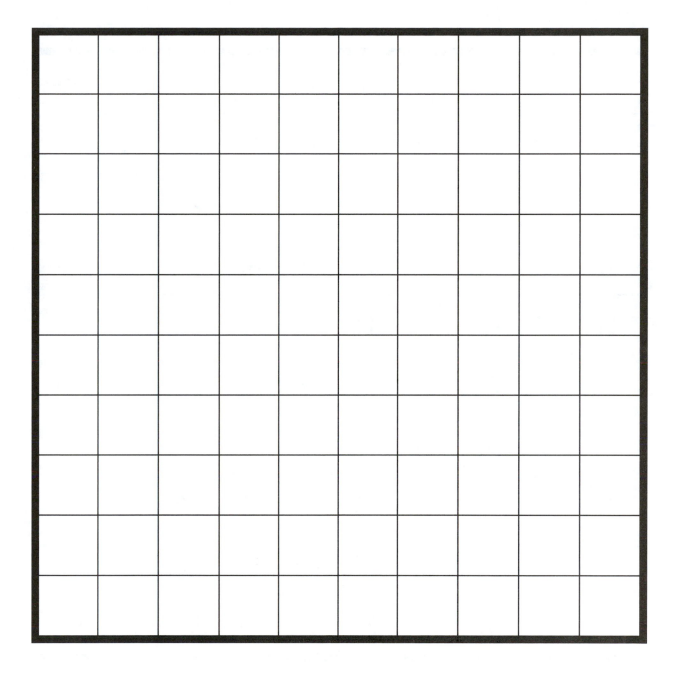

Blank hundreds
chart (10 × 10 square) — 21

1	2	3	4	5	6	7	8	9	10
11	12	13	14	15	16	17	18	19	20
21	22	23	24	25	26	27	28	29	30
31	32	33	34	35	36	37	38	39	40
41	42	43	44	45	46	47	48	49	50
51	52	53	54	55	56	57	58	59	60
61	62	63	64	65	66	67	68	69	70
71	72	73	74	75	76	77	78	79	80
81	82	83	84	85	86	87	88	89	90
91	92	93	94	95	96	97	98	99	100

Hundreds chart —22

1	2	3	4	5	6	7	8	9	10
11	12	13	14	15	16	17	18	19	20
21	22	23	24	25	26	27	28	29	30
31	32	33	34	35	36	37	38	39	40
41	42	43	44	45	46	47	48	49	50
51	52	53	54	55	56	57	58	59	60
61	62	63	64	65	66	67	68	69	70
71	72	73	74	75	76	77	78	79	80
81	82	83	84	85	86	87	88	89	90
91	92	93	94	95	96	97	98	99	100

1	2	3	4	5	6	7	8	9	10
11	12	13	14	15	16	17	18	19	20
21	22	23	24	25	26	27	28	29	30
31	32	33	34	35	36	37	38	39	40
41	42	43	44	45	46	47	48	49	50
51	52	53	54	55	56	57	58	59	60
61	62	63	64	65	66	67	68	69	70
71	72	73	74	75	76	77	78	79	80
81	82	83	84	85	86	87	88	89	90
91	92	93	94	95	96	97	98	99	100

1	2	3	4	5	6	7	8	9	10
11	12	13	14	15	16	17	18	19	20
21	22	23	24	25	26	27	28	29	30
31	32	33	34	35	36	37	38	39	40
41	42	43	44	45	46	47	48	49	50
51	52	53	54	55	56	57	58	59	60
61	62	63	64	65	66	67	68	69	70
71	72	73	74	75	76	77	78	79	80
81	82	83	84	85	86	87	88	89	90
91	92	93	94	95	96	97	98	99	100

1	2	3	4	5	6	7	8	9	10
11	12	13	14	15	16	17	18	19	20
21	22	23	24	25	26	27	28	29	30
31	32	33	34	35	36	37	38	39	40
41	42	43	44	45	46	47	48	49	50
51	52	53	54	55	56	57	58	59	60
61	62	63	64	65	66	67	68	69	70
71	72	73	74	75	76	77	78	79	80
81	82	83	84	85	86	87	88	89	90
91	92	93	94	95	96	97	98	99	100

Four small hundreds charts—23

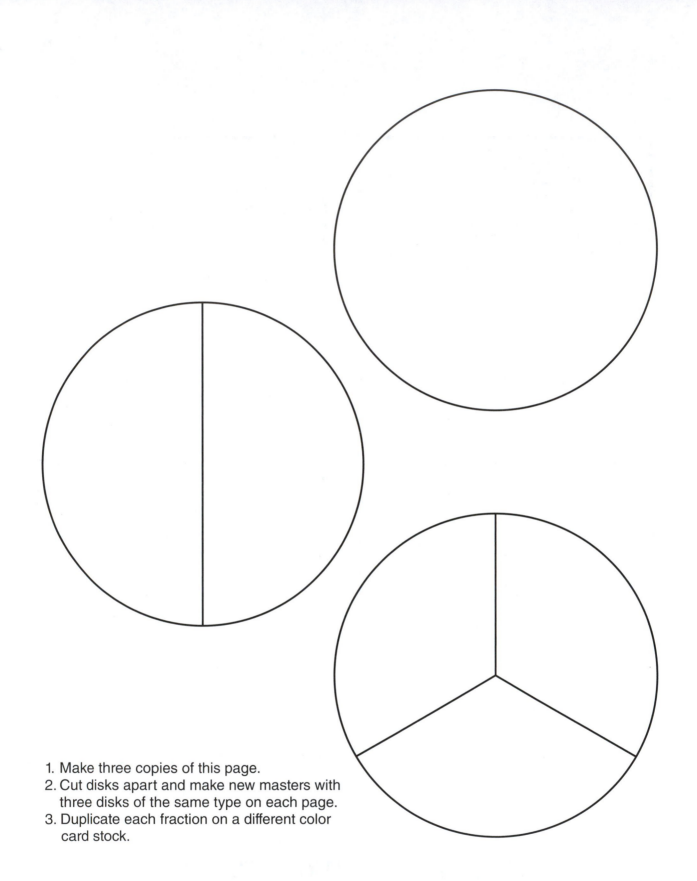

1. Make three copies of this page.
2. Cut disks apart and make new masters with three disks of the same type on each page.
3. Duplicate each fraction on a different color card stock.

Circular fraction pieces —24

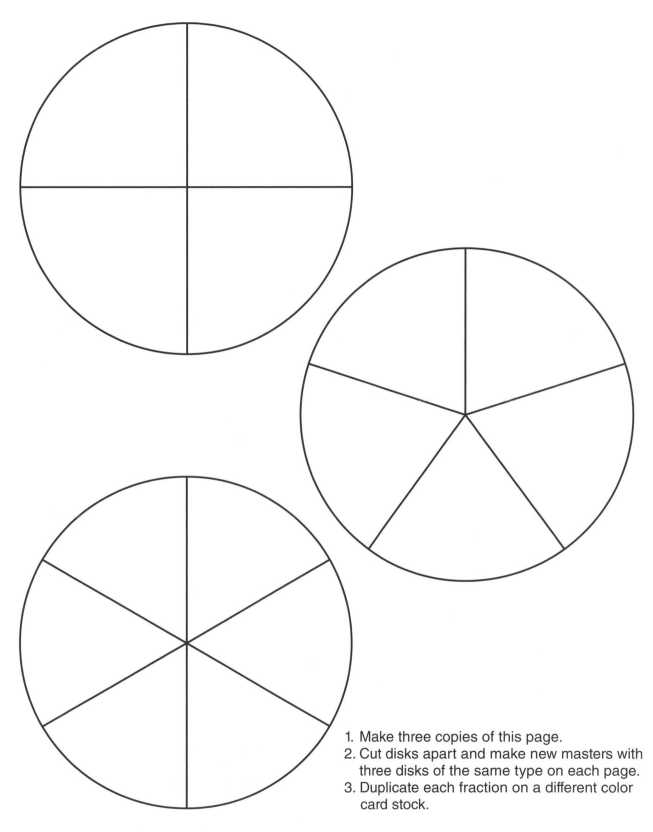

1. Make three copies of this page.
2. Cut disks apart and make new masters with three disks of the same type on each page.
3. Duplicate each fraction on a different color card stock.

Circular fraction pieces —25

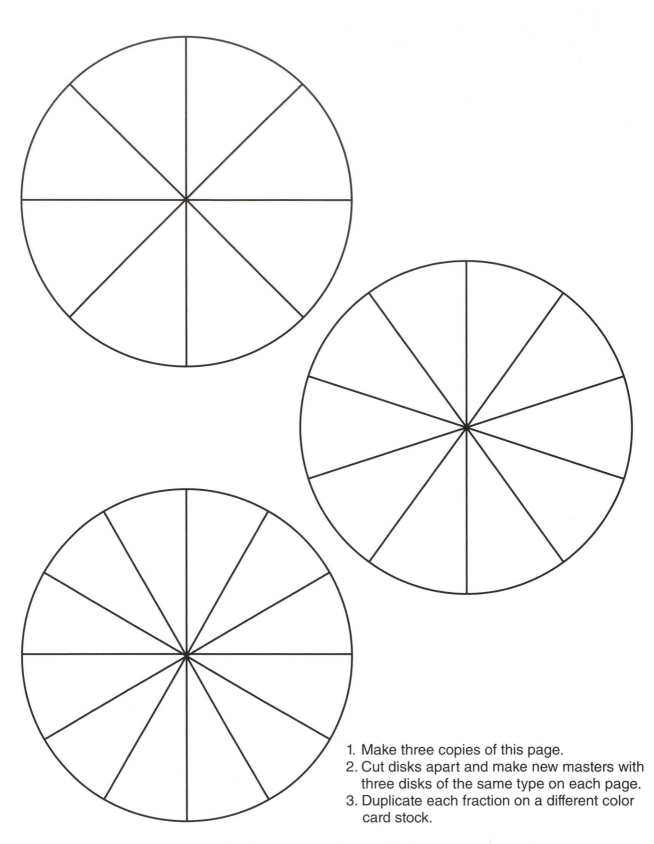

1. Make three copies of this page.
2. Cut disks apart and make new masters with three disks of the same type on each page.
3. Duplicate each fraction on a different color card stock.

Circular fraction pieces —26

10 × 10 grids — 27

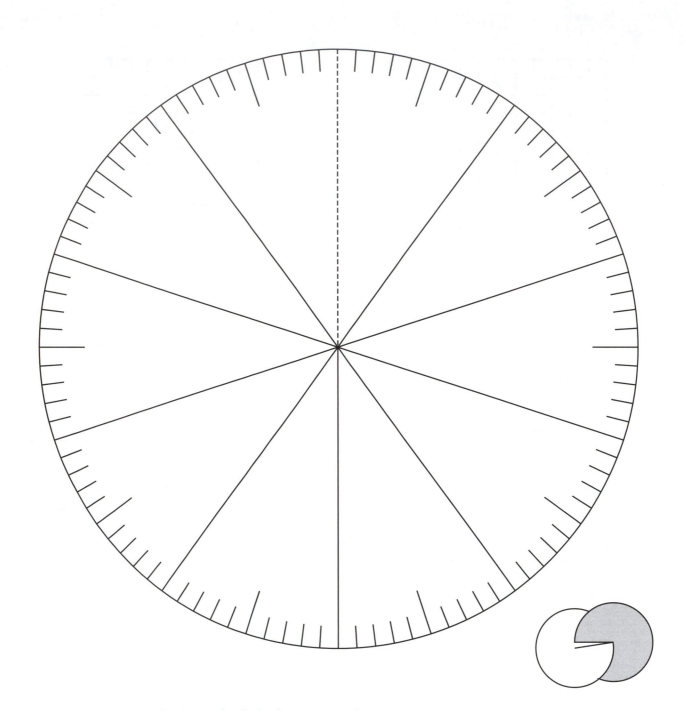

Rational number wheel — 28

Field Experience Guide: Resources for Teachers of Elementary and Middle School Mathematics © Pearson Education, Inc., 2013

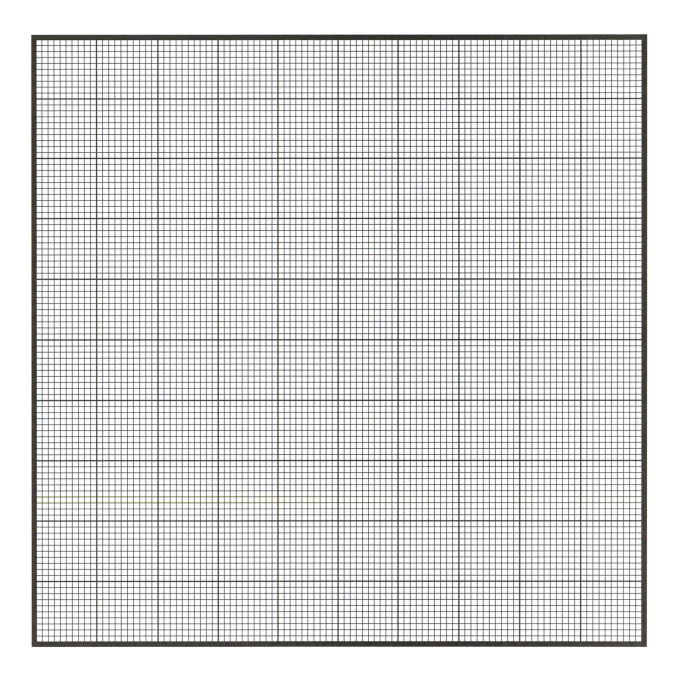

10,000 grid — 29

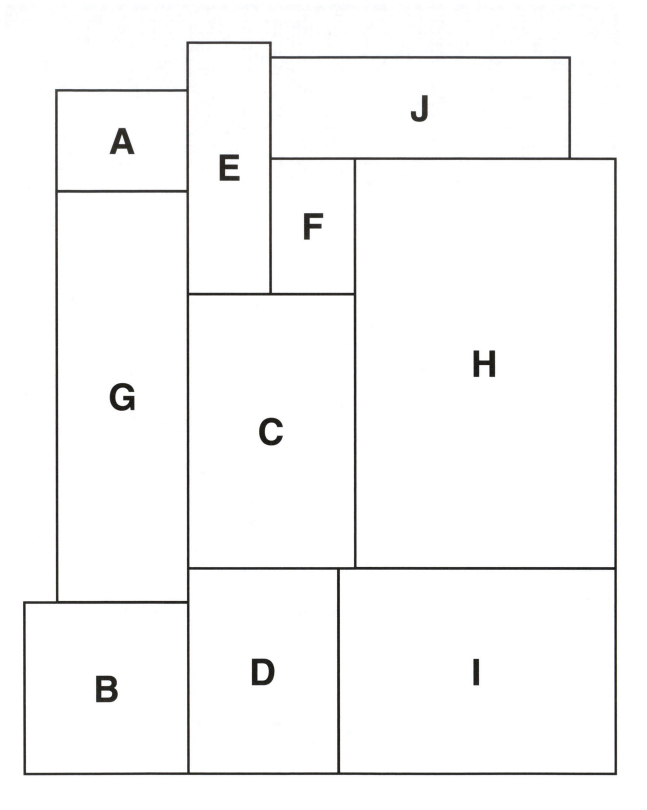

Look-alike rectangles—30

Look-Alike Rectangles
Three Groups and an Odd Ball

Rectangles Group 1 (Letter of rect.)	Measures in cm		Ratio of sides
	Long side	Short side	Short/Long

Rectangles Group 2 (Letter of rect.)	Measures in cm		Ratio of sides
	Long side	Short side	Short/Long

Rectangles Group 3 (Letter of rect.)	Measures in cm		Ratio of sides
	Long side	Short side	Short/Long

Odd Ball (Letter of rect.)	Measures in cm		Ratio of sides
	Long side	Short side	Short/Long

Look-alike rectangles recording sheet—31

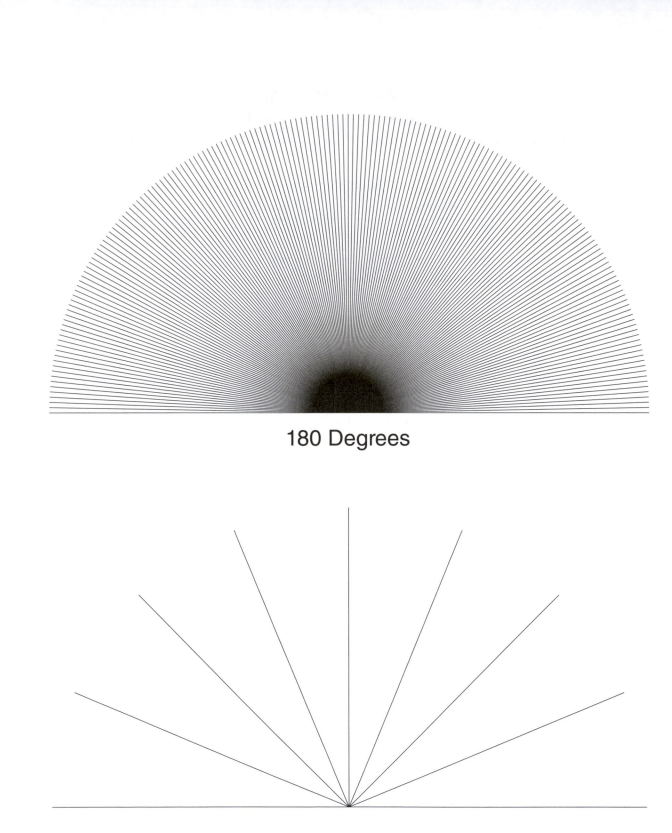

180 Degrees

8 Wedges

Degrees and wedges —32

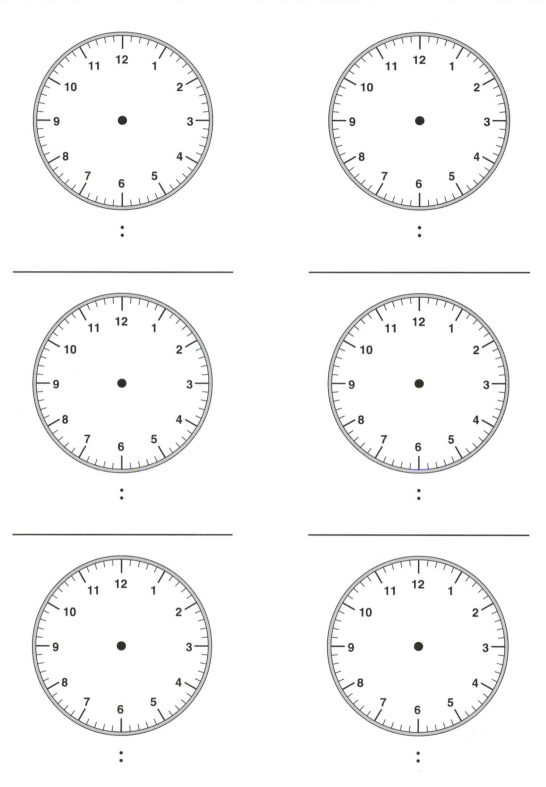

Clock faces—33

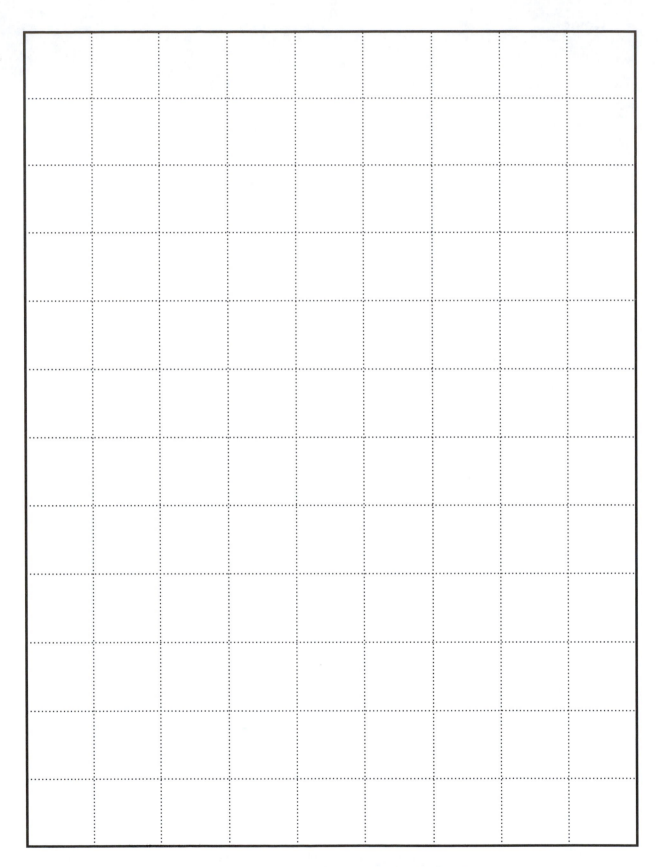

2-cm square grid —34

Field Experience Guide: Resources for Teachers of Elementary and Middle School Mathematics © Pearson Education, Inc., 2013

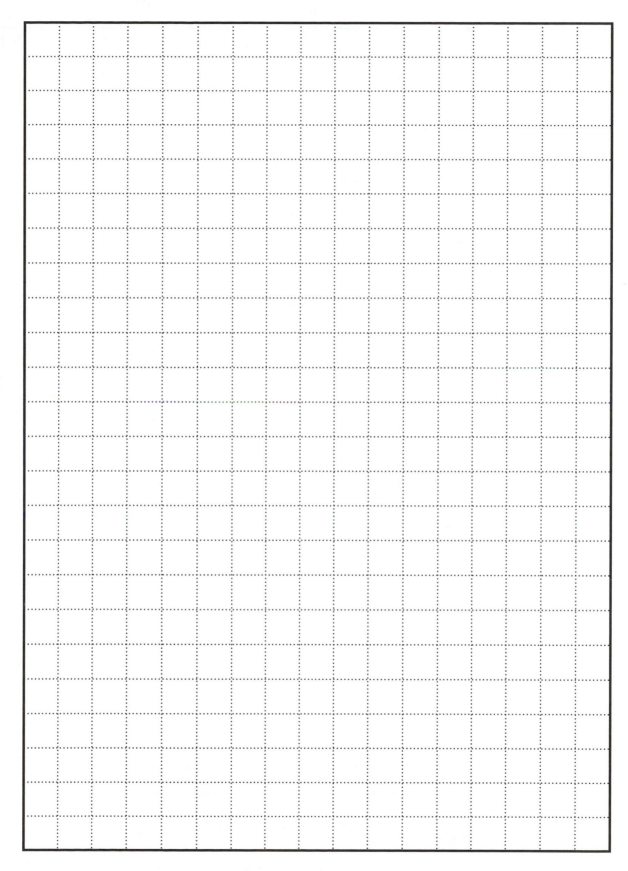

1-cm square grid —35

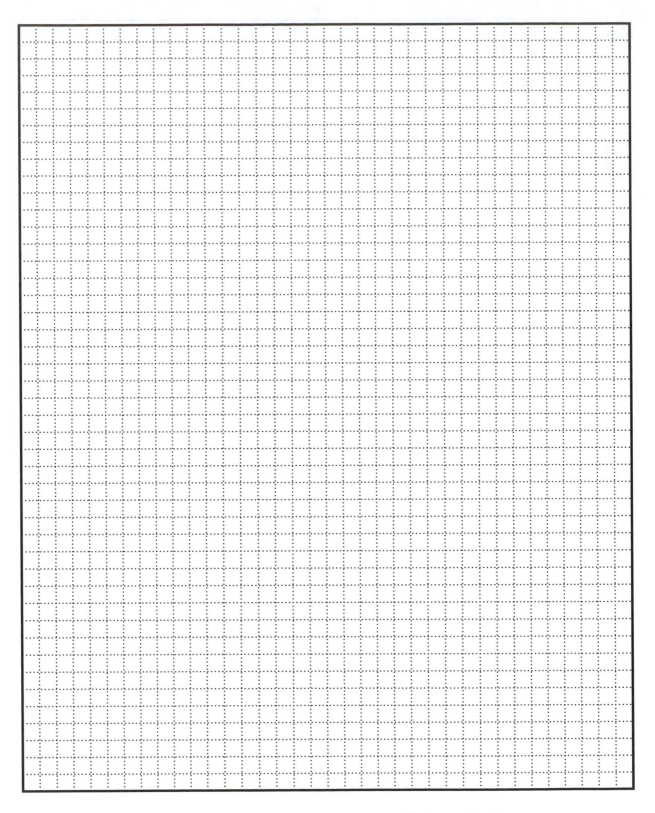

0.5-cm square grid —36

1-cm square dot grid — 37

2-cm isometric grid —38

Field Experience Guide: Resources for Teachers of Elementary and Middle School Mathematics © Pearson Education, Inc., 2013

1-cm isometric dot grid —39

1-cm square/diagonal grid —40

Field Experience Guide: Resources for Teachers of Elementary and Middle School Mathematics © Pearson Education, Inc., 2013

Assorted shapes —41

Assorted shapes —42

Field Experience Guide: Resources for Teachers of Elementary and Middle School Mathematics © Pearson Education, Inc., 2013

Assorted shapes —43

Assorted shapes —44

Field Experience Guide: Resources for Teachers of Elementary and Middle School Mathematics © Pearson Education, Inc., 2013

Assorted shapes —45

Assorted shapes —46

Assorted shapes —47

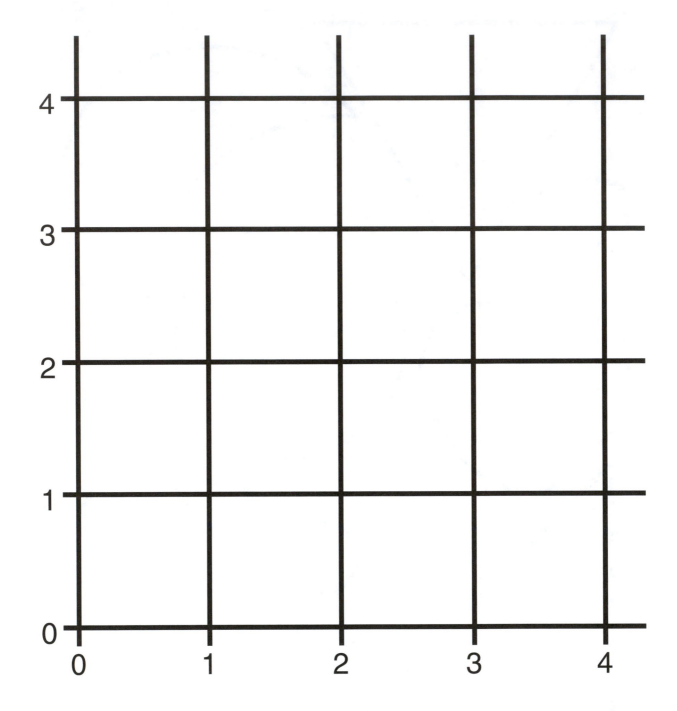

Coordinate grid —48

Field Experience Guide: Resources for Teachers of Elementary and Middle School Mathematics © Pearson Education, Inc., 2013

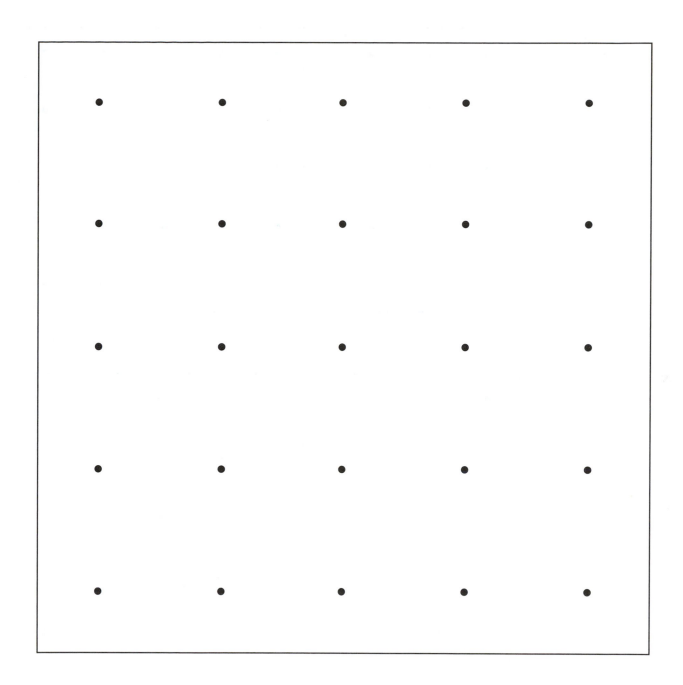

Geoboard pattern —49

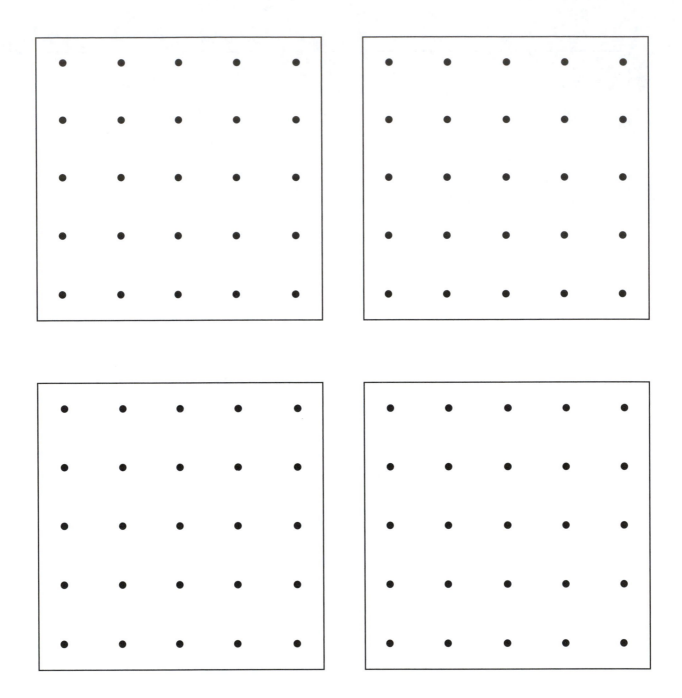

Geoboard recording sheets —50

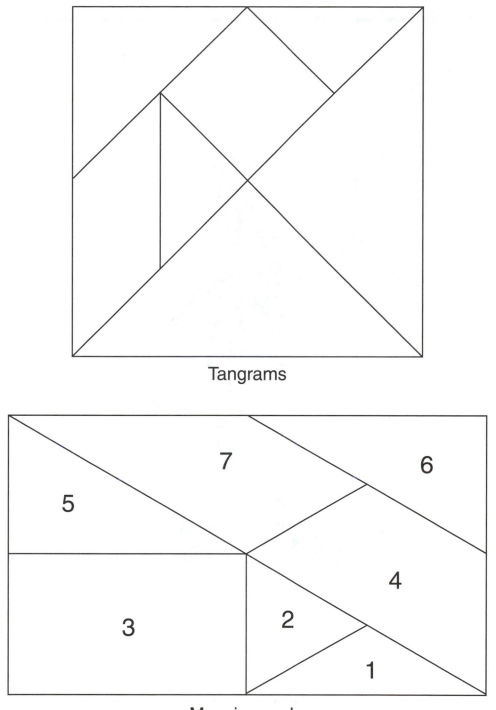

Tangrams

Mosaic puzzle

Tangrams and mosaic puzzle—51

Motion man—Side 1

Directions:

Make copies of Side 1. Then copy Side 2 on the reverse of Side 1. Check the orientation with one copy. When done correctly the two sides will match up when held to the light.

Motion man—52

Motion man—Side 2
(See directions on Side 1.)

Motion man—53

Parallelograms

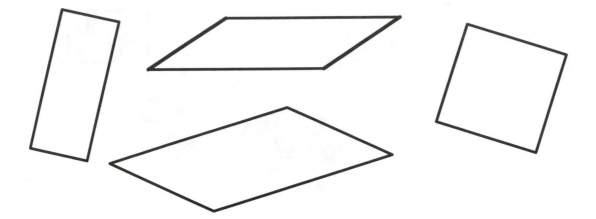

Properties of sides:

Properties of angles:

Properties of diagonals:

      Note: Diagonals are perpendicular or not

                   Bisected by the other or not

                   Congruent or not

Properties of symmetry (line and point):

Property lists for quadrilaterals —54

   Field Experience Guide: Resources for Teachers of Elementary and Middle School Mathematics © Pearson Education, Inc., 2013

Rhombuses

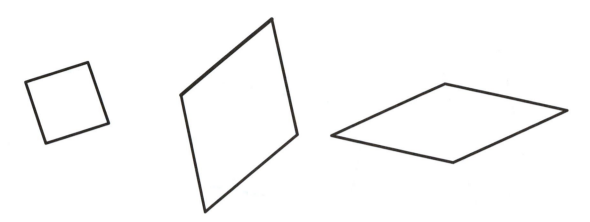

Properties of sides:

Properties of angles:

Properties of diagonals:
      Note: Diagonals are perpendicular or not
                 Bisected by the other or not
                 Congruent or not

Properties of symmetry (line and point):

Property lists for quadrilaterals — 55

Rectangles

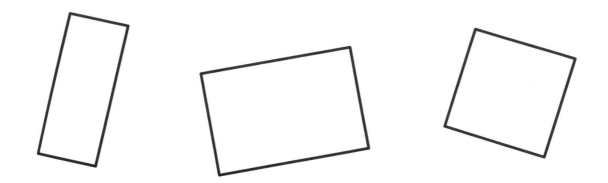

Properties of sides:

Properties of angles:

Properties of diagonals:
    Note: Diagonals are perpendicular or not
                Bisected by the other or not
                Congruent or not

Properties of symmetry (line and point):

Property lists for quadrilaterals —56

Squares

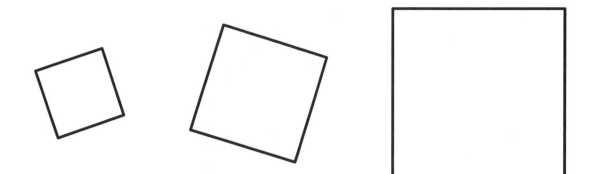

Properties of sides:

Properties of angles:

Properties of diagonals:
      Note: Diagonals are perpendicular or not
                  Bisected by the other or not
                  Congruent or not

Properties of symmetry (line and point):

Property lists for quadrilaterals —57

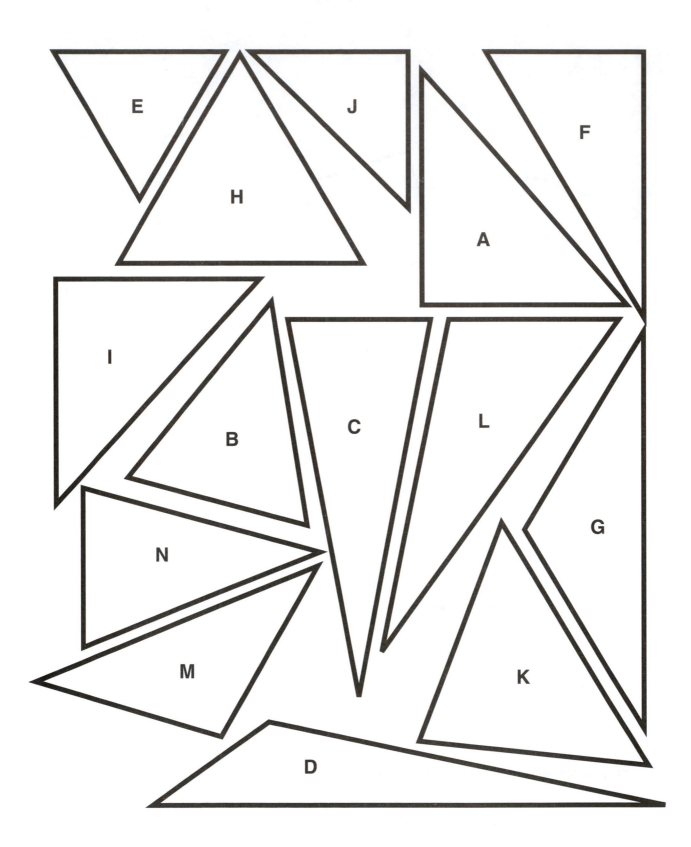

Assorted triangles—58

Field Experience Guide: Resources for Teachers of Elementary and Middle School Mathematics © Pearson Education, Inc., 2013

Woozle cards—59

Design a Bag

Name _____

Color: ☐

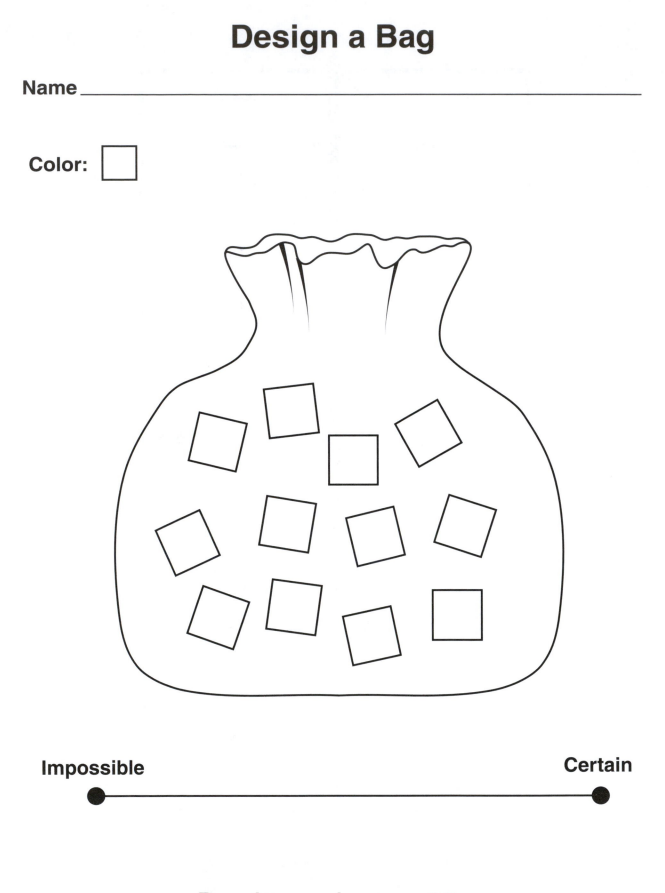

Impossible ●————————————————————————● **Certain**

Design a bag—60

What Are the Chances?

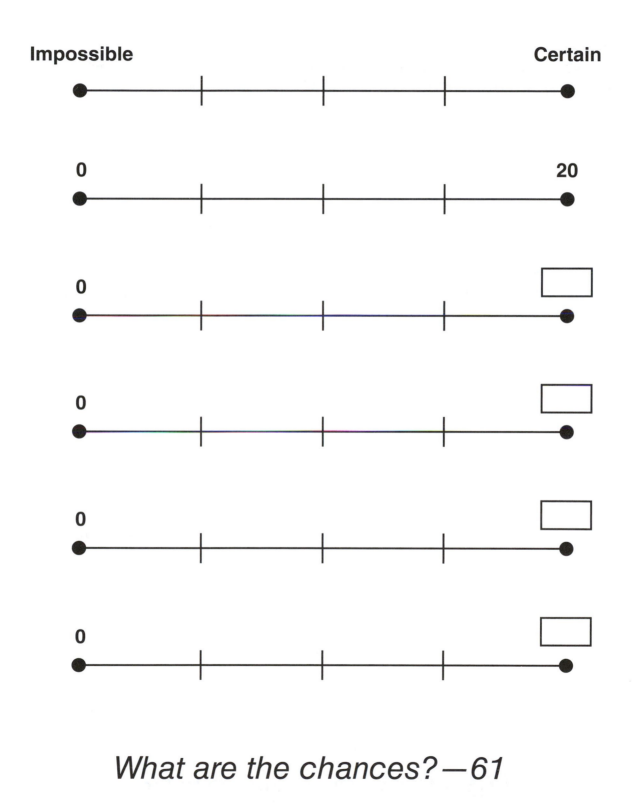

What are the chances?—61

Looking at Collections

Name _____

Collection #1

Danielle has 72 baseball cards in her collection. She has already put 35 of them into the plastic holders. How many more cards need to be placed in plastic holders?

Collection #2

Timothy collects Matchbox cars and has them on two shelves in his bedroom. He has 24 Matchbox cars in all. On the top shelf he has put 16 of the cars. How many will be placed on the bottom shelf?

Collection #3

Danielle and Timothy both like to collect state quarters. When they last visited, Danielle had 32 quarters and Timothy had 24 quarters. How many more does Danielle have than Timothy?

Looking at collections — 62

Field Experience Guide: Resources for Teachers of Elementary and Middle School Mathematics © Pearson Education, Inc., 2013

2 More Than

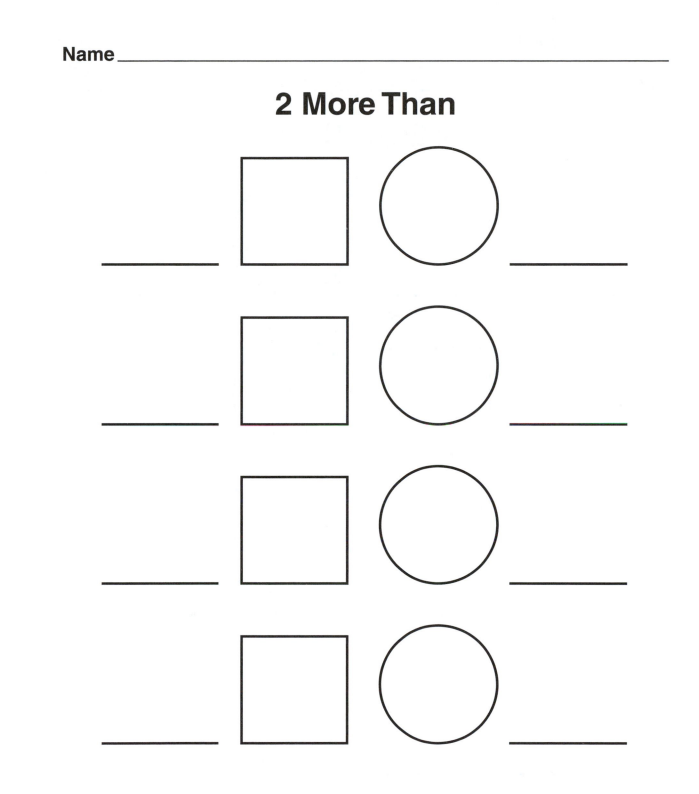

2 more than —63

2 Less Than

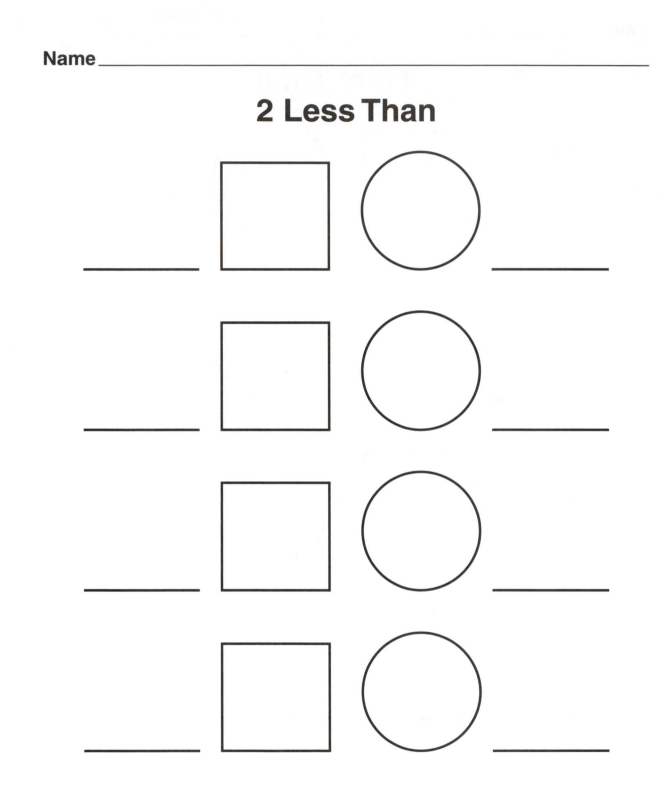

2 less than —64

Name _____

How Long?

Object	**Object** ....
Estimate	**Estimate**
.... tens .... ones	.... tens .... ones
Actual	**Actual**
.... tens .... ones	.... tens .... ones
....	....
number word	number word
....	....
number	number
Object	**Object** ....
Estimate	**Estimate**
.... tens .... ones	.... tens .... ones
Actual	**Actual**
.... tens .... ones	.... tens .... ones
....	....
number word	number word
....	....
number	number

How long? — 65

Name _____

Fraction Names

Find fraction names for each shaded region. Explain how you saw each name you found.

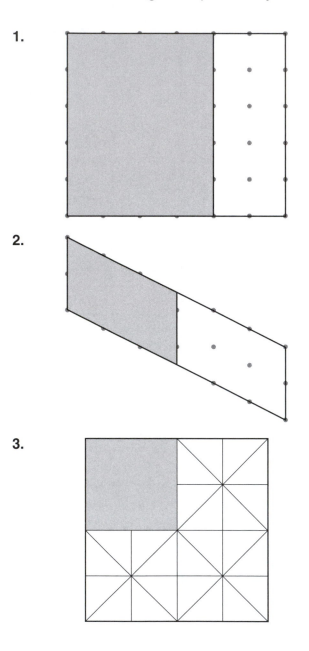

1.

2.

3.

Fraction names —66

Field Experience Guide: Resources for Teachers of Elementary and Middle School Mathematics © Pearson Education, Inc., 2013

Solving Problems Involving Fractions

Name _____

Solve these problems. Use words and drawings to explain how you got your answer.

1. You have ¾ of a pizza left. If you give ⅓ of the leftover pizza to your brother, how much of a whole pizza will your brother get?

2. Someone ate ¹⁄₁₀ of the cake, leaving only ⁹⁄₁₀. If you eat ⅔ of the cake that is left, how much of a whole cake will you have eaten?

3. Gloria used 2½ tubes of blue paint to paint the sky in her picture. Each tube holds ⅘ ounce of paint. How many ounces of blue paint did Gloria use?

Solving problems involving fractions—67

It's a Matter of Rates

Solve each of these problems. Use pictures and words to show how you solved it.

1. Terry can run 4 laps in 12 minutes. Susan can run 3 laps in 9 minutes. Who is the faster runner?

2. Jack and Jill were at the bottom of a hill, hoping to fetch a pail of water. Jack walks uphill at 5 steps every 25 seconds, while Jill walks uphill at 3 steps every 10 seconds. Assuming a constant walking rate, who will get to the pail of water first?

3. Some of the hens in Farmer Brown's chicken farm lay brown eggs and some lay white eggs. Farmer Brown noticed that in the old hen house, she collected 4 brown eggs for every 10 white eggs. In the new hen house, the ratio of brown eggs to white eggs was 1 to 3. If both hen houses produce the same number of eggs, in which henhouse will there be more brown eggs?

4. The Play-a-Lot Video Game Store charges $2.00 for every 15 minutes to play on their wide selection of video games. Wired-for-Action Video Store charges $3.00 for 20 minutes of play on their video games. Where would you choose to go if you were basing your decision on pricing?

It's a matter of rates—68

Field Experience Guide: Resources for Teachers of Elementary and Middle School Mathematics © Pearson Education, Inc., 2013

Windows

Name _____

Step	1	2	3	4	5	6	7		20
No. of sticks	4	7	10						

Describe the pattern you see in the drawing:

_____

_____

_____

Describe the pattern you see in the table:

_____

_____

_____

Use words to describe the rule for finding out how many sticks you need to make any length of window:

_____

_____

_____

_____

_____

Use numbers and symbols to write an equation for your rule:

_____

_____

Predict how many — 69

Dot Arrays

Name _____

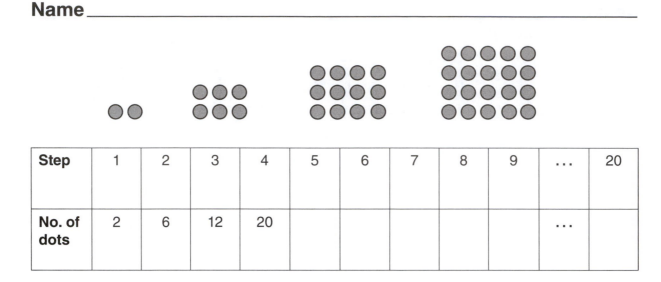

Step	1	2	3	4	5	6	7	8	9	. . .	20
No. of dots	2	6	12	20						. . .	

Describe the pattern you see in the drawing:

_____

_____

_____

Describe the pattern you see in the table:

_____

_____

_____

Use words to describe the rule for finding out how many dots you need to make any dot array:

_____

_____

_____

_____

_____

Use numbers and symbols to write an equation for your rule:

_____

_____

Predict how many—70

Create a Journey Story

If possible, create a story about a journey that the graph could represent. If not possible, explain.

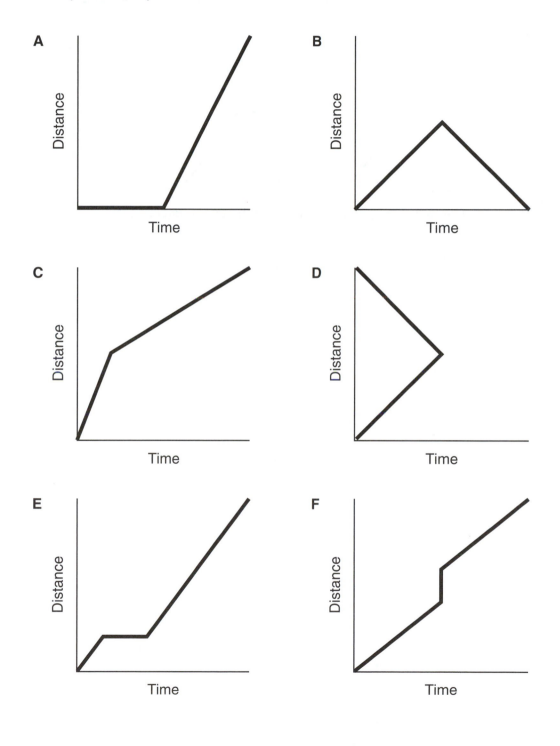

Create a journey story—71

Crooked Paths

Name_____

Circle the longer path. If they are the same, circle both.

How we decided: (Draw pictures)

Crooked paths — 72

Rectangles Made with 36 Tiles

Name _____

Rectangle Dimensions	Area	Perimeter

Rectangles made with 36 tiles—73

Fixed Area Recording Sheet

Name _____

Length	Width	Area	Perimeter

Fixed area recording sheet —74

Properties of Quadrilateral Diagonals

Name_____

Name of Quadrilateral	Congruent Diagonals		Diagonals Bisected			Intersection of Diagonals	
	Yes	No	Both	One	Neither	Perpendicular	Not

Properties of quadrilateral diagonals—75

Toy Purchases

 $8

 $12

 $3

 $5

 $7

 $1

Toy purchases—76

Field Experience Guide: Resources for Teachers of Elementary and Middle School Mathematics © Pearson Education, Inc., 2013

Toying with Measures

Name _____

	Mean	Median	Mode
Original Set of 6			

Make predictions based on these changes. Give reasons for your predictions.

Add a $20 toy			
Reasons			
Return the $1 toy			
Reasons			
Get a free toy			
Reasons			
Buy a second $12 toy			
Reasons			
Your change:			
Reasons			

Calculate the actual statistics for each of the changes.

Add a $20 toy			
Return the $1 toy			
Get a free toy			
Buy a second $12 toy			
Your change:			

Toying with measures—77